Bl £ 3/11-

D1255516

STRICT RESPONSIBILITY

AUSTRALIA
The Law Book Co. of Australasia Pty. Ltd.
Sydney : Melbourne : Brisbane

CANADA AND U.S.A.
The Carswell Company Ltd.
Toronto

INDIA
N. M. Tripathi Private Ltd.
Bombay

ISRAEL
Steimatzky's Agency Ltd.
Tel Aviv

NEW ZEALAND
Sweet & Maxwell (N.Z.) Ltd.
Wellington

PAKISTAN
Pakistan Law House
Karachi

STRICT
RESPONSIBILITY

BY

COLIN HOWARD, LL.B., LL.M., Ph.D.
Senior Lecturer in Law, University of Adelaide
Ezra Ripley Thayer Teaching Fellow, Harvard Law School, 1963–64

LONDON
SWEET & MAXWELL
1963

*Published in 1963 by
Sweet & Maxwell Limited of
11 New Fetter Lane, London,
and printed in Great Britain
by Staples Printers Limited
of London and Rochester*

I dedicate this book
to
My Wife
for putting up with me
while I was writing it

v

PREFACE

IN the opinion of one well placed to make such a judgment, there is room for "books which explore in depth some small segment of law, particularly if that segment is usually regarded as a mere orphan of the greater divisions of the law, to be given grudging house-room in an obscure corner of a standard textbook".[1] This book falls into that category. It is about the doctrine of strict responsibility for regulatory or, as they are often called, public welfare offences. Its theme is that the antithesis between *mens rea* and strict responsibility is unnecessary in this part of the law because responsibility based on negligence is better suited than either to the requirements of this type of legislation.

Throughout the book two parallel themes are pursued: one, what the law is, and the other, what the law might be. The extent to which any particular passage falls under the one head or the other often depends on the standpoint of the reader. For example, the doctrine of reasonable mistake of fact which I should like to see governing all regulatory offences is to a large extent in being in Australia. To an Australian reader, therefore, the chapters on this subject appear mostly as an account of the law as it is, whereas for an English or American reader the same chapters illustrate the law as, in general, I think it ought to be. Other passages, such as the analysis of the American Law Institute's Model Penal Code, are entirely essays in the law as it might be.

Of the many adverse criticisms which can no doubt be justly made of this book, I am able to anticipate three. The first is that some readers may find the organisation of Chapter One, along the lines of a medieval disputation, irritating and perhaps unrealistic. The problem facing me here was that the arguments put forward in support of strict responsibility commonly derive a spurious cogency from being interwoven with one another. The pedestrian mode of analysis adopted in Chapter One seemed to me to be the best way of dispelling this intellectual fog once and for all.

Secondly, there is a certain amount of repetition or overlapping between chapters. This also has been done deliberately for clarity of

[1] R. E. Megarry, (1958) 74 *Law Quarterly Review* 112.

Preface

exposition. It has been well said, by a far more experienced author than myself, that "readability is even more important than brevity, which can sometimes be attained at too great a price".[2]

Thirdly, and more seriously, many will think that I go too far in my advocacy of judicial interpretation of statutes to produce adherence to a uniform principle of criminal responsibility. For example, I am quite ready to see the *prima facie* meaning of such words as "permit" and "knowingly" diluted to allow conviction for negligence (in regulatory prosecutions only). To this criticism I can reply only, *mea culpa*. I am of opinion that the courts should be much more enterprising than they usually are in the interpretation of penal statutes, and I hold this view because the courts are usually concerned in the cases which come before them with matters to which it is quite clear that Parliament has not directed its attention at all. The mental elements in "permit" and "knowingly" are excellent examples: permit or know exactly what?

I have to say that this book was first written as a thesis presented to the University of Adelaide for the degree of Doctor of Philosophy, in which capacity it was in 1962 also awarded the Bonython Prize for an original thesis on a legal subject. Minor revisions have been made for publication. I am happy to acknowledge the kind permission of the American Law Institute to reproduce passages from the Model Penal Code and the commentary. Thereto; and of the editors of the *Columbia Law Rewiew* and the *Wisconsin Law Review* to quote from material published in these journals.

C. H.

Harvard Law School
October, 1963

[2] L. C. B. Gower, *Modern Company Law* (1st ed.), vi.

viii

CONTENTS

Preface . . . . *page* vii

Table of Statutes xi

Table of Cases xiv

1. INTRODUCTION 1
   Strict responsibility 1
   Background 3
   Legislative intention 9
   History 13
   Necessity 15
   Implementation 18
   Deterrence 24
   Public interest 27

2. SANCTIONS AND BURDEN OF PROOF . . 29
   Introduction 29
   The relevance of the sanction . . . 29
   The meaning of "serious punishment" . . 32
   Conclusion on sanctions 35
   The meaning of *mens rea* 36
   Mens rea and public interest . . . 36
   Negligence and strict responsibility . . 38
   Burden of proof 39
   Conclusion on burden of proof . . . 44
   Ignorance and mistake 44

3. STATUTORY WORDS 46
   Introduction 46
   Status offences 46
   A rule for status offences 50
   Illustrations 51
   Particular words 53
   Conclusion 66

4. THE MACHINERY OF CHANGE . . . 68
   Introduction 68
   Statute 68
   Conclusion on statutes 77
   Case-law 78
   Conclusion on case-law 83
   Statute and case-law combined . . . 84
   Administrative courts 84

Contents

5. REASONABLE MISTAKE OF FACT . . *page* 85
Introduction 85
Characteristics of the reasonable mistake rule . . 88
Other jurisdictions 109

6. REASONABLE MISTAKE AND PARTICULAR
WORDS 113
Introduction 113
Neutral words 114
Status offences 125
Knowingly: wilfully 132
Permit: suffer: allow 133
Cause 140
Fraudulent 141
Evade 142
Statutory defences 143

7. THE AUSTRALIAN CRIMINAL CODES . . 145
Introduction 145
Interpretation 145
Case-law 156
Conclusion 166

8. THE MODEL PENAL CODE . . . 167
Introduction 167
The definition of violation 172
Culpability requirements 179
Punishment 185
Burden of proof 187
Conclusions 187

9. THE GENERAL DEFENCES 189
Introduction 189
Strict responsibility and the mental element in crime . 190
Infancy 192
Coverture 192
Compulsion 193
Insanity and automatism 199
Intoxication 201
Other personal incapacity 203
Necessity, impossibility, inevitable accident . . 204

Bibliography 209

Index 213

TABLE OF STATUTES

UNITED KINGDOM

1872 Licensing Act (35 & 36
Vict. c. 94)
ss. 13, 16 (2) . 8
1883 Trial of Lunatics Act
(46 & 47 Vict. c. 38)
s. 2 . . . 199
1887 Merchandise Marks Act
(50 & 51 Vict. c. 28)
s. 2 (2) . . 19
1900 Commonwealth of Aus-
tralia Constitution
Act (63 & 64 Vict.
c. 12) . . . 85
1926 Fertilisers and Feeding
Stuffs Act (16 & 17
Geo. 5 c. 45)
s. 7 (1) . . 19
1937 Factories Act (1 Edw. 8
and 1 Geo. 6 c. 67)
s. 137 (1) . . 19
1952 Magistrates' Courts Act
(15 & 16 Geo. 6 and
1 Eliz. 2 c. 55)
ss. 19 (15), 25 (1) . 30
1st Sched. . . 30

1953 Licensing Act (1 & 2
Eliz. 2 c. 46)
s. 120 (3) . . 21
1954 Mines and Quarries Act
(2 & 3 Eliz. 2 c. 70)
s. 157 . . . 19
1955 Food and Drug Act
(4 & 5 Eliz. 2 c. 16)
s. 113 . . . 19
1956 Road Traffic Act (4 & 5
Eliz. 2 c. 67)
s. 20 (2) . . 42
1957 Homicide Act (5 & 6
Eliz. 2 c. 11) . . 78
1960 Road Traffic Act (8 & 9
Eliz. 2 c. 16)
s. 104 (1) (b) . 21
Offices Act (8 & 9 Eliz. 2
c. 47)
s. 1 (6) . . 19
Administration of Jus-
tice Act (8 & 9 Eliz. 2
c. 65)
s. 1 (1) (a) . . 80

AUSTRALIA

Commonwealth Audit Act,
1901
s. 64 (1) (a) . . . 141
Commonwealth Customs Act,
1901–1920
s. 234 142
Commonwealth Distillation
Act, 1901–1931
s. 74 (4) . 51, 126–127

Commonwealth Judiciary Act,
1903
s. 80 163
Commonwealth Maternity
Allowance Act, 1912
s. 10 (a) . . . 115
National Security Act (C'th),
1939–1940
s. 10 121
War Precautions Act (C'th),
1914–1916 . . . 119

New South Wales

Impounding Act, 1898
s. 9 134
Landlord and Tenant (Amendment) Act, 1948–1949
s. 35 122

Licensing Act, 1912
s. 63 (4) . . . 128
Liquor (Amendment) Act, 1905
s. 19 (4) . . . 125

Table of Statutes

Masters and Servants Act, 1902
  s. 4 116
Motor Traffic Act, 1909
  s. 6 (1) (c) (v) . . 138
Motor Traffic Act, 1909–1956
  s. 3 136

Poisons Act, 1952–1956
  s. 12 21

Sydney Harbour Trust Act,
1901 56

Northern Territory

Aboriginal Ordinance, 1918–
1947
  ss. 3, 3A . . . 97
Licensing Ordinance, 1939–
1952
  s. 141 . . . 97, 105

Observance of Law Ordinance,
1921
  s. 11 (a) . . 122–123

Queensland

Aboriginals Protection and
Restriction of the Sale of
Opium Act, 1897
  s. 22 . . . 156–158
Criminal Code, 1889 . . 74
  s. 23 . 75, 142, 145–159,
          162, 164–166
  s. 24 . 75, 145, 147, 150–
          155, 159–166
  s. 36 . 146, 157, 158, 161
  ss. 291, 301 . . . 151
  s. 466 156
  s. 576 152

Criminal Code Act, 1899
  s. 2 . . 74, 146, 161
  s. 8 146
  s. 23, 24 . . . 75
  s. 36 74

Divisional Boards Act, 1887 . 157
Traffic Act, 1905 . . . 158
Traffic Acts, 1949–1957
  s. 49 (1) (q) . . . 158
Weights and Measures Act
  s. 28 (3) (ii) . . 158–159

South Australia

Health Act, 1898
  s. 109 . . . 117–118
Impounding Act, 1920–1947
  s. 46 . . . 52–53
Landlord and Tenant (Control
of Rents) Act, 1942
  s. 33 89
Licensing Act, 1917
  ss. 94 (2), 185 . . 135
Licensing Act, 1932–1945
  s. 170 104
Licensing Act, 1932–1960
  s. 77 (2) . . . 21

Lottery and Gaming Act,
1917–1930
  s. 48 (a) . . . 129
  s. 63 (3) . . . 51
Motor Vehicles Act, 1959
  s. 91 124
Police Act, 1936–1951
  s. 74 (1) . . 131, 194
Police Offences Act, 1953
  s. 35 (1) . . . 140
Road Traffic Act, 1934–1939
  s. 30 . . . 60, 88
Road Traffic Act, 1934–1959
  s. 38a (1) a . . . 21

Tasmania

Criminal Code, 1924 . 74, 145
  s. 13 147
Criminal Code Act, 1924
  s. 8 78

Traffic Act, 1925–1947
  s. 14 138

Table of Statutes

Victoria

Dairy Supervision Act, 1915
  s. 44 (g) . . 205–206
Factories and Shops Act, 1915
  s. 226 119
Forests Act, 1957
  s. 95 (h) . . . 90
Game Act, 1928
  s. 5 (2) 90
Health Act, 1956
  ss. 291, 298, 300 . . 19
Licensing Act, 1890
  s. 182 115
Licensing Act, 1928–1934
  s. 161 96
  s. 178 130
  s. 206 204
Licensing Act, 1958
  s. 142 21

Licensing (Amendment) Act, 1953
  s. 26 204
Melbourne Harbour Trust Act, 1928 . . 67, 124
Police Offences Act, 1915
  s. 17 (9) . . . 137
Police Offences Act, 1928
  s. 155 130
Police Offences Act, 1958
  s. 32 136
Poisons Act, 1958
  s. 9 21
State Electricity Commission Act, 1928 . . . 89
Transport Regulation Act, 1933
  s. 39 (1) (c) . . . 136

Western Australia

Criminal Code, 1902
  s. 7 162
  s. 23 . 142, 145–159, 162, 164–166
  s. 24 . 145, 147, 150–155, 159–166
  s. 36 . . 146, 162–163
  ss. 268, 278 . . . 151
  s. 595 152
Criminal Code Act, 1902 . 146
Forests Act, 1918 . . . 162

Licensing Act, 1911–1951
  s. 147 (1) . . . 166
Sale of Liquors Amendment Act, 1897
  s. 7 165
State Transport Co-ordination Act, 1933
  ss. 15, 51 . . . 165
Wines, Beer and Spirit Sale Act, 1880 165

CANADA

Criminal Code, 1955
  s 7 (2) 78

Saskatchewan

Vehicles Act, 1957
  s. 113 (1) (b) . . . 110

NEW ZEALAND

Crimes Act, 1961
  s. 20 (1) . . . 78
Poisons Act, 1934
  ss. 18, 19 . . . 21

Transport Act, 1949
  s. 41 21

UNITED STATES OF AMERICA

Anti-Narcotic Act, 1914
  s. 2 20

Illinois

Criminal Code, 1961 . . 167

xiii

TABLE OF CASES

page

Adams *v.* State (1928) 110 Tex.Cr. 20 20
Adelaide Corporation *v.* Australasian Performing Right Association
Ltd. (1928) 40 C.L.R. 481 137
Aitken [1942] St. R. Qd. 57 156
Alford *v.* Riley Newman Ltd. (1934) S.R. (N.S.W.) 261 . . 49
Allen *v.* Whitehead [1930] 1 K.B. 211 49
Anderson *v.* Nystrom [1941] St. R. Qd. 56 . 146, 152, 153, 157,
159, 160, 162
Anstee *v.* Jennings [1935] V.L.R. 144 143
Ashbury *v.* Reid [1961] W.A.R. 49 164
Att.-Gen. for Northern Ireland *v.* Gallagher [1963] A.C. 349 94, 202

Bank of New South Wales *v.* Piper [1897] A.C. 383 . . 79, 100
Barker *v.* Callaghan [1941] V.L.R. 15 143
—— *v.* Levinson [1951] 1 K.B. 342 49
Barnes *v.* State (1849) 19 Conn. 398 6
Barrett *v.* Sullivan [1900] S.A.L.R. 48 143
Barrister, *Re a* (1957) 31 A.L.J.R. 424 148
Bear *v.* Lynch (1909) 8 C.L.R. 592 . . 48, 125, 128, 129, 142, 207
Beaver *v.* The Queen (1957) 118 C.C.C. 129 80
Beckwith *v.* Nicol Bros. [1916] V.L.R. 261 . . . 205, 207
Belling *v.* O'Sullivan [1950] S.A.S.R. 43 . . . 61, 104, 124
Bentley [1960] 7 C.L. 355 . . . . . . 200, 201
Bergin *v.* Khyat [1953] V.L.R. 695 . . . . 48, 125, 143
—— *v.* Stack [1952] A.L.R. 810; (1953) 88 C.L.R. 248 . 61, 96, 98,
102, 104, 122, 124, 131
—— *v.* Thompson [1953] V.L.R. 408 97
Bernhard [1938] 2 K.B. 264 98
Bollmeyer *v.* Daly [1933] S.A.S.R. 295 120
Bond *v.* Clarke [1938] S.A.S.R. 55 120
—— *v.* Evans (1888) 21 Q.B.D. 249 55
—— *v.* Foran (1934) 52 C.L.R. 364 . . 48, 51–52, 63, 120, 128, 132
—— *v.* Reynolds [1960] V.R. 601 . . . . . 135, 136
Bonnor [1951] V.R. 227 102
Bratty *v.* Att.-Gen. for Northern Ireland [1963] A.C. 386 .148, 200, 201
Brend *v.* Wood [1946] 62 T.L.R. 462 3
Briginshaw *v.* Briginshaw (1938) 60 C.L.R. 336 . . . 108
Brimblecombe *v.* Duncan [1958] Qd.R. 8 . 152, 153, 159, 160, 162
Broad *v.* Parish (1941) 64 C.L.R. 588 137
Broadhurst *v.* Cockroft [1937] V.L.R. 159 143
—— *v.* Larkin [1954] V.L.R. 541 136
Brown *v.* Board of Education (1954) 347 U.S. 483 . . . 82
—— *v.* Green (1951) 84 C.L.R. 285 . . . . 20, 122
—— *v.* Shennick (1908) 10 W.A.L.R. 107 165
Bruce, *Ex p.* (1957) 74 W.N. (N.S.W.) 452 . . . 136
Burke *v.* Williams [1918] St. R. Qd. 118 159

Cases

	page
Burney [1958] N.Z.L.R. 745	111
Buttons v. Melbourne Justices (1890) 16 V.L.R. 604	133, 204
Callaghan [1942] St. R. Qd. 40	146
—— v. R. (1952) 87 C.L.R. 115	153
Canty v. Buttrose [1912] V.L.R. 363	132, 205, 207
Carswell [1926] N.Z.L.R. 321	111
Carter [1959] V.R. 105	183, 200, 201
Chajutin v. Whitehead [1938] K.B. 506	20, 33
Charlesworth v. Federal Hotels Ltd. [1943] V.L.R. 88	129
—— v. Kissling [1943] V.L.R. 129	48, 130
—— v. Penfolds Wines Pty. Ltd. [1943] V.L.R. 76	137
Charlson [1955] 1 W.L.R. 317	200, 201
Chia Gee v. Martin (1906) 3 C.L.R. 649	47
Chisholm v. Doulton (1889) 22 Q.B.D. 736	3
Coates v. R. (1957) 31 A.L.J.R. 34	148
Cochrane v. Tuthill (1908) V.L.R. 549	132
Cogden (1950) unreported	200
Coleman v. Richards (1941) 43 W.A.L.R. 21	163
Colyer (1897) 8 Q.L.J. 27	132
Commissioner of Taxes v. King [1950] N.Z.L.R. 202	111
Cooper v. McKenna [1960] Qd. R. 406	148, 200
Cornish v. Elliott (1873) 4 A.J.R. 152	133
Cottle [1958] N.Z.L.R. 999	111, 200, 201
Coysh v. Elliott [1963] V.R. 114	61
Crudginton v. Cooney [1902] St. R. Qd. 176	156
Cullen v. Ware (1897) 3 A.L.R. (C.N.) 65	132
Cundy v. Le Cocq (1884) 13 Q.B.D. 207	8, 117
D'Audney v. Marketing Services (N.Z.) Ltd. [1962] N.Z.L.R. 51	111
Davies v. O'Sullivan No. 2 [1949] S.A.S.R. 208	133
Dawson v. Jack (1902) 28 V.L.R. 634	114
Dayman v. Proudman [1941] S.A.S.R. 87 (see also Proudman v. Dayman)	53, 89, 131
De La Rue v. McNamara [1940] V.L.R. 128	48, 129
Dendle v. Williams [1918] St. R. Qd. 50	159
Derry v. Peek (1889) 14 App. Cas. 337	102
Dineen v. Nicholson [1922] S.A.S.R. 1	125, 144
D.P.P. v. Smith [1961] A.C. 290	101
Dixon v. Seiler [1928] St. R. Qd. 93	159
Dotson v. State (1878) 62 Ala. 141	102
Doulin v. Coulton (1938) 55 W.N. (N.S.W.) 131	133
Dowling v. Bowie (1952) 86 C.L.R. 136	61, 97, 105, 107, 122
Doyle v. Sparling (1881) 3 A.L.T. 63	133
Dugdale v. Dight [1906] V.L.R. 783	114
Duncan v. Ellis (1916) 21 C.L.R. 379	21, 26, 85, 119
—— v. Keppert (1900) 26 V.L.R. 182	133
Dunn, Ex p. (1902) 19 W.N. (N.S.W.) 38	132
—— v. Monson (1911) 30 N.Z.L.R. 399	111
Durham v. Ramson (1907) 9 W.A.L.R. 76	164
Dymond [1920] 2 K.B. 260	101

Cases

page

Earl v. Jakus [1961] V.R. 143 136
Eccles v. Richardson [1916] N.Z.L.R. 1090 111
Eclipse Motors v. Milner [1950] S.A.S.R. 1 . . . 125, 143
Engineers' Case (1920) 28 C.L.R. 129 82
Erson [1914] V.L.R. 144 . . . . . 79, 115, 117, 132
Ewart (1905) 25 N.Z.L.R. 709 . . . 63, 64, 73, 109, 111, 127
—— v. Fox [1954] V.L.R. 699 193

Fenwick v. Boucaut [1951] S.A.S.R. 290 133
Ferrier v. Wilson (1906) 4 C.L.R. 785 . 56–57, 111, 133, 134, 135,
137, 138, 139, 140, 142
Fiorella v. Birmingham (1950) 35 Ala. App. 384 1
Foreman v. Bowser (1918) 12 Q.J.P.R. 108 153
Foster v. Aloni [1951] V.L.R. 481 . . . 61, 89, 90, 92, 93, 94
—— v. Damyon (1932) 38 A.L.R. 477 141
Foy [1960] Qd. R. 225 200
Francis v. Rowan (1941) 64 C.L.R. 196 . . . 85, 120, 121, 123,
124, 138
—— v. Smith (1886) 2 W.N. (N.S.W.) 82 133
Fraser v. Dryden's Carrying Co. [1941] V.L.R. 103 . 49, 125, 144
Freeman v. C. T. Warne Pty. Ltd. [1947] V.L.R. 695 . . . 143

Gardner v. Akeroyd [1952] 2 Q.B. 743 121
Garside (1884) 6 A.L.T. 152 133
Gaumont British Distributors Ltd. v. Henry [1939] 2 K.B. 711 . 64
Gee v. Wills (1945) 47 W.A.L.R. 24 163
Georgeff v. Ryan [1954] S.A.S.R. 234 . . . . . 61, 124
Gepp v. Anderson [1949] S.A.S.R. 135 . . . . . 61, 124
Gherashe v. Boase [1959] V.R. 1 . . . . 61, 90, 92, 124
Gilbert v. Gulliver [1918] V.L.R. 185 134
Gill v. Williams (1916) 12 Tas. L.R. 67 . . . . 126, 137
Gleeson v. Hobson [1907] V.L.R. 148 . . . . . 115, 203
Gordon v. Schubert [1956] N.Z.L.R. 431 111
—— v. State (1875) 52 Ala. 308 103
Gould & Co., Ltd. v. Cameron [1951] N.Z.L.R. 314 . . . 111
Green v. Sergeant [1951] V.L.R. 500 . 61, 90, 91, 92, 98, 132
Griffin v. Larum (1915) 32 W.N. (N.S.W.) 10 . . 48, 128, 144
—— v. Wilson (1935) 52 C.L.R. 260 47
Gurney (1869) 11 Cox 414 102

Hall v. Bartlett (1898) 24 V.L.R. 1 119
Hamilton v. State (1930) 115 Tex. Cr. 96 102
Hammond v. King (1908) 137 Iowa 548 1
Hardgrave v. The King (1906) 4 C.L.R. 232 . . 53, 100, 141, 146
Harding v. Price [1948] 1 K.B. 695 . . . . . 3, 64
Harrison-Owen [1951] 2 All E.R. 726 200
Hawthorn v. Bartholomew [1954] V.L.R. 28 . . 61, 124, 132
Hazelwood & Co., Ltd. v. Richardson [1948] N.Z.L.R. 1204 . 111
Heading v. McCubbin [1936] V.L.R. 159 120
Heaslop v. Burton [1902] St. R. Qd. 259 . . . . 105, 154
Henty v. Hardwick (1866) Argus Newspaper, July 4 . . . 133
Hesford v. Gilliam (1898) 4 A.L.R. (C.N.) 90 114

	page
Hickinbotham *v.* Dawson [1935] V.L.R. 47	120
Hill *v.* Baxter [1958] 1 Q.B. 277 . . 148, 183, 200, 201	
—— *v.* Douglas [1959] N.Z.L.R. 121	111
—— *v.* Richardson (1904) 6 W.A.L.R. 85	159
Hillard *v.* Fitzpatrick (1901) 27 V.L.R. 380 . . .	133
Hinchley *v.* Rankin [1961] 1 W.L.R. 421	49
Hirst [1932] N.Z.L.R. 300	111
Hobbs *v.* Winchester Corporation [1910] 2 K.B. 471 . . 21, 80, 117	
Holland *v.* Peterkin [1961] N.Z.L.R. 769	111
Holmes [1960] W.A.R. 122	200
Hop Sing, *Ex p.* (1887) 4 W.N. (N.S.W.) 59 . . .	141
Horseman *v.* Cavanagh [1930] S.A.S.R. 1 . . . 56, 135	
Howell *v.* Bullen [1915] V.L.R. 445	141
Hubbard *v.* Beck (1947) 64 W.N. (N.S.W.) 20 . . .	120
Hudson *v.* Hanlon (1913) 30 W.N. (N.S.W.) 91 . . .	134
Huggins (1730) 2 Ld. Raym. 1574	23
Hunt *v.* Maloney [1959] Qd. R. 164 . . . 19, 152, 157	
Hussie *v.* Williamson [1955] Q.W.N. 48 . . . 158–159	
Innes *v.* McKinley [1954] N.Z.L.R. 1054	111
Innes (C. L.) & Co., Ltd. *v.* Carrol [1943] N.Z.L.R. 80 . .	111
Irving *v.* Gallagher [1903] St. R. Qd. 121 . . .	114
Isherwood *v.* O'Brien (1920) 23 W.A.L.R. 10 . . .	164
Jackson *v.* Butterworth [1946] V.L.R. 330 . . . 23, 108, 133	
Jaffrey *v.* Sanders [1923] S.A.S.R. 276	53
Jolly *v.* Virgo [1927] S.A.S.R. 188 . . . . 56, 135	
Kasperek (1951) 101 C.C.C. 375	200
Kasriel Neumann (1947) unreported	47
Kay *v.* Butterworth [1945] 61 T.L.R. 452	148
Kelly *v.* Wigzell (1907) 5 C.L.R. 126	159
Kilbride *v.* Lake [1962] N.Z.L.R. 590 . . . 205, 206, 207	
Lambert, *Ex. p.* (1905) 22 W.N. (N.S.W.) 130 . . .	133
—— *v.* California (1957) 355 U.S. 225	98
Larsonneur (1933) 24 Cr. App. R. 74 . 24, 47, 51, 183, 184, 193,	
	194, 206
Laughton *v.* Master Butchers Ltd. (1915) S.A.L.R. 3 . 117, 131, 132	
Lawrence *v.* Lake [1921] Q.W.N. 30 . . . 156, 157	
Lewis *v.* Brown (1931) 48 W.N. (N.S.W.) 196 . . 49, 129, 132	
Lim Chin Aik *v.* The Queen [1963] A.C. 160 . . .	110
Linnett *v.* Commissioner of Police [1946] K.B. 290 . .	49
Linssen *v.* Hitchcock (1915) 34 N.Z.L.R. 545 . . .	111
Lipshut *v.* McKay [1950] V.L.R. 57 . . . 61, 124, 132	
Little, *Ex p.* (1902) 2 S.R. (N.S.W.) (L) 444 . . .	133
Loch *v.* Deakin [1925] St. R. Qd. 237	158
Lomas *v.* Peek [1947] 2 All E.R. 574	66
Loveday *v.* Ayre [1955] St. R. Qd. 264 . . . 159, 160	
Lowe [1917] V.L.R. 155	133

Cases

page

Macarthur *v.* Hing [1909] St. R. Qd. 179 156
McAteer *v.* Lester [1962] N.Z.L.R. 485 47
McCarthy *v.* Codd [1959] V.R. 88 204
McCrae *v.* Downey [1947] V.L.R. 194 . . . . 61, 105, 124
McDermott, *Ex. p.* (1901) 18 W.N. (N.S.W.) 231 . . . 132
M'Kinnon, *Ex p.* (1853) 1 Legge 792 133
M'Queen (1875) 1 V.L.R. (L) 18 133
Maher *v.* Musson (1934) 52 C.L.R. 100 . 51, 100, 103, 104, 113, 120,
                                       122, 126, 128, 130, 132

Mahoney *v.* Le Page (1900) 6 A.L.R. 23 137
Maloney *v.* Clifford (1890) 6 W.N. (N.S.W.) 125 . . . 133
Manuels *v.* Crafter [1940] S.A.S.R. 7 193
Marsh *v.* Newton (1927) 44 W.N. (N.S.W.) 28 . . . 133
Marshall (1830) 1 Lew. 76 101
—— *v.* Foster (1898) 24 V.L.R. 155 116
Martin (1904) 4 S.R. (N.S.W.) 720 114
—— *v.* McGinnis (1894) 20 V.L.R. 556 133
—— *v.* Whittle [1922] V.L.R. 207 . . . . . 48, 129
Melling *v.* Melbourne Justices (1895) 17 A.L.T. 205 . . 133
Miller *v.* Hilton (1937) 57 C.L.R. 400 140
—— *v.* Hood [1921] N.Z.L.R. 998 111
Minor (1955) 112 C.C.C. 29 . . . . . 148, 200, 201
Moffat *v.* Hassett [1907] V.L.R. 515 133
Mollison (1876) 2 V.L.R. (L.) 144 116
Molloy *v.* Hallam [1903] St. R. Qd. 282 156
Morissette *v.* United States (1952) 342 U.S. 246 . . . 1, 3
Mouritzen *v.* White (1910) 12 W.A.L.R. 158 . . . 164
Mousell Bros. *v.* L. & N.W. Rly. [1917] 2 K.B. 836 . 23, 49, 50
Mowling *v.* Hawthorne Justices (1891) 17 V.L.R. 150 . . 133
Mullen *v.* The King [1938] St. R. Qd. 97 154
Murphy [1957] V.R. 545 124
—— *v.* Innes (1877) 11 S.A.L.R. 56 114
Myers *v.* Crabtree [1956] V.L.R. 431 . . . 49, 125, 143
Myerson *v.* Collard (1918) 25 C.L.R. 154 . . . 85, 119

Narrandera Pastures *v.* Coote (1961) 78 W.N. (N.S.W.) 697 . 206
Neilsen, *Ex. p.* (1903) 20 W.N. (N.S.W.) 4 . . . 133
Nelson *v.* Braisby (No. 2) [1934] N.Z.L.R. 559 . . . 111
Nelson (O. F.) & Co., Ltd. *v.* Police [1932] N.Z.L.R. 337 . . 111
Newton (G.), Ltd. *v.* Smith [1962] 2 Q.B. 278 . . . 80

O'Brien *v.* Skinner [1962] N.S.W.R. 575 61
O'Sullivan *v.* Fisher [1954] S.A.S.R. 33 . 47, 49, 131, 193, 194, 195,
                                       196, 197, 198
—— *v.* Friebe [1956] S.A.S.R. 89 . . . . . 125, 144
—— *v.* Harford [1956] S.A.S.R. 109 . . 61, 62, 132, 138
—— *v.* Truth & Sportsman Ltd. (1957) 96 C.L.R. 220 . 54, 140, 141

Pankhurst *v.* Porter (1917) 23 C.L.R. 504 . . . . 118, 121
Parker *v.* Alder [1899] 1 Q.B. 20 . . . . 21, 26, 207
Pelham *v.* Harris [1944] S.A.S.R. 224 . . . . . 89, 92
Persse *v.* Smith (1878) 4 V.L.R. (L.) 201 114

page

Peterson *v.* Curran [1950] Tas. S.R. 9 . . . . .61, 138
Piro *v.* Boorman [1958] S.A.S.R. 226 55
Plessy *v.* Ferguson (1896) 163 U.S. 537 82
Pocock *v.* Elliott [1923] S.A.S.R. 271 53
Potts *v.* Knox (1907) 24 W.N. (N.S.W.) 91 . . . 56, 134
Prince (1875) 2 C.C.R. 154 . . . . . . 64, 100
Proudman *v.* Dayman (1941) 67 C.L.R. 536 (*see also* Dayman *v.*
    Proudman) . 60–61, 86, 88–92, 95, 97, 99, 103–105, 110–111,
             113–114, 120–125, 128, 130–131, 137, 138–140

Quality Dairies *v.* Pedley [1952] 1 All E.R. 380 . . . . 49, 59

R. *v.* Australasian Films Ltd. (1921) 29 C.L.R. 195 . . . 23, 49
—— *v.* Governor of Metropolitan Gaol [1963] V.R. 61 . . 47
—— *v.* St. Margarets Trusts Ltd. [1958] 1 W.L.R. 522 . . 79, 80
—— *v.* Woodrow (1846) 15 M. & W. 404 13
Rees (1956) 115 C.C.C. 1 66
Reidy *v.* Herry (1897) 23 V.L.R. 508 193
Reynolds *v.* G. H. Austin & Sons Ltd. [1951] 2 K.B. 135, 149
                        24, 49, 64, 79, 109
Richards *v.* Grant [1958] V.R. 241 204
Riley [1896] 1 Q.B. 309 40
Ritchie, *Ex p.* (1896) 12 W.N. (N.S.W.) 109 . . . 141
Robinson *v.* Torrisi (1938) 40 W.A.L.R. 62 . . . 165
Roddy *v.* Perry No. 2 [1958] S.R. (N.S.W.) 41 . . . 97,98
Rogers *v.* Arnott [1960] 2 Q.B. 244 58
Roper *v.* Taylor's Central Garages Ltd. [1951] 2 T.L.R. 284 53, 64, 65
Ross *v.* Sickerdick (1916) 22 C.L.R. 197 . . . 118, 142
Rowan, *Ex p.* (1891) 8 W.N. (N.S.W.) 35 132
Russel *v.* Shand [1956] N.Z.L.R. 654 111
Ryall *v.* Carroll (1959) 102 C.L.R. 162 122

Sanderson (1910) W.A.L.R. 92 164
Sangster *v.* Henry (1920) 37 W.N. (N.S.W.) 135 . . 56, 134
Savage *v.* Hungerford (1902) 4 W.A.L.R. 135 . . . 163
Sawicki *v.* The Queen (1960) 124 C.C.C. 386 . . 55, 56, 109, 110
Scarth [1945] St. R. Qd. 38 . . . . . 93, 146
Shakespeare *v.* Taylor (1890) 24 S.A.L.R. 51 . . . 140
Sharp *v.* Caratti (1922) 25 W.A.L.R. 133 . . . 162, 163
Sherras *v.* De Rutzen [1895] 1 Q.B. 918 . . . 8, 64, 117
Shuter (1883) 9 V.L.R. (L.) 204 133
Slatcher *v.* Smith [1951] 2 K.B. 631 24
Smith *v.* California (1959) 361 U.S. 147 98
—— *v.* Manno [1961] S.A.S.R. 17 124
—— *v.* O'Grady [1953] V.L.R. 303 . . . . 67, 124
Snell *v.* Ryan [1951] S.A.S.R. 59 . . . 49, 52, 53, 131
Snow *v.* Cooper (1944) 57 W.A.L.R. 92 162
Sodeman *v.* The King (1936) 55 C.L.R. 192 . . . 43, 108
Somerset *v.* Wade [1894] 1 Q.B. 574 55
Sorsky (1944) 30 Cr. App. R. 84 20
Spooner *v.* Alexander (1912) 13 C.L.R. 704 . . 104, 116, 144
State *v.* Blue (1898) 17 Utah 175 3

Cases

	page
Steele *v.* Starr (1912) 29 W.N. (N.S.W.) 82	97
Stephens (1866) L.R. 1 Q.B. 702	14
—— *v.* Robert Reid & Co., Ltd. (1902) 28 V.L.R. 82 .	114, 132
—— *v.* Taufik Road (1908) 8 W.A.L.R. 183 . . .	164
Strong *v.* Dawtry [1961] 1 W.L.R. 841 . . . 24, 42, 203, 204
Sweeney *v.* Denness (1954) 56 W.A.L.R. 52	165
Technical Books Ltd. *v.* Collector of Customs [1957] N.Z.L.R. 490	111
Tennant *v.* Harris [1916] V.L.R. 557	137
Thomas *v.* Ivey (1892) 13 A.L.T. 190	133
—— *v.* McEather [1920] St. R. Qd. 166 . 146, 157, 159, 160, 162
—— *v.* The King (1937) 59 C.L.R. 279 . 3, 96, 101, 102, 120, 144, 146
Thompson *v.* Ewens [1958] S.A.S.R. 193 . . . . 61, 105, 124
—— *v.* Sampson [1930] V.L.R. 191 . . . . . 120, 204
Thorne *v.* Motor Trade Association [1937] A.C. 797 . . 101, 144
Tippett *v.* Heyman (1902) 19 W.N. (N.S.W.) 6 . . .	133
Tolson (1889) 23 Q.B.D. 168 . . . . . 3, 100, 144
Towers *v.* Gray [1961] 2 Q.B. 351	24
Transport Department *v.* McCutcheon [1962] N.Z.L.R. 675 .	111
Trenchard *v.* Ryan (1910) 10 S.R. (N.S.W.) 618 . . . 49, 125, 144
Tully *v.* O'Sullivan [1956] S.A.S.R. 106 . . . 48, 125, 143
Turnbull (1943) 44 S.R. (N.S.W.) 108 . . . . 10, 66, 132
Tustin (1908) 27 N.Z.L.R. 506	111
Twose (1879) 14 Cox 327	98
United States *v.* Ah Chong (1910) 15 Philippine 488 . . .	100
—— *v.* Balint (1922) 258 U.S. 250	20
Vallance *v.* The Queen (1961) 35 A.L.J.R. 182 . . .	147
Vickers [1957] 2 Q.B. 664	200
Wakefield (1958) 75 W.N. (N.S.W.) 66 . . . 148, 200, 201
Walker [1958] N.Z.L.R. 810	111
—— *v.* Chapman [1904] St. R. Qd. 330 . . . 146, 156, 160
Waterside Workers' Federation *v.* Birt [1918] St. R. Qd. 10 . .	153
Watmore *v.* Jenkins [1962] 2 Q.B. 572 . . . 183, 200, 201
Wells *v.* Noblet [1933] S.A.S.R. 134	129
West Coast Hotel *v.* Parrish (1937) 300 U.S. 379 . . .	82
Widgee Shire Council *v.* Bonney (1907) 4 C.L.R. 977 . 142, 146, 157
Wightman *v.* Copperwaite (1930) 32 W.A.L.R. 101 . .	163
Williamson *v.* Norris [1899] 1 Q.B. 7	3
Wilson *v.* Chambers (1926) 38 C.L.R. 131 . . . 96, 98, 142, 143
—— *v.* Dobra (1955) 57 W.A.L.R. 95	162
—— *v.* Inyang [1951] 2 K.B. 799	102
—— *v.* Murphy [1937] 1 All E.R. 315	49
Winton *v.* Wright (1941) 58 W.N. (N.S.W.) 181 . . .	138
Wolff, *Ex p.* (1939) 56 W.N. (N.S.W.) 33	133
Woodrow (1846) 15 M. & W. 404	6
Woolmington *v.* D.P.P. [1935] A.C. 462 . . . 82, 154, 200
Wulf *v.* Moore [1948] St. R. Qd. 95	158
Young *v.* Paddle Bros. Pty., Ltd. [1956] V.L.R. 38 . . 125, 143

CHAPTER 1

INTRODUCTION

Strict responsibility

It is customary and convenient to divide the constituents of an offence against the criminal law into two parts, *actus reus* and *mens rea*. The generally accepted sense in which these terms are used is that *actus reus* refers to the outward circumstances of the offence and *mens rea* to the mental state of the offender. Where, as is usual, a positive act is required, *actus reus* refers also to so much of the mental element, that is to say the volitional element, as is included in the definition of an act.[1]

Whereas at common law it was generally true to say that to convict D,[2] P had to prove both *actus reus* and *mens rea*, in modern times a doctrine has grown up that in certain classes of statutory offences, which may be called for convenience "regulatory offences",[3] D can be convicted on proof by P of *actus reus* only. This has come to be

[1] Glanville Williams, *Criminal Law: The General Part*, (2nd ed.), 22.
[2] D stands for the defendant to a criminal charge and P for the prosecutor.
[3] No mere name can convey an accurate impression of the varied group of offences referred to. Perkins, *Criminal Law*, 701–702, cites the following suggestions: public torts (35 *Harvard Law Review*, 462); public welfare offences (Sayre, 33 *Columbia Law Review*, 55); prohibitory laws (1 *Bl. Comm.*, * 58); prohibited acts (*Prince* (1875) L.R. 2 C.C.R. 154, 163); regulatory offences (*Morissette* v. *United States* (1952) 342 U.S. 246, 258); Sayre, 43 *Harvard Law Review*, 689, 720); police regulations (*Hammond* v. *King* (1908) 137 Iowa 548, 552; 114 N.W. 1062, 1063); administrative misdemeanours (Kirchheimer, 55 *Harvard Law Review*, 615, 636; *cf.* Schwenk, "The Administrative Crime, its Creation and Punishment by Administrative Agencies" (1943) 42 *Michigan Law Review*, 51, 86); quasi crimes (Stroud, *Mens Rea*, 11; *Fiorella* v. *Birmingham* (1950) 35 Ala. App. 384, 387; 48 So. 2d. 761, 764); civil offences (Gausewitz, 12 *Wisconsin Law Review*, 365; Perkins, *Criminal Law*, 692, and 100 *University of Pennsylvania Law Review*, 832). The Model Penal Code of the American Law Institute uses the term "violations": Proposed Official Drafts. 1.04(5).
Of these various suggestions, "regulatory offences" has been preferred in the text because the type of offence referred to is usually part of a legislative scheme for the administrative regulation of society. Sayre, (1933) 33 *Columbia Law Review*, 55, 73, classifies regulatory offences into the following categories:
(1) Illegal sales of intoxicating liquor;
    (*a*) sales of prohibited beverage;
    (*b*) sales to minors;
    (*c*) sales to habitual drunkards;
    (*d*) sales to Indians or other prohibited persons;
    (*e*) sales by methods prohibited by law;
(2) Sales of impure or adulterated food or drugs;
    (*a*) sales of adulterated or impure milk;
    (*b*) sales of adulterated butter or oleomargarine;

1

called the doctrine of strict, or absolute,[4] responsibility.[5] It is the source of much difference of opinion. Supporters of the doctrine regard it as a necessary evil. Their opponents agree about the evil but not about the necessity. Neither view having prevailed so far, this part of the law presents a picture of almost universal confusion. It is the object of this book, not to make yet another survey of the confusion,[6] but to seek out and analyse such practical possibilities of introducing order as have appeared in the common law countries up to the present time. As a preliminary, to which the remainder of this chapter will be devoted, the background and present scope of the

> (3) Sales of misbranded articles;
> (4) Violations of anti-narcotic acts;
> (5) Criminal nuisances;
>   (a) annoyances or injuries to the public health, safety, repose, or comfort;
>   (b) obstructions of highways;
> (6) Violations of traffic regulations;
> (7) Violations of motor vehicle laws;
> (8) Violations of general police regulations, passed for the safety, health, or well-being of the community.

This classification is supported by an exhaustive citation of cases in an appendix (*ibid.*, 84–88), but is open to the criticism that some of the categories are tendentiously described to conform with the title of Sayre's article, "Public Welfare Offenses": see 5 (a) and 8. It is cited here only to give an indication of the scope of the subject.

[4] It is immaterial which term is used. The word "strict" is used here as conveying a more accurate impression. Crimes of strict responsibility are those in which "the necessity for *mens rea* or negligence is wholly or partly excluded. There is no indication in the authorities that other defences are excluded such as infancy and duress". (Williams, *Criminal Law: The General Part*, (2nd ed.), 215.) If there were no possible defence, "absolute" would be more accurate.

[5] Strict responsibility is not unknown in other parts of the criminal law, for example in relation to knowledge of age of the victim in certain sexual offences, or, in some jurisdictions, in relation to material constituents of bigamy. As a general doctrine, however, it is confined to the so-called regulatory offences and it is only the general doctrine which is under discussion here. *Cf.* Hall, *General Principles of Criminal Law* (2nd ed.), 326.

[6] Every modern general text on the criminal law includes a section on strict responsibility, but see particularly the following discussions: Williams, *Criminal Law: The General Part* (2nd ed.), Ch. 6; Hall, *General Principles of Criminal Law* (2nd ed.), Ch. X – Appendix; Perkins, *Criminal Law*, Ch. 7 (5) (reprinted from 100 *University of Pennsylvania Law Review*, 832); Edwards, *Mens Rea in Statutory Offences*; Sayre, "Public Welfare Offenses" (1933) 33 *Columbia Law Review*, 55; Sayre, "Mens Rea" (1932) 45 *Harvard Law Review*, 974, 1016–1026; Stallybrass, "The Eclipse of Mens Rea" (1936) 52 *Law Quarterly Review*, 60; Turner, "The Mental Element in Crimes at Common Law" (1936) 6 *Cambridge Law Journal*, 31, and Jackson, "Absolute Prohibition in Statutory Offences", *ibid.*, 83 (both reprinted in *The Modern Approach to Criminal Law*, ed. Radzinowicz and Turner, Ch. 13 and Ch. 14); Laylin and Tuttle, "Due Process and Punishment" (1922) 20 *Michigan Law Review*, 614; Starrs, "The Regulatory Offense in Historical Perspective" in *Essays in Criminal Science*, ed. Mueller, Ch. 9; Mueller, "Mens Rea and the Law Without It" (1955) 58 *West Virginia Law Review*, 34; Hart, "The Aims of the Criminal Law" (1958) *Law and Contemporary Problems*, 401; Devlin, "Statutory Offences" (1958) 4 *Journal of the Society of Public Teachers of Law* (n.s.), 206 Wasserstrom, "Strict liability in the Criminal Law", (1960) 12 *Stanford Law Review* 731; Packer, "Mens Rea and the Supreme Court", [1962] *Supreme Court Review* 107.

doctrine of strict responsibility will be briefly described and consideration given to the arguments put forward in its support. These arguments will be rejected.

Background

For many centuries the criminal law developed round the concept that no man should be convicted of an offence unless not only *actus reus*, but also *mens rea*, were proved against him. This rule remains a cardinal principle of criminal responsibility at the present day.[7] It is true that in early law there appears to have been an emphasis on the nature and degree of harm done rather than on the moral guilt of the defendant; but the consensus of learned opinion is that at no stage did the law dispense altogether with the *mens rea* concept, the early stress on physical results being no more than a phenomenon natural to a relatively primitive phase of legal development.[8] By about the

---

[7] "It is a general principle of our criminal law that there must be as an essential ingredient in a criminal offence some blameworthy condition of mind. Sometimes it is negligence, sometimes malice, sometimes guilty knowledge – but as a general rule there must be something of that kind which is designated by the expression *mens rea*." (*Chisholm* v. *Doulton* (1889) 22 Q.B.D. 736, 741, *per* Cave J.) "Now the general rule of law is that a person cannot be convicted and punished in a proceeding of a criminal nature unless it can be shown that he had a guilty mind." (*Ibid.*, 739, *per* Field J.) "The full definition of every crime contains expressly or by implication a proposition as to a state of mind. Therefore, if the mental element of any conduct alleged to be a crime is proved to have been absent in any given case, the crime so defined is not committed." (*Tolson* (1889) 23 Q.B.D. 168, 187, *per* Stephen J.) "To prevent the punishment of the innocent, there has been ingrafted into our system of jurisprudence, as presumably in every other, the principle that the wrongful or criminal intent is the essence of crime, without which it cannot exist." (*State* v. *Blue* (1898) 17 Utah 175, 181; 53 Pac. 978, 980, *per* Bartch J.) "The general rule of English law is, that no crime can be committed unless there is *mens rea*." (*Williamson* v. *Norris* [1899] 1 Q.B. 7, 14, *per* Lord Russell C.J.) "It is of the utmost importance for the protection of the liberty of the subject that a court should always bear in mind that, unless a statute either clearly or by necessary implication rules out *mens rea* as a constituent part of a crime, the court should not find a man guilty of an offence against the criminal law unless he has a guilty mind." (*Brend* v. *Wood* (1946) 62 T.L.R. 462, 463, *per* Lord Goddard C.J.; repeated in *Harding* v. *Price* [1948] 1 K.B. 695, 700). *Thomas* v. *The King* (1937) 59 C.L.R. 279. *Morissette* v. *United States* (1952) 342 U.S. 246.

[8] "In seeking to determine the part played by intent in the early criminal law . . . one must guard against drawing too sweeping conclusions from evidence which is admittedly extremely meager. What the recorded fragments of early law seem to show is that a criminal intent was not always essential for criminality and many malefactors were convicted on proof of causation without proof of any intent to harm. But it also appears that even in the very earliest times the intent element could not be entirely disregarded, and, at least with respect to some crimes was of importance in determining criminality as well as in fixing the punishment." (Sayre, "Mens Rea" (1932) 45 *Harvard Law Review*, 974, 982.) See generally Sayre, *op. cit.*, 975–982; Holmes, *The Common Law*, Lecture 1; Wigmore, "Responsibility for Tortious Acts" (1894) 7 *Harvard Law Review*, 315; Winfield, "The Myth of Absolute Liability" (1926) 42 *Law Quarterly Review*, 37, reprinted in Winfield, *Select Legal*

thirteenth century the idea of a mental element in crime, or at least in the more serious crimes, such as homicide and larceny, was taking shape in the embryonic criminal law as a factor distinct from the mere performance of the forbidden act.[9] With the appearance in Coke's *Institutes*[10] of the maxim *actus non facit reum nisi mens sit rea* as a well-established principle of law, the now familiar distinction between the physical and mental elements in crime at common law took on its modern form.

Looking back on this development, two propositions may be advanced. The first is that the development of *mens rea* represented the growing influence in the criminal law of ethical considerations, of morality. The second is that the law was thereby improved. Since the view taken in this book is that any departure from ethical motivations in the theory or practice of the criminal law, however trivial, is against the interest of the community, it may be as well to elaborate a little on these two propositions.

As to the first, that *mens rea* is a legal manifestation of an ethical concept, it is, of course, not suggested that the law is to be identified with any particular moral code in any but the most general terms; still less that it is, or ought to be, identical with such a code. It is platitudinous that the application of a system of law depends upon the political identification of the community to which it applies; and that political identifications rarely coincide with communal divisions based on ethical or religious belief. Moreover, individual members of a group professing the same moral beliefs frequently differ over the detailed interpretation of those beliefs, and it is not practicable to reflect this degree of individual variation in a law common to all. But to admit these facts is not to deny that the criminal law should be based on moral considerations.

If we were all perfect, there would be no need for a criminal law. The reason for its existence is no doubt to keep the community in order. Yet, to concede, as all do, that merely keeping the community in order is unsatisfactory as an end in itself, is to admit at the same time that the application of the criminal law must be limited by the moral sense of the community, for there is no other basis for limitation. If merely keeping the peace were the sole end of criminal law, it

Essays, 15–29; 2 Holdsworth, *History of English Law*, Ch. 2; 2 Pollock and Maitland, *History of English Law*, 447–509; Hall, *General Principles of Criminal Law* (2nd ed.), 77–83.

[9] Sayre, *op. cit.*, 988–989.

[10] 3rd *Institute*, 6, 107, (1641).

would be simple, and doubtless effective, to rule that anyone who did any prohibited act should be put to death. It is quite probable that the problem of illegal parking would swiftly be solved if on mere proof of *actus reus* the defendant were removed permanently from the scene. The reason why this drastically simple solution to many problems of law-enforcement is not adopted is that it would be repugnant to the moral sense of the whole community. No sane man could accept such a law, for common to all civilised communities is a profound respect for human life.

This is an ethical consideration, and its power is demonstrated by the history of the death penalty, which for two centuries has been one of steadily lessening public support.[11] Similarly, an increasing revulsion against the use of corporal punishment less than death has been a marked feature of modern penology.[12] These phenomena reflect the general opinion that an offender should not be punished beyond the requirements of the case, whatever those requirements may be thought to be. The rise of the concept of *mens rea*, which antedates both of the developments just mentioned, is similarly a reflection in the law of the related belief that unless a man is at fault he should not be punished at all.

The second of the two propositions put forward above, that the criminal law was improved by the development of its moral content through the *mens rea* concept, implies that the evolution of *mens rea* as a prerequisite for conviction has rendered the modern criminal law a more effective instrument of social regulation than its primitive forerunner. In the long run, effective law-enforcement depends upon the support of the community. It has already been observed[13] that as far back as the Anglo-Saxons, long before the emergence of a general theory of *mens rea*, the lawmakers deemed it advisable to accord official recognition to the distinction between intentional and unintentional wrongs. It can scarcely be doubted that a law which seeks to distinguish between just and unjust punishment is more readily obeyed, and therefore more effective, than a law which strikes in blind disregard of the *mores* of the community.

[11] Radzinowicz, *A History of English Criminal Law*, Vol. I; *Report of the Royal Commission on Capital Punishment*, 1949–1953, (U.K.) Cmd. 8932; *Report of the Commission of Inquiry on Capital Punishment*, 1959, (Ceylon) Sessional Paper XIV.
[12] Tappan, *Crime, Justice and Correction*, Ch. 20; *Report of the Departmental Committee on Corporal Punishment*, 1938, (U.K.) Cmd. 5684; *Report of the Advisory Council on the Treatment of Offenders*, 1960, (U.K.) Cmnd. 1213.
[13] Above, n. 8.

It is against this background that the rise of the modern doctrine of strict responsibility[14] for minor statutory offences must be viewed. The historical facts are well known and need not be repeated in any detail here.[15] The starting point is generally taken to be the English case of *Woodrow*[16] in 1846, in which a licensed tobacco dealer was convicted of having adulterated tobacco in his possession even though it was proved that the tobacco had been adulterated in the course of manufacture and that the dealer, who had bought it in good faith, neither knew nor had any reason to suspect the adulteration. Contemporaneously, but apparently independently,[17] the same judicial attitude towards statutory offences of a similarly regulatory nature began to manifest itself in the U.S.A.

In a little over a century this new doctrine, that *mens rea* forms no part of the definition of a regulatory offence, has gone from strength to strength. At the present day it embraces a vast area of law of immediate concern to almost every member of the community capable of incurring criminal responsibility. Sayre, writing in 1933,[18] divided regulatory offences into seven broad classes, with nine sub-classes, but even then found himself obliged to add an eighth, comprising "violations of general police regulations, passed for the safety, health, or well-being of the community", as a sort of catch-all for the unclassifiable. The draftsmen of the American Law Institute's Model Penal Code, merely by way of giving "some indication of the range"[19] of strict responsibility at the present day, cite cases from the U.S.A., England, Canada and Australia to illustrate forty-two distinct types of offences within its scope. At a United Nations seminar on the role of the criminal law held in Tokyo in May 1960, lawyers from countries so diverse as Australia, Cambodia, China, Hong Kong,

---

[14] Hall, *op. cit.*, 326, regards the term "strict responsibility" as applicable even to an analysis of negligence. This, it is submitted, is confusing. As the terms "strict responsibility" and "negligence" are customarily used, while it is true that both refer to responsibility without advertence, negligence implies a defence of due care but strict responsibility does not. The customary usage will be adhered to in the text, so that strict responsibility means liability to conviction on proof of *actus reus* only, without proof of intention, recklessness or negligence.

[15] The classical account is by Sayre, "Public Welfare Offences" (1933) 33 *Columbia Law Review*, 55, 56–67. See also Starrs, "The Regulatory Offense in Historical Perspective" in *Essays in Criminal Science* (ed. Mueller), Ch. 9.

[16] (1846) 15 M. & W. 404; 153 E.R. 907.

[17] Sayre, *op. cit.*, 67. He sees the American development as starting with *Barnes* v. *State* (1849) 19 Conn. 398, in which it was held that the offence of selling liquor to a common drunkard was committed even if the seller did not know that the buyer was a common drunkard. (*Ibid.*, 63.)

[18] Sayre's classification is reproduced in n. 3 above.

[19] Tentative Draft No. 4, s. 2.05, Comment 141–145.

India, Indonesia, Korea, Japan, New Zealand, Philippines, Sarawak and Thailand contributed to the discussion on this subject.[20] A depth study of Wisconsin statutes in 1956[21] revealed that of 1,113 statutes creating criminal offences[22] which were in force in 1953, no less than 660 used language in the definitions of the offences which omitted all reference to a mental element, and which therefore, under the canons of construction which have come to govern these matters, left it open to the courts to impose strict responsibility if they saw fit.

The social importance of strict responsibility in the criminal law is therefore clear beyond argument. The question is whether it goes beyond the necessity of the case. Faced with a widespread acceptance of the doctrine by the judiciary, and the apparent acquiescence of the legislature, as evidenced by the Wisconsin study, in this judicial attitude over a range of offences which now almost certainly out-numbers offences requiring *mens rea* or negligence,[23] it is tempting to conclude that the doctrine is justified by its very success. This, indeed, appears to have been the view of Professor Sayre, who seems to have felt that since strict responsibility arose in the context of certain social conditions, it was therefore justified by those conditions.[24] Similarly, in his most recent reference to the subject, Dean Roscoe Pound adheres[25] to the view that strict responsibility for

---

[20] United Nations Seminar on the Role of Substantive Criminal Law in the Protection of Human Rights and the Purposes and Legitimate Limits of Penal Sanctions, Tokyo, Japan, May, 1960, *Proceedings*, 28–34.

[21] Remington, Robinson and Zick, "Liability Without Fault Criminal Statutes" [1956] *Wisconsin Law Review*, 625, 636, Table V.

[22] Defined as offences rendering the offender liable on conviction to fine or imprisonment or both. (*Ibid.*, 626, n. 2.)

[23] The Wisconsin study also demonstrated that by far the highest density of neutral language (*i.e.*, language omitting all reference to a mental element) in the definitions of offences was to be found in just those areas of administrative regulation of society in which modern legislatures are most prolifically active. "Such a concentration is found at the tension points of modern society: Business regulation, public health and safety, and the conservation of resources for planned futures." (*Ibid.*, 636.)

[24] "The decisions permitting convictions of light police offences without proof of a guilty mind came just at the time when the demands of an increasingly complex social order required additional regulation of an administrative character unrelated to questions of personal guilt; the movement also synchronised with the trend of the day away from nineteenth century individualism toward a new sense of the importance of collective interests. . . . The interesting fact that the same development took place in both England and the United States at about the same time strongly indicates that the movement has been not merely an historical accident but the result of the changing social conditions and beliefs of the day." (*Op. cit.*, 67.) "With respect to public welfare offences involving light penalties the abandonment of the classic requirement of *mens rea* is probably a sound development." (*Ibid.*, 84.)

[25] For an earlier statement see *The Spirit of the Common Law*, 52: "The good sense of courts has introduced a doctrine of acting at one's peril with respect to statutory crimes which expresses the needs of society." (1921.)

regulatory offences is based on "the social interest in the general security",[26] without, however, demonstrating either that this social interest is best served in this way, or that the advantages outweigh the disadvantages.

Now, this opinion may be right: it may indeed be that liability to conviction without proof of *mens rea* is necessary nowadays to the efficient regulation of society. But taking into account that it is the machinery of the criminal courts which is being used for this social regulation, and that for many centuries those courts have administered a law in which the *mens rea* concept has become increasingly prominent, one is entitled to inquire what may be the reasons on which the opinion is based, what the arguments designed to convince the reader that the modern phenomenon of strict responsibility not only is, but also ought to be.

The arguments which have been put forward are not lightly to be brushed aside. They have convinced generations of judges and many academic scholars that strict responsibility is here to stay because it serves a useful and necessary purpose in adapting the criminal law to current social pressures. Nevertheless, they have not convinced everyone. Persistent and continuing conflicts of opinion in the courts are reflected in the growing volume of mutually irreconcilable decisions, some in favour of strict responsibility, others, often distinguishable only on some trivial difference in the facts or between two similar statutes, against it.[27] Outside the courts scholars of the highest eminence are not wanting to support the view that strict responsibility entailing penal sanctions, however slight, has not been shown justified in either theory or practice.[28] Their criticisms of the

[26] I *Jurisprudence*, 448 (1959).
[27] A perfect example, often cited, is the contrast between *Cundy* v. *Le Cocq* (1884) 13 Q.B.D. 207, and *Sherras* v. *De Rutzen* [1895] 1 Q.B. 918. In *Cundy* v. *Le Cocq* the charge was laid under the Licensing Act, 1872, s. 13: "If any licensed person . . . sells any intoxicating liquor to any drunken person, he shall be liable to a penalty." These words were held to create strict responsibility, so that ignorance by the licensee that his customer was drunk was no defence. In *Sherras* v. *De Rutzen* the charge was laid under s. 16 (2) of the same Act: "If any licensed person . . . supplies any liquor . . . to any constable on duty . . . he shall be liable to a penalty." These words were held to imply a requirement of *mens rea*, so that ignorance by the licensee that his customer was a policeman on duty was a defence. Only the most trivial distinctions can be drawn between the two cases by reference either to the statute or to the facts. The determinative factor seems to have been that Stephen and Mathew JJ., who decided *Cundy* v. *Le Cocq*, approved of strict responsibility, whereas Day and Wright JJ., who decided *Sherras* v. *De Rutzen*, did not.
[28] Glanville Williams, *Criminal Law: The General Part* (2nd ed.), 255–261; Hall, *General Principles of Criminal Law* (2nd ed.), 342–351; Hart, "The Aims of the Criminal Law" (1958) 23 *Law and Contemporary Problems*, 401, 422–425.

arguments in favour of the doctrine are cogent. These arguments, and their refutations, are as follows.

Legislative intention

(i) *Argument*

Pride of place should certainly be given to the argument from legislative intention, according to which strict responsibility is the creation of the legislature and not the courts. "Most of what has been written heretofore has dealt largely with analysis and rationalisation of appellate decisions. This is justified only if the court plays the dominant role in the determination of whether fault is a prerequisite of criminal responsibility."[29]

A moment's reflection will show that in this area the courts do not and cannot play the dominant role commonly credited to them. Their function is to interpret statutes, not to improve upon the actions of the sovereign legislature by inserting into penal statutes words which would improve them in point of justice.[30] If the legislature, presumably as an act of policy, creates and defines a new statutory offence of a "merely admonitory"[31] kind without inserting into the definition any words indicative of an intention that no one should be convicted of that offence unless proved to have been at fault, then it is beyond the proper constitutional function of the courts to imply any such words in defiance of the plain statement in the statute.

Moreover, if the courts embark upon a process of modifying penal legislation in accordance with currently fashionable notions of justice, what was at the time of its enactment a clear, easily comprehensible law will come to be surrounded with quite unnecessary uncertainty, the future attitude of the courts to that and similar laws becoming unpredictable in the absence of direct authority. Indeed, failure on the part of the courts hitherto to adhere consistently to the principle that the legislature should be taken to mean only what it says has led to just that situation at the present time.

"In the present connection the courts have manifested an increasing readiness to assume the role of legislators, and to fill imagined lacunae in penal statutes by the conjectural emendations of judges. The result

---

[29] [1956] *Wisconsin Law Review*, 625.
[30] *Myerson* v. *Collard* (1918) 25 C.L.R. 154, 168, *per* Higgins J.
[31] [1946] *Wisconsin Law Review*, 172.

has been lamentable. Penal statutes have acquired appendages of judge-made law based upon the conjectures of judges as to what the Legislature would have provided if it had addressed its mind to a matter, where there is nothing to suggest that the Legislature ever thought about it at all or that the appendage would have survived if it had been included as part of the bill. A fertile field of litigation has been created; multitudes of reported cases have come into existence, many of them irreconcilable, in which the common law rule has been treated as excluded or not excluded upon judge-made indicia derived from cases in which there has often been a difference of opinion as to so-called necessary implications; and no one can now be reasonably sure of the effect of a penal statute until it has been tested by prosecutions."[32]

Interference by the courts with the plain words of penal statutes is thus not merely unconstitutional but undesirable also when tested pragmatically by reference to the results to which it has led. To inquire whether the doctrine of strict responsibility as worked out in the courts is justified or goes beyond the necessity of the case is therefore beside the point, for the doctrine is not primarily the work of the courts.

(ii) *Refutation*

The objection to the view that unless the definition of a statutory offence includes a specific reference to a mental element it is to be presumed that the legislature did not intend such an element to form part of the offence, is that it arbitrarily and artificially limits the legal context by reference to which the meaning of the words actually used must be discovered.

"Every criminal statute is expressed elliptically. It is not possible in drafting to state all the qualifications and exceptions that are intended. One does not, for instance, when creating a new offence, enact that persons under eight years of age cannot be convicted. Nor does one enact the defence of insanity or duress.[33] The exemptions belong to the general part of the criminal law, which is implied into specific offences. . . . [W]here the criminal law is codified . . . this general part is placed by itself in the code and is not repeated for each individual crime. Now the law of *mens rea* belongs to the general

---

[32] *Turnbull* (1943) 44 S.R. (N.S.W.) 108, 110, *per* Jordan C.J.
[33] The applicability of the general defences to a criminal charge to an offence of strict responsibility is discussed below, Ch. 9.

part of the criminal law, and it is not reasonable to expect [the legislature] every time it creates a new crime to enact it or even to make reference to it."[34]

Since there is no doubt that in reference to nearly all[35] statutory crimes other than regulatory offences the courts do without hesitation imply the general part of the criminal law, including the doctrine of *mens rea*, unless expressly excluded by the definition of the offence in question, the adoption of a different and intellectually unimpressive mode of interpretation for regulatory offences must be justified on grounds other than legislative intention as gathered from the literal words used.

This contention is strongly reinforced by the conclusions reached in the 1956 depth study of Wisconsin statutes already referred to.[36] The first five of these conclusions were as follows:

(1) A large percentage of criminal statutes in Wisconsin do not expressly require proof of fault for conviction.[37]
(2) There is no statute which expressly provides for liability without fault.
(3) There is practically no information available as to what the legislature actually intended when a particular statute was passed.
(4) Criteria proposed by courts and analysts for determining whether fault is required fail to explain adequately the pattern found in current criminal statutes in Wisconsin.
(5) The dominant characteristic of the criminal statutes of Wisconsin is their ambiguity on the issue of the requirement of fault.

The importance of the Wisconsin study to the general problem of strict responsibility in the criminal law can hardly be overestimated. In this chapter the conclusion will be reached that all of the arguments hitherto put forward in favour of imposing strict responsibility for regulatory offences are either demonstrably wrong or else, and this is the important point in relation particularly to legislative intention, rest upon unproved assumptions. A dominant characteristic of nearly all factual assertions so far made in discussing this

---

[34] Glanville Williams, *Criminal Law: The General Part* (2nd ed.), 259–260.
[35] Not all: see n. 5, above.
[36] [1956] *Wisconsin Law Review*, 625.
[37] "In this study, 'subjective fault' requires in general that the actor be aware of the nature of his conduct or of the harmful results which he has caused or the danger which he has created." (*Ibid.*, 628. See also Table V, 636.)

part of the law has been the total absence of evidence either in support or in refutation.

From this point of view, attention is particularly directed to conclusions (2), (3) and (5). If it is accepted, as it reasonably may be, that Wisconsin statutes are typical of the general pattern of legislation in this area, then the argument that strict responsibility is merely the application by the courts of a clearly expressed legislative intention must be rejected as inconsistent with the only available evidence. Not only is there no statute which in terms imposes responsibility without fault: there is practically no information available as to what the legislature did intend, and the obvious source of such information, the statutory wording itself, is vitiated by ambiguity. Ambiguity brings the court back to where it started in the search for a meaning; in which case no reason can be gathered from the *legal* implications of the statutory words why the general part of the criminal law, including the doctrine of *mens rea*, should not be implied into penal sections in accordance with the usual rule. If no justification for abandoning the usual rule is to be found by reference to the purely legal implications of the statutory words, such justification must be sought outside the statute.

One further comment may be made on the argument from legislative intention as presented herein. Responsibility for the present and continuing, judicial conflict on how best to ascertain the intention of the legislature, with consequential confusion in the law, was placed at the door of those who have tried to read *mens rea* requirements into minor penal statutes instead of following the simpler course of literal interpretation.[38] It can now be seen that, if anything, the contrary is the case: confusion and doubt have been spread, not by those who have tried to adhere to well-established principles of the criminal law, but by those who, for reasons which are inadequate so far as the law itself is concerned, have displaced the traditional canons of construction without providing a coherent and acceptable doctrine in their stead. Moreover, it is not the case that the present confusion, which all agree to be undesirable, can be effaced only by adopting the literal approach. Any approach would produce order, although not necessarily justice, so long as it satisfied the tests of comprehensibility and consistency.

---

[38] It is just another oddity of this very odd part of the law that strict construction of penal statutes, normally a valuable safeguard for the defendant, here results in a formidable extension of criminal responsibility.

History

(i) *Argument*

If the argument from legislative intention is accepted, it absolves the courts from the charge of creating unnecessary injustice. It does not, however, on any view dispose of the further question whether strict responsibility, whoever invented it, is defensible on its merits as a measure of social protection. The first line of defence on this issue is the argument from history. According to Sayre, "the interesting fact that the same development took place in both England and the United States at about the same time strongly indicates that the movement has been not merely an historical accident but the result of the changing social conditions and beliefs of the day."[39]

To the fact of original temporal coincidence may now be added the equally impressive fact of geographical distribution which has already been commented upon.[40] When a socio-legal phenomenon arises with apparently independent spontaneity in two different societies at the same stage of development, flourishes rapidly in those societies, and then spreads with equal success to other countries in response to similar social pressures, it is idle to inquire whether the phenomenon in question serves a useful purpose. Unless its utility were considerable, its appearance would be neither so inevitable nor so widespread.

(ii) *Refutation*

The short answer to the argument from history is that it is at best an explanation and not a justification. To sustain this view is not necessary to maintain, contrary to the apparent fact, that strict responsibility for minor regulatory offences owed its original appearance in *Woodrow*[41] to nothing more impressive than accident. The truth of the matter is that no one knows *why* the doctrine appeared when it did, or at all; we know only *how* it appeared.

Sayre conjectured[42] that strict responsibility grew up as "the not unnatural result of two pronounced movements which mark twentieth-century criminal administration, *i.e.*, (1) the shifts of emphasis from the protection of individual interests which marked nineteenth-century criminal administration to the protection of public and social

[39] 33 *Columbia Law Review*, 67.
[40] See n. 20, above.
[41] (1846) 15 M. & W. 404; 153 E.R. 907.
[42] 33 *Columbia Law Review*, 67–70.

interests and (2) the growing utilization of the criminal law machinery
to enforce, not only the true crimes of the classic law, but also a new
type of twentieth-century regulatory measure involving no moral
delinquency".

Even taken at the level of an explanation this account fails to
convince, for on his own showing Professor Sayre believed that the
general "growth of a distinct group of offences punishable without
regard to any mental element dates from about the middle of the
nineteenth century";[43] that "the conscious beginning in England of
the movement to do away with the requirement of *mens rea* for petty
police offences" began with *Stephens*[44] in 1866;[45] and that "the
new doctrine became firmly established in Massachusetts" also in
the 1860s.[46]

It may be, of course, that Sayre's contentions in this regard can be
reconciled by reading him as meaning that conditions which emerged
in the nineteenth century persisted in the twentieth century, although
this is not what he said. Even so, and even if it be accepted without
further demonstration that the two movements he mentions did in
fact influence the rise of strict responsibility, as opposed to being
merely contemporaneous therewith, his findings do not help the
cause of strict responsibility at the present day. In the first place, it
does not follow that *because* there has been a shift of emphasis from
private right to public interest, *therefore* the public interest in the
context of the regulatory offence is best served, or even satisfactorily
served, by abandoning the requirement of fault as a prerequisite for
conviction. No more does it follow, what is implied by the mere
juxtaposition of private right and public interest, that there is any
necessary conflict between the two. Evidence, as usual, is lacking.

The importance of the contention that the machinery of the
criminal law is being utilised to carry out work for which it was not
originally designed is that it underpins the justification for abandoning *mens rea* on the ground that there is no time to inquire into states
of mind. This argument will be dealt with next. It is pertinent to
observe at this point, however, that once again it is at least doubtful
whether the assertion that the criminal courts were not intended for
the administration of minor regulatory offences is supportable. Sayre

[43] *Ibid.*, 56.
[44] (1886) L.R. 1 Q.B. 702.
[45] 33 *Columbia Law Review*, 59.
[46] *Ibid.*, 64.

himself conceded[47] that punishment of those obstructing the King's highway was among the early functions of the criminal law. What is the basis of a parking offence if not obstruction of the public highway?[48] The true problem seems to be that the courts nowadays have too much work to do, not that they are being presented with work outside their traditional function.[49]

Necessity

(i) *Argument*

Proponents of strict responsibility recognise, of course, that the argument from history comes to an end with history. The world at any given time is composed entirely of relics of the past. Even if the historical argument is accepted as far as it goes, it might be maintained that however inevitable the doctrine may have been in bygone times, strict responsibility at the present day is an unjust anachronism standing against the mainstream of development of the criminal law. This contention calls forth the argument from necessity, whereby it is asserted that owing to the great pressure of work upon the minor criminal courts nowadays, it has become impracticable to inquire into *mens rea* in each prosecution for a regulatory offence.

"Criminal courts are today swamped with great floods of cases which they were never designed to handle; the machinery creaks under the strain. . . . The numbers of such cases are rapidly increasing. . . . It is needless to point out, that swamped with such appalling inundations of cases of petty violations, the lower criminal courts would be physically unable to examine the subjective intent of each defendant. . . ."[50]

Unless the machinery of law enforcement in this area is to break down altogether, some simplification of the process of prosecution must be found. The obvious step to take is to jettison the requirement of a guilty mind, for this requirement is inappropriate to petty violations of the kind in question.[51] It is all very well for the

[47] *Ibid.*, 69.
[48] Cynics may answer that the object of parking offences is indirect taxation.
[49] It is in fact entirely clear that at least from Tudor times many of the duties of justices of the peace have been purely regulatory in nature. For a recent general survey see Osborne, *Justices of the Peace, 1361–1848. A History or our Magistracy during Five Centuries.* See also I Holdsworth, *History of English Law* (7th ed., revised by Goodhart and Hanbury), 285–298; Starrs, "The Regulatory Offense in Historical Perspective" in *Essays in Criminal Science* (ed. Mueller), Ch. 9.
[50] Sayre, 33 *Columbia Law Review*, 69.
[51] "The ready enforcement which is vital for effective petty regulation on an extended scale can be gained only by a total disregard of the state of mind." (Sayre, *op. cit.*, 70.)

theoretician to argue from moral doctrines appropriate to serious criminal guilt. Let him watch a minor criminal court working hard against time, trying to dispose of its business against ever-increasing odds in the discharge of its duty to protect the day-to-day interests of the community: then he will become aware of the true nature of the problem. There is simply no time for *mens rea*.

(ii) *Refutation*

It is to be conceded that even if one disagrees with the view that regulatory offences are outside the traditional business of the criminal courts,[52] the argument from necessity is not thereby invalidated, for it may still be true that pressure of work prevents *mens rea* inquiries. However, when this argument is stripped of historical trappings it stands revealed in all its immoral simplicity. In no other context has the contention been solemnly advanced that if the law takes up too much time, the courts are entitled to jettison such part of it as they find tedious to administer.

It may be said that this is unfair exaggeration; that the true conflict here is not between justice and injustice but between competing methods of achieving substantial justice; that the question is whether the public interest is better served by the speedy disposal of what are, after all, minor offences which the defendant would probably like to face up to and forget about as soon as possible, or by a meticulous inquiry into the perhaps largely theoretical question whether the defendant can properly be said to have been at fault. If the latter, why not introduce the whole panoply of judge and jury instead of mere summary justice?

There are a number of objections to this plausible rationalisation of the present state of affairs. The first is that, no matter how the argument is presented, the courts have no power to achieve speed of administration at the expense of substantive law. It is no answer to this point to say that since strict responsibility is undoubtedly with us, the courts must now have such a power as far as regulatory offences are concerned, whatever the constitutional position may have been before the doctrine appeared. Certainly strict responsibility is with us. But the question now under discussion is not whether strict responsibility is with us, but whether its continued existence can be justified by reference to the argument from necessity in so far as that argument rests on the simple fact that the courts have too much work

---

[52] See n. 49, above.

to get through. It is submitted that it obviously cannot be: the courts do not have, and at no relevant time[53] have had, any power to modify the law to facilitate the flow of judicial business.

The second objection to the argument from necessity is that the courts in fact do have regard to the moral blameworthiness of the defendant, for they take it into account in deciding on the appropriate sentence. It is not the case that the maximum sentence is invariably imposed on conviction of a regulatory offence, or indeed the minimum sentence or any other fixed proportion of the possible.[54] If automatic maxima are not imposed, it follows, unless anyone be hardy enough to argue that the amount of the sentence for a regulatory offence is a matter of chance inclination by the court, that some criterion must be used to determine the sentences which are actually imposed. The point need not be laboured that this criterion is customarily the court's estimate of the gravity and anti-social significance of the defendant's behaviour in the circumstances charged. Moreover, the defendant is entitled to address the court in mitigation of sentence as much for a regulatory offence as for any other offence. Since the court's time can be and frequently is, taken up by *mens rea* considerations for one purpose, it is singularly unconvincing to argue that the court is unable to take it into account for another purpose in the same case.

The third, and concluding, objection to be made to the argument from supposed necessity is that it is misconceived. The considerations adduced in support show one thing and one thing only: that there should be an improvement in the administration of petty criminal justice, either by creating more courts of the same kind as already exist to cope with the increased volume of work, or by transferring the trial of regulatory offences to a new structure of courts or administrative agencies altogether.[55] This demonstration has nothing to do with *mens rea*.

---

[53] This reservation is made to allow for the possibly imperfect differentiation in early times between the legislature and the judiciary. *Cf.* Richardson and Sayles, "Parliaments and Great Councils in Medieval England" (1961) 77 *Law Quarterly Review*, 213 and 401.

[54] It is true that the court cannot take blameworthiness into account where there is a fixed statutory penalty, as commonly with a fine for a parking offence; and that in this situation abandonment of *mens rea* may result in saving of time. But this consideration still fails to meet the objection that the courts have no power to do any such thing. Moreover, the great majority of regulatory offences do not carry fixed penalties.

[55] Sayre, *op. cit.*, 69; Hall, *General Principles of Criminal Law* (2nd ed.), 359.

Implementation

(i) *Argument*

One of the main planks in the argument from necessity was the contention that the requirement of a guilty mind is inappropriate to minor regulatory offences. In its expanded form this contention is the argument from implementation, which is closely related to the argument from legislative intention and runs as follows.

It is the duty of the courts, having decided what a statute means according to its plain words, to use their best endeavours to implement the legislative purpose thus revealed. Clearly the object of regulatory offences is to enforce compliance with the statutes to which they belong. The duty of the courts is therefore to facilitate rather than obstruct this enforcement. It is the fact that in the vast majority of regulatory precautions, it would be impossible for the prosecutor to produce evidence of the state of the defendant's mind at the relevant time. What hope has the prosecutor of proving that a man who exceeded the parking limit in a restricted area intended to do so, or did so with knowledge of all the relevant facts? None whatever. Therefore, for the courts to require such proof would amount to nullifying the legislation they are supposed to be enforcing. That is one reason why *mens rea* is inappropriate to regulatory offences. There are two others.

The first relates to the penalty. If a man is charged with an offence, such as murder, which carries a long term of imprisonment, or death, on conviction, it is entirely proper that care should be taken to ensure that the act he is accused of committing was no accident or excusable error. But the punishment for a regulatory offence is light, often almost trivial, such as a small fine. Its object is not to deal with a formidably dangerous enemy of society[56] but to administer a sharp rebuke to an ordinary citizen who has lapsed a little in his standards of public responsibility. A searching inquiry into his precise state of mind when lapsing is out of all proportion to the demands of the occasion.

The second remaining argument on the inappropriateness of *mens rea* is that the authorities, partly out of a natural sense of fairness and partly because they are too busy to do otherwise, do not prosecute except in clear cases. This means that conviction is virtually a fore-

---

[56] Although it may be quite rational to regard those who fail to comply with food and drug regulations as a considerable social menace. *Cf.* Ross, *Sin and Society* (reference from Hall, *op. cit.*, 331, n. 23).

gone conclusion in regulatory offence prosecutions. To prolong the process by requiring proof of *mens rea* is an irresponsible waste of time and trouble.

(ii) *Refutation*

The argument from implementation rests on three assertions: that proof of *mens rea* by the prosecutor in the normal case would be impracticable, and that to require such proof would therefore nullify the legislation; that the penalty on conviction of a regulatory offence is too slight for conscientious inquiry into moral guilt to be reasonably proportionate to the seriousness of the question at issue; and that the authorities in fact prosecute only in clear cases where *mens rea* can be taken for granted.

The first of these assertions raises issues which are more conveniently discussed later on in connection with possible remedies for the present situation. Briefly, the objection here is twofold. In the first place, the mere fact that the prosecution may find its task of establishing guilt difficult is of itself no reason for depriving the defendant of his customary safeguards. "No doubt prosecutors would have their tasks made easy if no defence were possible; but the desirability (if it be desirable) of such a state of affairs has not yet been recognised as a principle of interpretation of statutes."[57]

Secondly, it does not follow that even if proof of *mens rea* is impossible in certain types of cases, the only solution is to go to the other extreme by denying the mental state of the defendant any relevance to the question of responsibility at all. There are plenty of possibilities between these alternatives. For example, there would be nothing discernibly detrimental to the administration of justice in relieving the prosecutor of the task of proving *mens rea*, or any lesser degree of fault, but leaving it open to the defendant to exculpate himself by establishing the absence of *mens rea* on the balance of probability.[58]

[57] *Hunt* v. *Maloney* [1959] Qd. R. 164, 171, *per* Stanley J.
[58] This point has already been conceded in some legislatures by the introduction of statutory defences enabling D to escape liability for some particular offence by proving the fault of a third party, or that he took all reasonable precautions, or that he took a warranty from a vendor that material sold complied with statutory standards. For recent examples see Food and Drugs Act, 1955 (Eng.), s. 113; Health Act, 1956 (Vic.), ss. 291, 298, 300; Offices Act, 1960 (Eng.), s. 1 (6). The idea is not at all new: Factories Act, 1937 (Eng.), s. 137 (1); Fertilisers and Feeding Stuffs Act, 1926 (Eng.), s. 7 (1); Merchandise Marks Act, 1887 (Eng.), s. 2 (2). For a variation by way of a defence of impracticability see Mines and Quarries Act, 1954 (Eng.), s. 157.

The assertion, in effect, that the penalty on conviction of a regulatory offence is too slight to be worth worrying about is entirely without foundation. There is overwhelming evidence not only that strict responsibility is applied in cases where the possible penalty includes a very large fine, or even imprisonment, but also that such penalties actually have been imposed after conviction on a strict responsibility basis.

One of the most conspicuous examples is the leading case of *United States* v. *Balint*[59] in which the Supreme Court of the United States applied strict responsibility to section 2 of the Anti-Narcotic Act of 1914 which made it an offence, *inter alia*, to sell narcotics otherwise than in accordance with the terms of that section. The maximum penalty on conviction was five years' imprisonment or a fine of $2,000 or both. In an English case, *Chajutin* v. *Whitehead*,[61] strict responsibility was applied to an offence of possessing an altered passport contrary to the Aliens Order, the effect being that the defendant was convicted without proof that he knew of the alteration. The punishment imposed was deportation, a result which might well have been even more serious for the defendant than a heavy fine or imprisonment. In another English case, *Sorsky*,[62] the question was whether conspiracy to commit an offence of strict responsibility was itself such an offence. After a confused discussion, which started from the premise that *mens rea* need not be proved against the defendant but ended inconclusively, the Court of Criminal Appeal upheld the conviction. The sentence imposed was imprisonment for twelve months, a fine of £1,000, and liability for one-half of the costs of the prosecution. In the Australian case of *Brown* v. *Green*,[63] *mens rea* was held excluded from the offence of a landlord receiving from a tenant a rent in excess of the amount lawfully chargeable, the maximum penalty for which was a fine of £250 and imprisonment for six months.

There are but four examples from a multitude. It is not possible, consistently with the evidence which for once is available on a strict

---

[59] (1922) 258 U.S. 250; 42 Sup. Ct. 301.
[60] Sayre, *op. cit.*, 81, could justify the decision "only on the ground of the extreme popular disapproval of the sale of narcotics"; in other words, only on the ground of popular prejudice. He gives some other striking American decisions at 80–83.
[61] [1938] K.B. 506.
[62] (1944) 30 Cr. App. R. 84.
[63] (1951) 84 C.L.R. 285. The question whether reasonable mistake of fact would have been a defence to the charge was left open as there was no evidence of a reasonable mistake.

responsibility point, to argue that conviction of a regulatory offence cannot have serious consequences in terms of penalty. Moreover, it is obvious that in such cases as the foregoing, the damage of conviction does not end with the formal punishment.[64] It has been pointed out[65] that one of the most serious consequences of an error of justice in strict responsibility offences of the order now under discussion is the moral obloquy, not to mention highly material disadvantage, of merely going on record as convicted. It is not infrequently, and quite properly, enacted that conviction of a certain number of offences against the liquor licensing laws results in automatic loss of the defendant's trading licence.[66] Even more familiar are laws that conviction a certain number of times under the motor traffic legislation results in automatic disqualification from driving.[67] A business reputation may be impaired, and certainly will not be enhanced, by conviction for some trading offence; an example would be a pharmacist convicted of failing to keep a proper record of the disposal of dangerous drugs in his possession.[68] To bring about secondary consequences of this kind without giving the accused person the opportunity to defend himself underlines the absurdity of defending strict responsibility on the ground that the penalty is small.

It is possible that some might wish to transfer the more obviously indefensible examples of injustice in this part of the law to the category of regrettable but necessary sacrifices for the common good, confessing the undesirability of individual injustice but avoiding the obvious inference on the ground that it is outweighed by the benefit

---

[64] A point overlooked in the not infrequent judicial statements that where the defendant is morally innocent, the penalty should be merely nominal (*e.g.*, *Parker* v. *Alder* [1899] 1 Q.B. 20, 26; *Hobbs* v. *Winchester Corporation* [1910] 2 K.B. 471, 485). In *Duncan* v. *Ellis* (1916) 21 C.L.R. 379, the High Court of Australia went so far as to penalise the successful prosecutor in costs.

[65] Glanville Williams, *Criminal Law: The General Part* (2nd ed.), 255. It is this consideration which has led the framers of the American Law Institute's Model Penal Code to adopt the new term "violation" for an infraction of penal law which ought not to carry the moral stigma of conviction for crime; Tentative Draft No. 4, Comment 140; Tentative Draft No. 2, Comment 9. See also Gausewitz, "Reclassification of Certain Offenses as Civil instead of Criminal" (1937) 12 *Wisconsin Law Review*, 365; Conway, "Is Criminal or Civil Procedure Proper for Enforcement of Traffic Laws" [1959] *Wisconsin Law Review*, 418; Perkins, "The Civil Offense" (1952) 100 *University of Pennsylvania Law Review*, 832 (reprinted in *Criminal Law*, 692–710).

[66] For example, Licensing Act, 1953 (Eng.), s. 120 (3); Licensing Act, 1958 (Vic.), s. 142; Licensing Act, 1932–1960 (S.A.), s. 77 (2).

[67] For example, Road Traffic Act, 1960 (Eng.), s. 104 (1) (*b*); Transport Act, 1949 (N.Z.), s. 41; Road Traffic Act, 1934–1959 (S.A.), s. 38*a* (1) *a*.

[68] For example, Poisons Act, 1934 (N.Z.), ss. 18, 19; Poisons Act, 1952–1956 (N.S.W.), s. 12; Poisons Act, 1958 (Vic.), s. 9.

to the general public interest. This is the last of the arguments made out in favour of strict responsibility. As such, it will be dealt with in its proper sequence. It is pertinent to observe at this point, however, that even if attention is thereby focused on the many regulatory offences, such as parking infringements, which undoubtedly do carry only an almost nominal sanction, the argument from the slightness of the penalty is not helped. There is no necessary connection between liability to conviction and extent of punishment. It is a pernicious and unsound doctrine that liability to conviction should be decided with one eye on the possible consequential punishment.

If it be thought that to exclude questions of punishment from questions of liability to conviction is too theoretical for the practical world, where both judges, magistrates and jurymen are likely to be affected in their deliberations by the probable consequences of their decisions, then it ought at least to be conceded that such considerations should influence the criminal law only in favour of the defendant, never against him. It is one thing to say, "If this man is convicted, a long sentence of imprisonment hangs over him; therefore let us be careful to ensure that every possibility of erroneous conviction is reduced to a minimum." It is quite another to say, "If this man is convicted, he will suffer at most a small fine which he can well afford to pay; let us therefore not worry too much about whether he deserves to be convicted at all." *As such*, the slightness of the penalty for a regulatory offence, even where the penalty is indeed slight, provides no ground whatever for abandoning the safeguards normally available to a defendant in criminal proceedings. It is only when slightness of penalty is linked with some other consideration, such as the need for speed in the administration of justice, that the argument wears even an appearance of plausibility.

Another consideration which may be conveniently interpolated here relates to the removal from the defendant to a regulatory offence charge in some jurisdictions of safeguards other than *mens rea* which are normally available to him in criminal proceedings. The usual rule of criminal law is that one is not responsible for the acts of another in the absence of such agreement or acquiescence in the actions of that other as would ground liability as principal in the second degree,[69] accessory before the fact, or conspirator; in other

---

[69] Or, of course, as principal in the first degree acting through an innocent agent or in pursuance of a common purpose.

words, in the absence of an appropriate *mens rea*.[70] It follows that if the *mens rea* requirement upon which this limitation of criminal responsibility is based is removed, there is no reason for not applying the doctrine of *respondeat superior*.[71] This is indeed the case: the defendant to a regulatory offence charge is not protected by the rule excluding vicarious responsibility from other parts of the criminal law.[72] Another safeguard denied him in the U.S.A.[73] is the requirement elsewhere in the criminal law that the case for the prosecution be proved beyond reasonable doubt. The American rule in regulatory offence cases is that no more than the balance of probability need be proved against the defendant.[74]

It is not clear why, when the defendant to a regulatory offence charge already has his position drastically weakened by the initial denial to him of the *mens rea* requirement, with the logical consequence that he is thereby incidentally exposed to vicarious responsibility for the wrongful acts of others, he should be put in a yet more hopeless situation by easing the normal standard of proof on a prosecutor. It is, however, clear that the damage done by the doctrine of strict responsibility is not confined to abrogation of *mens rea*. These additional liabilities to conviction which now go with that doctrine should also be borne in mind when evaluating its use to the community.

The third assertion upon which the argument from implementation relied was that the authorities prosecute only in cases of clear fault, so that denial of the *mens rea* requirement is a theoretical rather than a practical injustice. The first answer to be made to this contention is that, even if it is the fact that the authorities prosecute only in clear cases, this is no argument for modifying the substantive law. A guess may be hazarded that the police normally prosecute more serious

---

[70] *Huggins* (1730) 2 Ld. Raym. 1574; 92 E.R. 518. For a general discussion of vicarious responsibility in the criminal law see Sayre, "Criminal Responsibility for the Acts of Another." (1930) 43 *Harvard Law Review*, 689.

[71] *Mousell Bros.* v. *L. & N.W. Rly.* [1917] 2 K.B. 836; *R.* v. *Australasian Films Ltd.* (1921) 29 C.L.R. 195.

[72] The rule is the same in the U.S.A. See Perkins, *Criminal Law*, 696, n. 18.

[73] The courts have made no corresponding departure from principle in the British Commonwealth, although it is becoming common for the burden of proof of exculpation to be removed to the defendant by statute. See n. 58 above.

[74] This appears to be a consequence of the general American tendency to regard regulatory offences as civil rather than criminal proceedings. There is an analogy with the English rule imposing strict responsibility for public nuisances. For American authority see Perkins, *Criminal Law*, 696, n. 21. In one Australian case, *Jackson* v. *Butterworth* [1946] V.L.R. 330, a taxation prosecution was held to be a civil proceeding for burden of proof purposes.

offences only in cases which they think to be pretty clear for the good reason that both pressure of work and public relations militate against the opposite course; yet no one has been heard to argue that *mens rea* should be dropped from the definition of petty larceny, either on this ground or on the ground that the offence is trivial.[75] It is entirely improper to argue that the discretion of minor executive officials should replace the safeguards of substantive law, however slight the offence.

The second answer to the assertion is that, as with all other assertions in support of strict responsibility for which relevant evidence is available, it is demonstrably contrary to the fact. The law reports abound with judicial crocodile tears shed in cases where the convicted defendant was admitted on all sides to be entirely without moral fault.[76] This consideration has not prevented the authorities from prosecuting in these cases.[77]

Deterrence

(i) *Argument*

The penultimate argument put forward by the defenders of strict responsibility is that strict enforcement of regulatory statutes is a peculiarly effective deterrent to potential wrongdoers of the kind envisaged by this legislation. "Such statutes are not meant to punish the vicious will but to put pressure upon the thoughtless and inefficient to do their whole duty in the interest of public health or safety or morals."[78]

If a person knows that any error of judgment or failure to prevent prohibited acts on his part at all will lead to conviction, he is going to be as careful as it is humanly possible to be, more careful than if he knows that an excusable misfortune may be excused.

[75] *Cf.* Mannheim, "Mens Rea in German and English Law" (Part III) (1936) 18 *Journal of Comparative Legislation*, 78, 90.
[76] The English law reports are particularly rich in convictions of innocent people. For three recent examples see *Slatcher* v. *Smith* [1951] 2 K.B. 631; *Towers* v. *Gray* [1961] 2 Q.B. 351; and *Strong* v. *Dawtry* [1961] 1 W.L.R. 841. The English courts were also responsible for the most celebrated instance of arbitrary injustice in this whole field of law: *Larsonneur* (1933) 24 Cr. App. R. 74.
[77] *Cf.* Conclusion 8 in the Wisconsin study referred to above: "Though they have the power, administrators as a rule refrain from applying the criminal sanction unless they believe the offender to have been at fault. However, we know too little about the actual criteria employed by administrators in applying this type of criminal statute." [1956] *Wisconsin Law Review*, 626.
[78] Roscoe Pound, *The Spirit of the Common Law*, 52, quoted by Devlin J. in *Reynolds* v. *Austin* [1951] 2 K.B. 135, 149.

(ii) *Refutation*

The assertion that a potentially inefficient or thoughtless member of society will more effectively mend his ways if he knows that no excuse will be allowed for failure to achieve the statutory standard of behaviour than if he knows merely that a standard of care is exacted which is high but not perfect, is no more than an assumption for which no evidence can be produced in support. No one has ever carried out a controlled experiment whereby the incidence of a particular regulatory offence in a defined area was exactly measured under both a *mens rea* and a strict responsibility régime, police prosecuting practice remaining constant throughout the experimental period. This being so, the fact is that we have no idea what the social effect of strict responsibility has been. There is simply no relevant knowledge.[79]

This familiar state of affairs, however, does not preclude argument from general principles or by analogy from information in other fields. As far as information from other fields is concerned, the only conclusion to be drawn from what has been discovered so far about our assumptions in regard to deterrence is that where they are not based upon exact information they are almost invariably wrong. The most conspicuous examples are capital and corporal punishment, both of which have been shown to have no significant effect upon the rate of incidence of the crimes for which they have been imposed.[80] This should make us very hesitant to assert dogmatically that strict responsibility is self-evidently an effective deterrent in any field. We should become even more cautious when we remember that still less is there evidence of the effectiveness or otherwise of measures lying between the extremes of strict responsibility being imposed on the defendant and full *mens rea* being required to be proved by the prosecution, such as putting the burden of self-exculpation, by disproving *mens rea*' on the defendant.

Argument from general principle leads similarly to the conclusion that there is no ground for the belief that strict responsibility is a peculiarly effective deterrent. It must be admitted that if there is any substance in the deterrence theory at all, there must be knowledge on the part of the person aimed at that his actions may have either

---

[79] "May I add that I have never seen any evidence which supports the rationalisations made in support of such liability in penal law, especially that it actually raises standards and protects the public." (Hall, "The Three Fundamental Aspects of Criminal Law" in *Essays in Criminal Science* (ed. Mueller), 159, 163.)

[80] See nn. 11 and 12, above.

the threatened result or some similar consequence. It is scarcely maintainable that the vast majority of regulatory offence defendants have any thoughts on the matter at all until they are prosecuted.[81] Moreover, the present uncertainty about the range of the regulatory offences would render the best-informed defendant's opinions unreliable. General deterrence may therefore be dismissed as a serious argument.

Special deterrence confined to the particular defendant has no more substance. It is true that conviction on a strict responsibility basis may make the individual defendant more careful in future, but this possibility alone does not justify strict responsibility. In the first place, it applies only where the defendant has in fact been less careful than he might have been. It cannot make any improvement in a man who is shown to have taken all reasonable, or even all possible, care to prevent the proscribed occurrence.[82] Secondly, even where the defendant has been inefficient or thoughtless, there is no reason to suppose that his conduct in future cannot be improved by some method less unintelligently drastic than making it clear to him that in the instant case he would have been punished even if he had been very careful. Indeed, it can be plausibly argued that strict responsibility, by inducing an understandable cynicism, is more likely to produce a lowering of standards than a raising of them. Especially is this the case with the defendant who has taken every care to avoid transgressing the law.

On the question of punishment it is interesting to note here one of the more conspicuous of many inconsistencies between the arguments in favour of strict responsibility. It was argued that the purpose of the regulatory offence was not to punish so much as to put pressure on the thoughtless and careless. But if the penalties imposed were normally as slight as it is sometimes maintained that they are, the pressure applied would be singularly gentle; and if it were indeed true that they were scarcely worth worrying about, they would be

[81] Where, as is often the case, a regulatory offence affects a particular branch of trade or industry, a certain amount of publicity will be given to decisions of the courts through trade journals. There is also the general public awareness that wrongdoing is likely to infringe the criminal law. To this extent it may be argued that general deterrence can be operative, but there is no evidence that some doctrine less drastic than strict responsibility might not be as effective in this respect, as in others. *Cf.* Hart, "The Aims of the Criminal Law" (1958) 23 *Law and Contemporary Problems*, 401, 423.

[82] As in *Parker* v. *Alder* [1899] 1 Q.B. 20; *Duncan* v. *Ellis* (1916) 21 C.L.R. 379. See also the cases cited in n. 76, above.

for all purposes, practical or theoretical, quite ineffective. It cannot be argued at one and the same time that a given punishment is a significant social regulator but too insignificant to produce consequences worth worrying about.

Public interest

(i) *Argument*

Finally, the possibility of injustice in the particular case has to be faced. This the defenders of strict responsibility concede to be an evil, but they regard it as a necessary and not a very great evil. The necessity arises out of a conflict between the public interest and the interests of individuals. "All criminal law is a compromise between two fundamentally conflicting interests, that of the public which demands restraint of all who injure or menace the social well-being and that of the individual which demands maximum liberty and freedom from interference."[83]

Where regulatory statutes are concerned it is clear that in any such conflict the interest of the public must prevail, for by definition such statutes are designed to promote the well-being of the community at large, not merely the well-being of the community through the protection of some individuals in it. The nature of the conflict has already been demonstrated: the importance of general deterrence as against the claim of the individual to have his subjective fault proved; the importance of the speedy administration of law in a multitude of cases as against the desire of each individual defendant to have the charge against him investigated at length. Moreover, the slightness of the penalty reduces to a minimum the discomfort of being sacrificed for the common good. Indeed, where it is clear that the defendant is entirely without fault, penalty may be remitted altogether.

(ii) *Refutation*

"It is becoming increasingly recognized that strict liability has no place whatever in the criminal law; indeed, that it smacks of barbarism to punish people despite the fact that there is no reason for blaming them at all."[84] At the last ditch the proponents of strict responsibility seek to meet this objection to their views by pointing

---

[83] Sayre, (1933) 33 *Columbia Law Review*, 55, 68.
[84] Hall, *Essays in Criminal Science* (ed. Mueller), 159, 162.

to a supposed conflict between the interests of individuals and the
interest of the public at large, maintaining that this conflict must be
necessarily solved by subordinating the individual, even if this entails
injustice.

There is no need to answer the contention at length. It is apparent
from the foregoing discussion of other arguments that no such
conflict of interest has been demonstrated because it has not been
proved that strict responsibility is a necessary instrument of social
regulation. In so far as this allegation of want of proof depends on
the possibility that less drastic methods would achieve the same ends
as are aimed at by the doctrine of strict responsibility, it will be
discussed in the next chapter.

Conclusion

The conclusion is that strict responsibility is prima facie objectionable because it envisages the punishment of innocent people; is not
justified by any of the arguments which have been put forward in its
favour; and is supported by none of the available evidence.

CHAPTER 2

SANCTIONS AND BURDEN OF PROOF

Introduction

The conclusion reached at the end of the previous chapter, that the doctrine of strict responsibility was not justified in the criminal law, means that it ought to be eliminated. The abolition of strict responsibility, however, would not bring with it the automatic solution of the underlying problems of which it is the outward sign. There would still remain such questions as whether it is desirable to try a person accused of a regulatory offence upon the same principles of criminal responsibility as are appropriate to more serious crimes; if not, upon what principles he should be tried; and in what courts he should be tried. Even when amendments to the law are agreed upon, there remains the formidable problem of how best to put them into effect.

These difficulties will be explored in general terms in this chapter and the two following. The conclusions will be reached that regulatory offences are not for all purposes to be equated with more serious crimes, and that the best method of effecting reform depends upon the structure of the courts in the jurisdiction concerned.

The relevance of the sanction

There is no reason to doubt that trial by jury is in nearly all cases more favourable to the defendant under the common law system than trial by a court of summary jurisdiction.[1] Nevertheless it is generally accepted that the interest of the defendant is not the only interest relevant to a system of criminal trial. One of the reasons why the relatively lengthy and complicated process of jury trial is retained for the more serious crimes is that conviction of such a crime exposes the

---

[1] The best account of the merits and demerits of the jury sustem under modern conditions is in Glanville Williams, *The Proof of Guilt*, (3rd ed.) Ch. 10. Although in certain particular situations, such as a highly coloured sex case, a jury may be an inadequate guarantee to the defendant of a fair trial, Williams's general conclusion is that "in one way or another the jury system tends to the acquittal of criminals who if tried under a purely professional system would be convicted". See also his Chapter 11 on summary jurisdiction.

defendant to very damaging consequences in terms of punishment and public opprobrium. It follows that the less serious the punishment for a crime, the less reason there is on this ground for granting the defendant the right to jury trial.

As the ladder of crime is descended from the more to the less serious offences, the general interest of the community in dispatch of business and avoidance of unnecessary public expense increases in importance in relation to the defendant's particular interest in being protected from wrongful conviction.[1a] At some point in the scale this changing relationship between relevant interests renders jury trial out of proportion to the gravity of the offence charged. At this point the interests of the defendant are to some extent[2] subordinated to the interests of society in that he is deprived of the right to jury trial and may be brought before a court of summary jurisdiction only. Allowance is made for reasonable doubts about the point on the scale where the line should be drawn by the creation of an overlapping group of offences where the defendant is normally tried summarily but may demand jury trial if he wishes.[3]

Up to a point an analogous process of reasoning is permissible with the principles of responsibility appropriate to the different crimes. The difficulty is to avoid the common error of pushing the analogy too far.

It was said above[4] to be a pernicious and unsound doctrine that liability to conviction should be decided with one eye on the possible consequential punishment. This must not be taken to mean that the punishment prescribed for a crime has no relevance at all to the mental element required for that crime. One may cite the doctrine of constructive murder as an instance, especially in jurisdictions which retain the death penalty. Although the idea of constructive crime is repugnant in any context, there is no doubt that much of the force of

---

[1a] For the sake of social stability the community also has an ultimate interest in the avoidance of wrongful convictions; but for the purpose of the discussion in the text an antithesis is properly drawn between the more immediate interests of society in general and the defendant in particular.

[2] This should perhaps read "to some further extent", for to some extent the interests of society always prevail over those of the individual in a criminal prosecution. For example, even an innocent man may properly be arrested and kept in prison until acquitted if there are reasonable grounds for thinking he has committed a serious crime. Of course, not everyone would necessarily think that summary trial is to the defendant's disadvantage as compared with jury trial. For one thing it is quicker. See also n. 1 above.

[3] *e.g.*, Magistrates' Courts Act, 1952 (Eng.), ss. 19 (5) and 25 (1) and First Schedule.

[4] Ch. 1, p. 22.

the arguments which can be directed against constructive murder in particular comes from its being undifferentiated from intentional murder in terms of punishment otherwise than by executive clemency. If constructive murder were made a comparatively trivial offence, a misdemeanour punishable with a small fine or a short term of imprisonment, it would become much less objectionable.

Clearly, therefore, the possible punishment is relevant to the mental element in regulatory offences; but this is not to say that the mental element should be determined by reference only to the possible punishment. The nature of the relevance of the sanction to the mental element in a new regulatory offence needs to be defined. It is submitted that the role of the sanction in determining the place to be occupied by a new offence in the general structure of the criminal law is by way of being a possible source of protection for the defendant. If the sanction is small its effect on the construction of the crime in terms of mental element should be neutral; it should sway the court in no direction. But if the sanction is large, this should be a strong influence in the direction of *mens rea*.

The danger to be guarded against is the tendency to argue that because the punishment is small, therefore the safeguards for the defendant normal in criminal law should be reduced. Where the safeguard of the requirement of a mental element in crime is concerned, this argument can, and often does, lead straight to strict responsibility. But there is a difference between saying that no one should be exposed to a long term of imprisonment without proof that he intended to commit the crime charged, and saying that because he is not so liable it should therefore not be necessary to prove such an intention. The difference is that the first proposition works positively in favour of the defendant whereas the second works positively against him. It is submitted that, since the first does not entail the second, the first should be accepted and the second rejected on the ground that the first is just and the second unjust.

The position reached would be the one stated above, namely, that where an offence carries a liability to serious punishment (the meaning of which expression is reserved for detailed discussion below), it should always be construed as requiring *mens rea* (the meaning of which is also reserved for further discussion); but that where an offence does not carry a serious punishment, the factor of possible punishment should be dismissed from consideration in deciding on the mental element appropriate to that offence.

The meaning of "serious punishment"

(i) *Imprisonment*

The foregoing statement of principle needs to be amplified by giving acceptable meanings to "serious punishment" and "*mens rea*". As to the former, it is submitted that imprisonment marks the line between serious and minor punishment so far as types of punishment are concerned. If an offence carries the possibility of any term of imprisonment[5] on conviction it should be classed as serious for the present purpose.[6] Any sanction more severe than imprisonment[7] would be *a fortiori* serious. The drawing of this line does not dispose of all the difficulties, however. Although for most crimes the effective choice is between imprisonment and fine, or a combination of the two, there are some crimes for which quite different sanctions are appropriate, such as deportation, or deprivation of a licence to drive or trade, forfeiture, or removal from office. There is also the question how large a fine has to be before it becomes comparable in seriousness with a term of imprisonment.

(ii) *Fines*

To take the second of these difficulties first, there does not seem to be any automatic way of differentiating between serious and petty fines. Where this part of the law is regulated by statute, as in the projected Model Penal Code of the American Law Institute, there is nothing to prevent an arbitrary line being drawn below which a fine is not to be equated with any term of imprisonment. This line is drawn in the Model Penal Code at $500,[8] but changing circumstances are certain to render any fixed sum unreal in the course of time. Where, as is usual, statute has nothing to say on the matter, other rules must be devised for distinguishing serious from non-serious fines.

The question can arise in the context of regulatory offences only under some statute. The obvious first rule to adopt therefore seems to be the following: wherever a fine alone is imposed in a statute, it

---

[5] Otherwise, of course, than consequentially upon non-payment of a fine. The test is whether imprisonment may be imposed as part of the original sentence on conviction.
[6] The same line is drawn in the Model Penal Code of the American Law Institute. See Tentative Draft No. 4, Comment 140, para. 1.
[7] Although there may be utilitarian arguments to the contrary, most people would regard corporal and capital punishment as more severe than imprisonment, and a fine as less severe.
[8] Proposed Official Draft, s. 6.03 (4), which has to be read in the light of the rule that by definition a violation is an offence for which imprisonment may not be imposed: s. 1.04 (5).

is to be considered a serious punishment in the present context if it is equal to or exceeds any fine which may be alternative or additional to imprisonment elsewhere in the same statute. This is not to say, of course, that a fine may not be serious even if it is not equal to or more than any fine under the same statute which may be imposed together with or instead of imprisonment. A regulatory statute may well envisage fines as the only sanction. In such a case it is useless to attempt to lay down a fixed rule. The courts would doubtless have regard to analogous statutes in arriving at an estimate of the seriousness of the punishment.

(iii) *Other sanctions*

There is another way of estimating the seriousness of a punishment which links up with the first of the two difficulties in this area, that of sanctions tailored to fit the crime, such as deportation, deprivation of a licence to drive or trade, forfeiture, or removal from office. This way is to inquire what the effect of the maximum punishment prescribed would be on the least blameworthy defendant to whom it could be applied.

The problem posed by these special punishments is that their seriousness is not to be measured in terms of the choice between imprisonment and a fine, for they are not strictly comparable with either of these alternatives. A strong example would be deportation.[9] To a refugee from a Communist country, deportation from the West might be a more serious punishment than almost any term of imprisonment. On a less spectacular level, the loss of a trading licence might be infinitely more damaging to the individual defendant than several months in prison or a quite substantial fine. If such punishments are measured in seriousness by their effect on the least blameworthy defendant to whom they could be applied under the relevant legislation, they clearly fall into the same class as imprisonment, with the consequence that the offences for which they may be imposed ought to include a requirement of *mens rea*.

Before inquiring into the implications of this conclusion it is as well to analyse further the suggestion that the seriousness of punishment for the present purpose ought to be measured in terms of its significance for the least blameworthy defendant on whom it might be imposed. It can be objected that this test is unreal, for if there is a choice of penalties open to the court between a maximum and a

[9] *Cf. Chajutin* v. *Whitehead* [1938] K.B. 506; Ch. 1, n. 61, above.

minimum, it is implied that variation between these extremes will be guided by the moral culpability of the individual defendant; that over-severe sentences can always be cured on appeal; and that courts normally have a power of absolute discharge to dispose of the case of the morally innocent defendant, the minimum punishment being in effect nothing.

These objections are persuasive but not, it is submitted, in the present context decisive. An unfortunate characteristic of strict responsibility for regulatory offences has been the readiness with which judges upholding the doctrine have given effect to the possible, however unjust, in preference to the probable. It is not probable that legislatures all over the world intended the conviction of morally innocent people on the scale which has occurred during the twentieth century; but it is certainly possible that this result was intended. It is quite probable that the maximum punishment will never be imposed in this part of the law upon the least blameworthy defendant; and that if it is, the injustice will be corrected on appeal. Nevertheless, the opposite consequences are certainly possible and should therefore be taken into account for the present purpose, which is to draw a line in terms of seriousness of possible punishment above which a statutory offence should never be interpreted in such a way as to exclude a requirement of *mens rea*.

It is submitted that in seeking to compare such punishments as deportation, deprivation of a licence to drive or trade, forfeiture, and removal from office with imprisonment in order to arrive at a scale of seriousness, the distinguishing feature of imprisonment of most value is the effect which it has of depriving the defendant of the power of earning his living. It is tentatively suggested that a punishment is to be classed as serious if the effect of imposing it may be to deprive the defendant of the means of livelihood, whether temporarily or permanently.

It is not intended that the result of this test should vary with the particular defendant. What is proposed is that if the sanction for an offence, read in the context of the statutory scheme of which that offence forms a part, could have the result of depriving the person upon whom it is imposed of the means of livelihood, and this result could follow equally for the least as for the most morally guilty, then that offence should require *mens rea* in D to be proved by P as an essential prerequisite for conviction.

If such a principle of interpretation were applied, there should be excluded from consideration the possibilities that any particular individual might be able to earn his living in some other way, or that in any particular case the defendant was not dependent upon that of which he might be deprived for his livelihood. The object would be to provide a touchstone of the justice of excluding *mens rea* from the definition of an offence, not merely a guide to mitigation of penalty.

(iv) *Fines and other sanctions combined*

Another difficulty to be foreseen and guarded against is presented by those offences for which a fine only is the penalty on first conviction, disqualification or other legal disability being discretionary or mandatory only after a given number of previous convictions.[10] It would be absurd to argue that until D is in present danger of such a punishment he is not entitled to the protection of *mens rea*. The rule should be that if conviction of the offence in question puts D in a position where he is more likely than he was before conviction to lose the means of livelihood through judicial penalties, he should be entitled to the protection of *mens rea*.[11]

Conclusion on sanctions

The result of the foregoing reasoning is to restrict the number of offences which do not require proof by P of *mens rea* in D to those which are punishable only by a small fine; for it is quite clear that the other familiar punishments, particularly disqualification from trading or driving, could have the effect of depriving D of his livelihood. Further than this, however, the analysis of punishments will not carry us.

There remains the question what principles are to be applied to those offences which on this approach do not qualify for the *mens rea* requirement.[11a] Before answering it, two other antecedent

---

[10] See Ch. 1, nn. 66 and 67, above, for examples.

[11] If both a fine and a "tailored" penalty can be imposed, then clearly the punishment falls into the serious class. A different view of the seriousness of the "tailored" sanctions is taken by the framers of the Model Penal Code. In the Code these punishments are equated with fines not exceeding $500 and are termed "civil penalties" as opposed, presumably, to "criminal punishments". See, *e.g.*, Proposed Official Draft, ss. 1.04 (5) and 6.03 (4). It is submitted that this is a grave underestimate of the importance of such punishments to persons who undergo them merely on the basis of strict responsibility.

[11a] It should be remembered that agreement on the principles to be applied to regulatory offences does not necessarily depend on agreement with the views previously expressed about the relative seriousness of different punishments. The latter relate primarily to the demarcation of the appropriate area of the law to which to apply the former. Although the two discussions are inter-related, they are not wholly interdependent.

questions must also be disposed of: the meaning of *mens rea* as used herein, and whether it is justifiable in the public interest to exclude any offences at all from the requirement of *mens rea*.

The meaning of mens rea

A long disquisition on the meaning of *mens rea* would be out of place here. So far as the problem of strict responsibility is concerned, the most important single characteristic of the various states of mind included for convenience under the customary term *mens rea* is knowledge by D of all the facts relevant to the definition of the offence with which he is charged at the time when he did or omitted to do the acts said by P to constitute that offence.

Negligence is excluded from *mens rea* because negligence includes a reference to some material degree of inadvertence, whereas inadvertence to a relevant fact or state of affairs can never amount to *mens rea* as that term is used herein. What is sometimes called advertent negligence is in this terminology a contradiction in terms. If conduct is indulged in with advertence to all the relevant facts but without desire or intention as to the forbidden result, which by definition is foreseen as likely, it amounts to recklessness for the present purpose and therefore to *mens rea*.

It will be seen that if a basically simple design is adopted with intention, or desire of consequences, at the top; recklessness, or foresight of consequences next; negligence, or lack of foresight of consequences next; and strict responsibility, wherein no question of intention, desire or foresight is considered relevant, at the bottom; the result follows that the line between *mens rea* and other possible legally relevant mental states, which do not appertain only to the physical voluntariness of an act, is drawn below recklessness and above negligence. This is the plan which will be acted upon in this book. A certain degree of elaboration will necessarily take place in ensuing discussions of mistake, negligence and *actus reus*.

Mens rea and public interest

It seems reasonable to say that if an offence is punishable with nothing more than a small fine, or even a quite substantial fine provided that imprisonment is not an alternative, the prosecutor should not be required to prove *mens rea*, simply on the balance of convenience as between the interests of D in so far as they are contrary to the general public interest, and the general public interest. As was observed at the beginning of this chapter in connection with the choice between trial by jury and summary trial, the public has a legitimate interest in dispatch of business, efficient law enforcement and saving of public money. The limits upon this interest are two: current ideas of justice, being the legal expression of current morality; and the avoidance of any measure which reduces efficient law enforcement by occasioning contempt for the law.[12]

It is tentatively suggested, without any pretension to special knowledge of current public views on justice or law enforcement, that this interest of the public is best served at the present day if it is limited through the operation of the doctrine of *mens rea* at the point where the possible punishment for an offence becomes serious in the sense indicated above. Where the possible punishment is not serious in that sense, the general public interest may properly prevail to some extent over the particular conflicting interest of D in avoiding wrongful conviction. Where the punishment is not serious, therefore, the doctrine of *mens rea*, in the form in which it requires P to prove *mens rea* in D, may be abandoned in some measure. If D is in danger only of forfeiting money in no disastrous amount, it is reasonable to argue that his position is sufficiently less deleterious to him for the protection of the *mens rea* requirement to be less necessary than where a stronger sanction is in issue.

It is probable that regulatory offences are at least as likely to be committed through negligence as through intentional wrongdoing, and it is certainly strongly arguable that unless the regulatory offence covers negligence, a large area of human conduct which ought in the public interest to be subjected to coercive pressure to comply with laws laid down for the general good will remain untouched. The statutes regulating the sale of food and drugs may be taken as an example.

No doubt a certain number of offenders are deliberate wrongdoers who hope to increase profits by failing to comply with minimum standards of quality or cleanliness. To strike at these people is a proper object of the legislation. But it is also a proper object of the legislation to render more aware of their social obligations those many others who fail to comply with minimum standards simply through carelessness, through negligently omitting to take the pre-

[12] The second of these limitations is really only a particular instance of the first; but it is sufficiently important and often enough overlooked to merit being stressed by separate mention.

cautions which in the public interest ought to be taken by anyone in that branch of trade. For each intentional wrongdoer in this context, it seems very likely that there is at least one negligent wrong-doer also. Even if there is not, the possibility of negligent wrongdoing remains and ought in the public interest to be taken into account in the administration of the legislation.

It is therefore the case that at just the point where diminution of punishment renders dependence on the *mens rea* requirement less necessary for D, a public interest in criminal responsibility for negligence emerges quite independently of questions of punishment. The suggestion therefore is that if the punishment for an offence is not serious in the sense indicated above, the basis of criminal responsibility may justifiably be widened to include responsibility for negligence, the reason being that at this point the interest of the public in prohibiting certain kinds of behaviour outweighs D's interest in not being punished for an inadvertent act or omission.

Negligence and strict responsibility

The two preliminary questions leading up to a discussion of the proper principles to be applied to offences of the definitions of which a requirement of proof of *mens rea* in D by P does not form a part having been disposed of, a wider discussion of the proper principles to be applied to such offences follows naturally. The first problem posed is whether it is necessary or desirable to enlarge the basis of responsibility merely to negligence, one step down in the scale sketched above, or better to go the whole way and jump from *mens rea* to strict responsibility.

This problem has been disposed of in the first chapter. There is no acceptable principle upon which the protection normally available to D upon a criminal charge may be reduced beyond the necessity of the case as established by evidence or reason. There is neither evidence nor reason to support the view that what may be accomplished by strict criminal responsibility cannot be accomplished at least as well, if not better, by the narrower responsibility for negligence.

It is true, as the scale of values above demonstrates, that if strict responsibility is imposed, those who commit offences negligently or with *mens rea* will be caught; but it is also true that the morally innocent will be caught as well. It has been shown in the first chapter that there is no evidence of any state of affairs which justifies the conviction of the innocent. This finding precludes further argument on the question whether criminal responsibility should under any circumstances extend further than negligence.

Burden of proof

If it be now accepted that criminal responsibility for regulatory offences demonstrably ought to rest on negligence, the next task is to turn that conclusion into a practical doctrine, particularly as to burden and quantum of proof. Should the burden remain upon P to prove negligence, and if so, should he be required to prove negligence beyond reasonable doubt or merely upon the balance of probability? If the burden of proof of exculpation is shifted to D, should he be assisted by reducing the quantum of proof of exculpation in all cases to the balance of probability? Should a burden of proof rest upon D only if he desires to exculpate himself by proving due care, or also in other circumstances, as if he denies some other fact relied on by P?

(i) *Quantum*: *initial reservation*

The way to the answers to the foregoing questions has to be traced with some care in order to avoid arguments which are found on inspection to be meaningless owing to an imprecise use of terms. For example, take the contrast between placing the burden of proof of his case upon P and the burden of proof of exculpation upon D. At first sight it seems reasonable to say that the quantum upon P remains beyond reasonable doubt but the quantum upon D ought not to exceed the balance of probability. Yet what can this mean?

Suppose that D is charged under an adulteration statute with having supplied sub-standard milk. P proves the fact of supply of sub-standard milk by D. D wishes to exculpate himself by proving that he took due care to see that all milk supplied by him was up to standard. It is self-contradictory to say that D must prove this due care on the balance of probability if it is at the same time maintained that P must prove his case beyond reasonable doubt, for D could cast a reasonable doubt upon P's case without by any means establishing some proposition affirmatively on the balance of probability. The effect of casting a reasonable doubt upon the proof advanced of some fact which is asserted is not to establish the fact contrary to the one

asserted, but to prevent any finding of fact upon that point at all.[13]
The statement, if it be made, that in one and the same proceeding
there can be a quantum beyond reasonable doubt upon P and a
quantum on the balance of probability upon D therefore has to be
qualified in some way before it can make sense.

(ii) *Evidentiary and persuasive burdens*

Another possible source of confusion is the distinction which
exists between what have been called the persuasive and the evidentiary burdens of proof.[14] The accepted distinction in criminal law
is as follows.

Both P and D bear the burden of introducing some evidence in
support of their contentions on the facts, although each may discharge this burden by pointing to something arising out of the
evidence advanced by the other. This is called the evidentiary burden
of proof. The persuasive burden of proof is the burden of persuading
the arbiter of fact in the court that some fact asserted is indeed likely
to be true, either likely on the balance of probability against improbability, or likely beyond reasonable doubt.

The term "burden of proof" is used herein to refer only to the
persuasive burden of proof.

(iii) *The burden on the defendant*

Bearing these *caveats* in mind, and therefore deferring questions
of quantum for the time being, the next question is whether D should
ever be required to discharge a burden of proof in order to defend
himself. Since the clearly established general rule of criminal law is
now that P, who undertakes the accusation, must prove the whole of
his case, which means everything that he asserts, it follows that to
change the rule in the present context means making an exception
to a powerful principle. The making of such an exception needs
weighty reasons in support. It is submitted that a case for such an
exception can be made out.

One has to remember that the offences being dealt with here are
those which carry the possibility only of a small fine as a sanction.
As with *mens rea*, although the smallness of the sanction is not of
itself a reason for abandoning a general rule of criminal law which

---

[13] *Cf. Riley* [1896] 1 Q.B. 309, 318, *per* Hawkins J., where it was said that a plea of
guilty was not an admission of facts.
[14] This distinction is discussed in detail in Glanville Williams, *Criminal Law: The
General Part* (2nd ed.), 876–886.

operates for the protection of D, yet it may be a factor contributing to the displacing of part of D's interests in favour of those of the public where these are in conflict.

It has been observed above that in the regulatory offence area the public probably has at least as great an interest in suppressing unjustifiable carelessness as in suppressing intentional or reckless wrongdoing. The circumstances under which regulatory offences are committed are normally obscure in a way that more serious offences are not. No one commits murder or larceny in a blaze of publicity if he can help it, but a murder or a larceny is nevertheless an exceptional occurrence, not to be compared in frequency of incidence with the bottling and distribution of milk or the parking of automobiles; not, in short, part of a lawful but closely regulated community activity.

The exceptional nature of serious crime renders it relatively easy of investigation. Facts connected with its commission are likely, if remembered or observed at all, to be recalled and established in court without undue difficulty. The outstanding characteristic of regulatory offences for the agencies of law enforcement, on the contrary, is the absence in nearly every case of a circumstance easily distinguishable from a normal lawful community activity upon the basis of which to prove culpability in D. There is nothing remarkable about a parked car or one of a thousand bottles of milk in a consignment. If the car is parked in a restricted area, or one bottle of milk in a thousand found to contain diluted milk, there is normally nothing in the available evidence enabling P to claim with any show of plausibility that he has proved negligence in D beyond reasonable doubt.

Unless P is to derive some further advantage in the prosecution as against D, for all practical purposes the *mens rea* rule might just as well be left intact for regulatory offences. Without some corresponding shift in the burden of proof, an extension of responsibility to include negligence would not reduce the practical difficulty of enforcing this part of the law.

It seems reasonable, therefore, to have a rule that if P establishes a prima facie case, by proving the facts constituting the *actus reus* of the offence charged, D should be convicted unless he affirmatively establishes that the situation proved occurred without fault on his part. To establish absence of fault it should be necessary for D to prove that he was not negligent in relation to the legal duty proved by P. At first sight this seems to put upon D the difficult task of proving a negative, but by closer analysis of what the law would actually require it is easy to show that nothing of the kind is contemplated.

In all cases the basis of the charge against D will be either an improper action on his part, such as selling something outside permitted hours, or an improper omission, such as a failure to remove his automobile from a metered parking spot after the permitted period of parking has expired. All that is required of D is that he show in either case that his behaviour, whether of omission or commission or both, was reasonable in the circumstances. Reasonableness would be determined by the court as a question of fact. The effect on the course of proceedings would be as follows.

P would place before the court an apparent instance of behaviour which was anti-social because it unjustifiably infringed a minor penal law. D would then argue, normally, but not necessarily, on the basis of evidence introduced by himself, that his behaviour was not in fact unjustifiable because in all the circumstances it was reasonable. P would be allowed the right to reply by way of arguing that on the evidence as it stood at the close of D's case he had demonstrably not behaved reasonably.

A striking instance of the practical utility of such a rule is furnished by a recent English decision, *Strong* v. *Dawtry*.[15] In that case D was charged with leaving his automobile in a metered parking space without making the initial payment for the right to park there; in other words, for parking without putting a coin in the meter. It was found as a fact that only after D had parked his car did he discover that he was without the appropriate piece of small change. He left his car and asked a nearby policeman (!) for change but the constable was unable to oblige. He then asked a taxi driver, who supplied him with change. On returning to the meter, with every intention of inserting the appropriate coin, he found that during his two minutes' absence a parking attendant had fixed a notice of infringement to the car. Notwithstanding immediate and adequately substantiated explanations, D was prosecuted and convicted, the conviction being upheld on appeal to the Divisional Court.

The basis of the defence was the contention that into the "absolute" wording of the statute[16] there must necessarily be read an implication

---

[15] [1961] 1 W.L.R. 841.
[16] Road Traffic Act, 1956 (Eng.), s. 20 (2): ". . . the initial charge shall be payable on the leaving of the vehicle in the parking place. . . ." It was the words "on the leaving" which the court regarded as imposing strict responsibility.

that a motorist be allowed a reasonable time to insert a coin into the meter. The court found itself unable to accept this common-sense suggestion. Yet if the task before the court had been, not an unrealistic inspection of the ambiguous words of a minor regulation, but the determination of the question whether in all the circumstances D had behaved reasonably, acquittal would surely have followed. It is difficult to believe that if D had been acquitted the public interest would have suffered.[17]

(iv) *Quantum: further analysis*

It is now appropriate to return to quantum. In every trial P has to establish a prima facie case. There is no reason why, in accordance with the usual rule, he should not have to establish the facts constituting this prima facie case beyond reasonable doubt. If the defence is a denial of the *actus reus* asserted by P, it should be open to D to deny P's case by casting a reasonable doubt upon the truth of the facts relied on by P, as in every other criminal trial. But if D's defence is that he acted reasonably, and therefore does not depend upon a denial of any of the facts asserted by P, there are three possibilities. D may argue on the basis either of the facts proved by P (and by hypothesis admitted by D); or of facts proved by D; or a combination of the two. In so far as D is not arguing from facts proved by P, he must prove the facts material to his argument himself. Here again there is no reason for a departure from the usual rule, which is that wherever a burden of proof rests upon the defendant to criminal proceedings, he is not required to establish any proposition more rigorously than upon the balance of probability.[18] Therefore D should establish any facts on which he relies as showing that he acted reasonably upon the balance of probability.

The question whether, on the basis of such facts as are proved

---

[17] At 843, expressing surprise that the magistrates had fined the defendant, the court suggested that perhaps absence of change was a common excuse. But the vestige of public interest thereby produced disappears when it is remembered that there was no need for the magistrates to believe the defendant's story if they thought it was a fabricated excuse. It may be suggested that by leaving his car in the parking space while he sought change D was suiting only his own convenience and therefore not behaving reasonably. Surely this approach to such legislation is over-rigid. Why should not intending customers be allowed reasonable latitude in providing their custom to the owners of the parking space?

[18] *Sodeman* v. *The King* (1936) 55 C.L.R. 192, 216, *per* Dixon J.: "Where by statute or otherwise the burden of disproving facts or of proving a particular issue is thrown upon a party charged with a criminal offence, he is not required to satisfy the tribunal beyond reasonable doubt. It is sufficient if he satisfies them in the same manner and to the same extent as is required in the proof of a civil issue."

either by P or by D, D is to be found to have acted reasonably, although a question of fact as opposed to a question of law, is scarcely susceptible of evaluation in terms of quantum of proof. If the concept of reasonableness as employed in the present context is properly applied, no question of quantum arises because this finding of fact is not objectively proved by D but is in reality an expression of opinion by the court itself. The facts advanced by D in support of his contention are susceptible of proof which may be evaluated in terms of quantum, but the opinion of the court which those facts are adduced to support clearly is not.

Conclusion on burden of proof

The position reached is as follows. Where D is charged with a regulatory offence, which in the present context means a statutory offence triable summarily for which the maximum possible penalty on conviction is a relatively small fine, it should not be incumbent upon D to prove *mens rea* in D. On the other hand, it should remain open to D to answer a prima facie case established by D by proving affirmatively that he acted reasonably in all the circumstances. Such facts as are relied on by P should be proved by him beyond reasonable doubt. Such further facts as are relied on by D should be proved by him on the balance of probability if he wishes to set up a defence of reasonable behaviour; but if he wishes to defend himself only by casting a reasonable doubt upon the facts relied on by P, it should be open to him to do so without assuming the burden of proving anything affirmatively.

It will be observed that although in one sense this rule establishes responsibility for negligence in relation to regulatory offences, this way of expressing the result is misleading, for it implies that P has to prove some degree of negligence, which is not the case. P does not have to prove any degree of negligence affirmatively, although it is of course open to him to do so if he so wishes in any particular case. It is for this reason that no question of degrees of negligence arises.

Ignorance and mistake

The allied problems of simple ignorance and mistake require separate mention. There is a distinction between simple ignorance and positive mistake,[19] although both are forms of ignorance. The

---

[19] Glanville Williams, *Criminal Law: The General Part* (2nd ed.), 151–152.

difference between the two is clear enough in theory although it may be difficult to distinguish them in some situations in practice. Simple ignorance is absence of knowledge, whereas mistake is a positively wrong belief. The distinction is of importance where the law is that D may exculpate himself when charged with a regulatory offence by proving affirmatively that he acted under the influence of a positive and reasonable but wrong belief, but cannot exculpate himself by proving merely that he was ignorant of a material fact, however reasonably.[20]

In this chapter, however, the nature of the distinction in both theory and practice may be passed over[21] because if a rule of exculpation on the ground of reasonable behaviour were adopted, the difference would be immaterial. The question would be whether it was either reasonable of D in the circumstances to be ignorant of the fact which he did not know, or reasonable of him to make the mistake which he did. In both cases, of course, if the court came to the conclusion that his ignorance or mistake was reasonable, there would still remain the further question whether he acted reasonably in the light of his actual state of mind. Only if this further question were answered in D's favour would he be entitled to acquittal.

[20] As may be the case in Australia. See Ch. 5, below.
[21] It will be taken up again in connection with the Australian law referred to in the previous footnote.

CHAPTER 3

STATUTORY WORDS

Introduction

The argument so far has proceeded on the implied assumption that the statutory words creating the offence are neutral in regard to *mens rea* in that they include no express reference to a state of mind in D. Under the canons of construction which are now universally accepted by the courts this would be the case with such formulations as "No person shall" do something, or "Every person who" does something "shall be liable to a penalty". These are the cases of so-called "plain words" upon which the doctrine of strict responsibility has thriven for a century or more.

So far as such neutral phrases are concerned, the present argument is that since the courts decline to derive any assistance from the words themselves and look to outside factors, such as comparison with other sections of the same statute or severity of punishment, for guidance on the question of *mens rea*, the outside factors to which they ought to address themselves and the results at which they ought to arrive are those which have been discussed in the previous chapter. There are, however, many common statutory words and phrases apt to be understood as referring to some degree of *mens rea* of which account must be taken in any attempt to lay down a general doctrine to replace strict responsibility.

The commonest such words in regulatory statutes at the present day are perhaps "permit", "cause" and knowingly". There are also what may be termed "status offences", the definitions of which tend more than any other statutory form of words in favour of strict responsibility. Status offences will be discussed before the problems arising out of particular words.

Status offences

A status offence is one which attaches criminal responsibility to someone merely by reason of his status, capacity, or physical situation apparently dispensing with the need for either act or omission as a prerequisite for conviction. Some of these offences, as interpreted by the courts, have come as near as the nature of things allows to the absurdity of crime without either *actus reus* or *mens rea*. Such a situation, as the cases which follow will show, is indefensible.

(i) *Being found*

The most famous instance of conviction for a status offence occurred in *Larsonneur*.[1] The defendant, who was a French subject, had been permitted to land in the United Kingdom from France on condition that she took no employment during her stay. This condition was subsequently varied by the addition of a requirement that she leave the United Kingdom by a certain date. The defendant complied on the due date by going to the Irish Free State, whence, however, she was promptly deported and handed back by the Irish police to the English police in the United Kingdom. Without being allowed out of police custody she was charged and convicted before a magistrate that she, "being an alien to whom leave to land in the United Kingdom has been refused was found in the United Kingdom". The conviction was affirmed by the Court of Criminal Appeal.

Neither the appellant nor the Court of Criminal Appeal seems to have regarded the word "found" as giving rise to difficulty. The appellant's argument[2] was based on the contention that she could not be said to have landed in the United Kingdom within the meaning of the condition in her passport since she had been forcibly brought there. This consideration the Court of Criminal Appeal[3] dismissed as "perfectly immaterial".[4] All concerned seem to have accepted that the appellant had certainly been found in the United Kingdom, even though this view entailed by implication the remarkable proposition

---

[1] (1933) 24 Cr. App. R. 74. There appears to be a similar unreported Northern Ireland case, *Kasriel Neumann* (1947): see (1958) 21 *Modern Law Review*, 379, n. 22. The account given in that note of the South Australian case of *O'Sullivan* v. *Fisher* [1954] S.A.S.R. 33, is inaccurate. It is not that case, but *Chia Gee* v. *Martin* (1906) 3 C.L.R. 649, which furnishes an Australian equivalent to *Larsonneur*. The headnote reads in part: "Where prohibited immigrants were discovered as stowaways . . . and brought ashore in custody, it is no defence to a subsequent prosecution for being prohibited immigrants found within the Commonwealth, that they were brought ashore in the custody of the law." *Chia Gee*, however, was a much less striking case than *Larsonneur* on the facts, for the defendants had stowed away with the plain intention of entering Australia illegally. See also *Griffin* v. *Wilson* (1935) 52 C.L.R. 260, 266, *per* Dixon J., and *R.* v. *Governor of Metropolitan Gaol* [1963] V.R. 61. It has been held in New Zealand that there cannot be an aider and abettor to an offence of being found: *McAteer* v. *Lester* [1962] N.Z.L.R. 485.
[2] (1933) 24 Cr. App. R. 74, 76–77.
[3] Lord Hewart C.J., Avory and Humphreys JJ.
[4] (1933) 24 Cr. App. R. 74, 78.

that the police could "find" someone who at all material times had been in their own custody. On this latter point the decision should certainly be regarded as wrong, but this is a relatively superficial matter compared with the true significance of the process of reasoning applied to the offence charged.

The relative unimportance of the improper interpretation of the word "found" in the case is easily demonstrated. Let it be supposed that the defendant in *Larsonneur* had not been deported from Ireland but had been returned to the United Kingdom by accident, as if the lady had been misdirected to the wrong aeroplane at an airport and had been unable to prevent herself being landed in England after she discovered the mistake. Under these circumstances she might well have been genuinely "found" by the English police whilst trying to board another aeroplane back to Ireland, but a conviction would have been none the less objectionable for that.

The true fault with the *Larsonneur* type of reasoning is that it takes no account of anything done or omitted to be done by D. There is no basis, on a literal view, for arguing even the need for a conscious, voluntary act. Once two statuses, the status of being a person refused permission to land and the status of being a person found in the forbidden country, are added together, conviction follows. Where the statute expresses an offence in this impersonal form it is possible to argue with a formidable show of logic that strict responsibility cannot be avoided, for the constituents of the offence require nothing of D except that he exist.

(ii) *Other status offences*

Status offences are not uncommon. Two of the most frequently recurring types to be found in the law reports are those which penalise a person for being either the occupier of premises[5] upon

---

[5] *e.g.*, *Bear* v. *Lynch* (1909) 8 C.L.R. 592: licensee of licensed premises upon which a person was found, outside permitted hours for the sale of liquor, otherwise than for a lawful purpose. *Griffin* v. *Larum* (1915) 32 W.N. (N.S.W.) 10: *ditto. Martin* v. *Whittle* [1922] V.L.R. 207: licensee of licensed premises upon which liquor was disposed of otherwise than during the hours authorised by the licence. *Bond* v. *Foran* (1934) 52 C.L.R. 364: occupier of a house used for betting. *De La Rue* v. *McNamara* [1940] V.L.R. 128: occupier of a house whereon a contrivance for gaming was kept. *Charlesworth* v. *Kissling* [1943] V.L.R. 129: secretary of a members' club on the premises of which liquor was drunk on a Sunday. *Bergin* v. *Khyat* [1953] V.L.R. 695: licensee of licensed premises upon which liquor was drunk on a Sunday. *Tully* v. *O'Sullivan* [1956] S.A.S.R. 106; occupier of premises used for unlawful gaming. The denominator common to this group of examples from one jurisdiction alone is that in each case an attempt was made, usually unsuccessfully, to raise a defence based on absence of knowledge of the unlawful state of affairs.

which some unlawful event occurs, or the owner of a chattel[6] which in some way infringes the law. Thus a licensee is often penalised merely by virtue of the two facts that at the material time he was the licensed occupier of premises and an unlawful game was played on those premises,[7] the statute failing to specify any necessary connection between these concurrent events as a prerequisite for conviction. Similarly the owner of a motor vehicle used for an unlawful purpose is frequently made criminally responsible merely by virtue of the fact that he happened to be the owner when the unlawful user took place.[8] Being drunk in a public place[9] falls into the same category, together with vagrancy and other such crimes.[9a] A recent English case[10] brought to light a less familiar variant on the same theme, the responsibility of a parent for the non-attendance at school of a child of school age, this responsibility attaching to D by virtue of the concurrent circumstances of parenthood and non-attendance only.

Vicarious responsibility in this part of the law furnishes another example of a class of status offences, although here the liability to conviction depends not on anything expressly stated in the statute, but on the doctrine formulated in *Mousell Bros.* v. *L.N.W. Rly.*[11] that where strict responsibility is to be applied to the person who actually performed the forbidden act, there is no difficulty in convicting also anyone on whose behalf he was acting provided that the offence was committed within the scope of the discretion delegated to him.[12] The basis of this extended liability is said to be that since

[6] *e.g., Trenchard* v. *Ryan* (1910) 10 S.R. (N.S.W.) 618: owner of a horse ridden or driven in a public street when unfit for the purpose. *Lewis* v. *Brown* (1931) 48 W.N. (N.S.W.) 196: owner of cattle trespassing on unauthorised land. *Fraser* v. *Dryden's Carrying Co.* [1941] V.L.R. 103: owner of a commercial goods vehicle operated on a public highway otherwise than in accordance with its licence. *Snell* v. *Ryan* [1951] S.A.S.R. 59: owner of cattle found straying in a public place. *Myers* v. *Crabtree* [1956] V.L.R. 431: owner of a motor vehicle used to carry a load in excess of the permitted maximum.

[7] See n. 5, above.

[8] See n. 6, above.

[9] *O'Sullivan* v. *Fisher* [1954] S.A.S.R. 33. This case is discussed in detail in Ch. 8, n. 13, below.

[9a] Lacey, "Vagrancy and Other Crimes of Personal Condition", (1953) 66 *Harvard Law Review* 1203; Enloe, "Criminal Sanctions for the 'Status' of Narcotics Addiction", (1963) 17 *South Western Law Journal* 134.

[10] *Hinchley* v. *Rankin* [1961] 1 W.L.R. 421.

[11] [1917] 2 K.B. 836, 845–846, *per* Atkin J. This doctrine has been applied in Australia: *R.* v. *Australasian Films Ltd.* (1921) 29 C.L.R. 195; *Alford* v. *Riley Newman Ltd.* (1934) S.R. (N.S.W.) 261.

[12] *Allen* v. *Whitehead* [1930] 1 K.B. 211; *Wilson* v. *Murphy* [1937] 1 All E.R. 315; *Linnett* v. *Commissioner of Police* [1946] K.B. 290; *Barker* v. *Levinson* [1951] 1 K.B 342; *Reynolds* v. *Austin* [1951] 2 K.B. 135; *Quality Dairies* v. *Pedley* [1952] 1 All E.R. 380·

the offence does not call for *mens rea*, it is immaterial that D did not know what his delegate was doing.[13] Nevertheless, in such cases D is being convicted merely by virtue of two concurrent circumstances, his employment of the delegate and a breach of the law by the employee.

A rule for status offences

The immediate problem is to find a satisfactory way of construing statutory offences which require for conviction only the concurrence of circumstances independent of any act or omission by D which will bring them within the ambit of such a general rule of exculpation for reasonable behaviour as was advanced above. Vicarious responsibility can be treated as a separate problem for this purpose since it does not turn, except in the most tenuous and uncertain way, upon the precise wording of the statute.

It is suggested that nothing more complicated is called for here than a reversal by the courts themselves of the tendency towards undue preoccupation with the literal meanings of statutory words which, on the whole, they at present exhibit. There is no ground at all for presupposing in the approach to status offences that the legislature intended to be unreasonable when creating them. Still less is there ground for such a presupposition when it is clear that in the vast majority of regulatory statutes, if not in all, the legislature cannot be realistically said to have had any intention whatever in regard to the minute niceties of wording in question here.

It is easily demonstrable that the statement of the elements of an offence in a statute normally constitutes a minimum, not a maximum, of what has to be proved against D. The apt comment of Dr. Glanville Williams, that criminal statutes are always expressed elliptically because it is not reasonable to expect the legislature to set out the whole of the general part of the criminal law afresh for each new offence created, has already been quoted,[14] and carries the point. If the opposite argument is pressed to a *reductio ad absurdum* it follows that no court has jurisdiction to try an offence unless that court is expressly given such power by a statute referring to that offence. Obviously the statutory statement of an offence, however minor, does not normally set out any more than a minimum set of conditions for conviction.

[13] *Mousell Bros.* v. *L.N.W. Rly.* [1917] 2 K.B. 836, 845–846, *per* Atkin J.
[14] Ch. 1, n. 34.

This general rule applies as much to status offences as to other crimes. The inference follows that merely because there is no express mention in the definition of an offence of such a basic prerequisite for criminal responsibility as *actus reus*, some conscious, voluntary act or omission by D, such a requirement is not necessarily to be excluded from that offence.[15] The mere fact that a statute makes no express mention of some act or omission by D is an utterly inadequate reason for failing to imply such a requirement.

Illustrations

There are three Australian decisions, two by the High Court, which illustrate very well that there is no need for the courts to be unduly impressed by the impersonal wording which characterises status offences.[16] The first in point of time is *Maher* v. *Musson*.[17] D was charged with an offence against the Commonwealth Distillation Act, 1901–1931, s. 74 (4), which said: "No person shall . . . have . . . in his custody . . . any illicit spirit."

On an unimaginatively literal reading, it can well be argued that there is no express requirement of either knowledge or act or omission in this offence. If D, wittingly or unwittingly, fulfils the requirements for the status of custodian of a container which contains spirit the status of which is illegality, the offence is committed; so that he might well be liable to conviction if someone secreted illicit spirit among his possessions without his knowledge. Four members of a court of five[18] firmly rejected such an interpretation of the statute, two of them bluntly on the ground that it would be "a palpable and evident absurdity".[19] The same can be said with some force of the result of *Larsonneur*.[20]

The second case is *Bond* v. *Foran*[21] where the charge was laid under the Lottery and Gaming Act, 1917–1930 (S.A.), s. 63 (3): "No person shall be the occupier of any . . . house, office, room, or place kept or used" for any of certain prohibited purposes, one of which was betting. The High Court held unanimously[22] that it was not enough

---

[15] The argument that the defendant's very possession of the offending statuses constitutes in some metaphysical way an *actus reus* is not worthy of serious consideration. At best it begs the question.

[16] See further, below, p. 125.

[17] (1934) 52 C.L.R. 100.

[18] Rich, Dixon, McTiernan and Evatt JJ., Starke J. dissenting.

[19] 52 C.L.R. 100, 109, *per* McTiernan and Evatt JJ.

[20] Above, n. 1.

[21] (1934) 52 C.L.R. 364.

[22] Rich, Starke, Dixon and McTiernan JJ.

for D to be merely the occupier of the premises in question whilst betting was taking place, although that was all that the section expressly said. A connection between the two events had to be established by proof that D knew of the unlawful user. *Bond* v. *Foran* is a particularly strong illustration of judicial refusal to become entangled in the irrelevant minutiae of statutory wording, for in that case the legislative history of the offence showed that formerly the word "knowingly" had been expressly included in the definition. It was open to the court to argue that the omission of so important a word in the later amending statute must have been deliberate, but the change was regarded, in effect, as immaterial.

The third case, *Snell* v. *Ryan*,[23] arose in the Supreme Court of South Australia, and is equally striking for adherence to reasonable principles of construction of statute law. D had been convicted summarily of an offence against the Impounding Act, 1920–1947 (S.A.), s. 46: "If any cattle are found straying ... in any street or public place, the owner thereof shall be liable to a penalty not exceeding five pounds."

He had depastured his cattle in a securely fenced paddock. Without his knowledge someone had opened and left open a gate through which a cow strayed on to the public road. The conviction was on the basis that the wording of the section was absolute, the manner in which the cow came to reach the road therefore being immaterial. One might have thought this decision inevitable, the impersonal wording of the statute being reinforced by the small maximum fine of five pounds. However, Napier C.J. of the South Australian Supreme Court declined to be persuaded by these small points. After remarking that he thought it "unnecessary to hold that the statute law is so arbitrary and unjust",[24] he continued:

"I have too much respect for the Legislature to suppose that it could have intended to penalize the owner of cattle, which are found straying, through no default or neglect upon the part of anyone for whom the owner is responsible, but as the result of the wrongful and possibly criminal act of a stranger.

"If the terms of the statute leave any escape from that predicament we are entitled to put an interpretation upon the Act, which avoids what I should describe as tyranny and injustice, and – speaking generally – this avenue of escape is opened by the presumption that

[23] [1951] S.A.S.R. 59.
[24] [1951] S.A.S.R. 59.

a person is not criminally responsible for an act which is done independently of the exercise of his will or by accident. . . .[25] The onus was, of course, upon the appellant to show how his cow came to be upon the road, but when it appears that he had done everything that any reasonable man could be expected to do, in the way of securing his cattle, and ensuring that they would be kept off the road, it is plain that he ought not to be convicted under this section."[26]

The decision was in fact even stronger than appears merely from the foregoing extract. Earlier cases[27] on this legislation had expressly decided that the offence under s. 46 required at least negligence in D. When those cases were decided in 1923, however, the offence had been "suffering" cattle to stray, and in 1926, perhaps as a result of those decisions, section 46 had been altered to the impersonal form which came before the court in *Snell* v. *Ryan*. Nevertheless, the impersonal wording was read as doing no more than shift to D the burden of proving that he was not negligent.

It is clear from such cases as these that there is no reason at all for the courts to be mesmerised by impersonal statutory wording into abandoning any of the safeguards normally available to a person accused of a criminal offence, however minor. That should be enough to dispose of the menace of the status offence.

Particular words

It is now time to take up the problems presented by particular words. The nature of the difficulty presented by the inclusion in the definition of a statutory offence of such a word as "permit", "cause", or "knowingly", is to decide what it means. Since the word is there, some significance should be attached to it by the courts, even if only, as has been said of the word "knowingly", by way of concluding that it does no more than "say expressly what is normally implied".[28] In status offences difficulty was occasioned by omission rather than inclusion of words, but the history of judicial decision upon the meaning of particular descriptive words in criminal statutes yields to no other part of the law in obscurity and inconsistency.[29]

---

[25] His Honour here referred to his own citation in *Dayman* v. *Proudman* [1941] S.A.S.R. 87, 97, of *Hardgrave* v. *The King* (1906) 4 C.L.R. 232, 237.

[26] [1951] S.A.S.R. 59, 60.

[27] *Pocock* v. *Elliott* [1923] S.A.S.R. 271; *Jaffrey* v. *Sanders* [1923] S.A.S.R. 276.

[28] *Roper* v. *Taylor's Central Garages Ltd.*, [1951] 2 T.L.R. 284, 288, *per* Devlin J.

[29] *Cf.* Edwards, *Mens Rea in Statutory Offences*, 52: "Travellers along the Queen's highway will probably agree that a plethora of signposts can sometimes be as disconcerting and misleading as a complete absence of directions indicating what lies

Of the multifarious words in common use in this connection,[30] "permit", "cause" and "knowingly" have been chosen as examples here, not only because they are nowadays the words perhaps most frequently before the courts, but also because in themselves they illustrate aptly the sorts of problems which arise and which obstruct the creation of a sound general rule for the interpretation of regulatory offences.

(i) *Causing*

To start with the simplest situation, there seems to be little doubt[31] now that for a conviction of "causing" some prohibited consequence, P must prove *mens rea*. The form of this *mens rea* has been precisely described by the High Court of Australia, after a careful analysis of the English cases, in the following passage:

"[W]hen it is made an offence by or under statute for one man to 'cause' the doing of a prohibited act by another the provision is not to be understood as referring to any description of antecedent event or condition produced by the first man which contributed to the determination of the will of the second man to do the prohibited act. Nor is it enough that in producing the antecedent event or condition the first man was actuated by the desire that the second should be led to do the prohibited act. The provision should be understood as opening up a less indefinite inquiry into the sequence of anterior events to which the forbidden result may be ascribed. It should be interpreted as confined to cases where the prohibited act is done on the actual authority, express or implied, of the party said to have caused it or in consequence of his exerting some capacity which he possesses in fact or law to control or influence the acts of the other. He must, moreover, contemplate or desire that the prohibited act will ensue."[32]

If such an interpretation of a single statutory word is to be accepted, it cuts across the scheme outlined above for the develop-

ahead. The same feeling of desperation may be experienced by examining the judicial interpretations during the past hundred and fifty years of statutory offences involving guilty knowledge."
[30] As to which see Edwards, *op. cit.*, *passim*, and especially at 52 and 53, n. 2.
[31] In Australia there is no doubt. As to this and the contrast with England, see the next footnote.
[32] *O'Sullivan* v. *Truth and Sportsman Ltd.* (1957) 96 C.L.R. 220, 228, *per* Dixon C.J., Williams, Webb and Fullager JJ. Kitto J. delivered a concurring judgment. For a discussion of English authority leading to substantially the same conclusion see Edwards, *op. cit.*, Ch. CI. The few English cases casting doubt on *mens rea* are reviewed by the same author at 150–155.

ment in regulatory offences punishable only with a small fine of a general rule of prima facie liability to conviction on proof of *actus reus*, subject to a general defence of reasonable behaviour; for it means that if the Legislature chances (and the present pattern of regulatory legislation leads one to suppose that the choice of these words often is a matter of chance)[32a] to employ the word "cause", *mens rea* is implied into the offence and the burden of proof therefore rests on P. This is an indication that although the general tenor of discussion, in this book and elsewhere, has been towards an extension of the safeguards for D, it does not necessarily follow that merely because one is against strict responsibility, therefore one is in favour of *mens rea* wherever possible.

Reasons have already been given for thinking that full *mens rea* and a total burden of proof on P are not always appropriate to just and effective law enforcement. Where regulatory offences are concerned there is much to be said for modifying the rules appropriate to the more serious crimes. This consideration leads as much to a restrictive interpretation of such words as "cause" against D as to the exclusion of strict responsibility in his favour.

(ii) *Permitting*

From this point of view the word "permit", with which may be included synonyms such as "suffers" and "allows",[33] is of absorbing interest. At the outset it is apparent that the *mens rea* problem with the word "cause", which arose only through judicial interpretation, is much more acute with "permit" because the very idea of permission tends to suggest advertence to the action or state of affairs permitted, which is not the case with the idea of causing. If there were no judicial dicta on the subject at all, one would still tend to expect that D could not be said to permit something unless he knew he was permitting. This, however, is too superficial a view.

(*a*) *One's own act.* The concept of permitting something to happen may vary according as attention is directed to something which D

[32a] Or at least of uncritical re-enactment of old statutory forms.
[33] As to "suffers", *Bond* v. *Evans* (1888) 21 Q.B.D. 249, 257, *per* Stephen J.; *Somerset* v. *Wade* [1894] 1 Q.B. 574, 576, *per* Mathew J. As to "allows", *Sawicki* v. *The Queen* (1960) 124 C.C.C. 386, 388, *per* Thomson J. After a detailed discussion of English authority Edwards, *op. cit.*, 125–129, comes to the conclusion that "the same conditions of liability pertain whether the offence is founded on suffering or on permitting". For a contrary Australian view see *Piro* v. *Boorman* [1958] S.A.S.R. 226, 230; but what the court really had in mind in that case was not any distinction between suffering and permitting, but the difference, discussed below, between allowing a state of affairs and allowing someone to do something.

personally did or something which someone else did. In the first case, the situation envisaged is where D sees that something either will certainly happen, or is likely to happen, or may happen, and fails to prevent its occurrence. There is no room for the notion of active authorisation if D is not dealing with another person. So far as his own acts or omissions are concerned, if a distinction is to be drawn between what he does and what he permits, this can take the form only of a distinction between what he does and what he fails to prevent.

If D fails to prevent that which he foresees will certainly happen unless he prevents it, then he has permitted that occurrence provided that his failure was voluntary. A legal problem arises over how far this responsibility extends beyond foresight of certainty; in particular, whether D may be convicted of permitting where he foresaw only that the prohibited occurrence was likely but not certain, or even only possible but not likely. To avoid difficulties such as an unrealistically precise definition of "likely", which in the present context would have to mean more than fifty per cent probable, a rule of no utility whatever in the summary prosecution of a regulatory offence, it is convenient to discuss this question together with the related problem of whether D should be required actually to have foreseen some consequence or may be convicted of permitting if he merely ought to have foreseen that consequence.

The question raised is very similar in substance to the problem of status offences. It will be recalled that the troubles occasioned by status offences melted away where the courts declined to immerse themselves in nice distinctions of verbal syntactical meaning, but directed attention instead to what would be a reasonable scope to give to the offence in question. The same can be done here. Once again a decision of the High Court of Australia furnishes a good example.

In *Ferrier* v. *Wilson*[34] D was charged that he "allowed" rubbish to fall into the waters of Sydney Harbour from a lighter of which he was the owner.[35] The lighter had been engaged in removing rubbish from a ship and had been left moored overnight. In the morning it was

[34] (1906) 4 C.L.R. 785.
[35] Reg. 39 of the regulations made under the Sydney Harbour Trust Act, 1901 (N.S.W.). *Ferrier* v. *Wilson* has been followed on the meaning of "allow" (which was treated in the case as being synonymous with "permit") in *Potts* v. *Knox* (1907) 24 W.N. (N.S.W.) 91; *Sangster* v. *Henry* (1920) 37 W.N. (N.S.W.) 135; *Jolly* v. *Virgo* [1927] S.A.S.R. 188; *Horseman* v. *Cavanagh* [1930] S.A.S.R. 1. For a Canadian case laying down the same rule see *Sawicki* v. *The Queen* (1960) 128 C.C.C. 386.

found capsized, but the cause did not appear. The High Court[36] held that the word "allow" was apt to create criminal responsibility for "the case where somebody by negligence allows the event which ought to be prevented to happen".[37] This approach to the problem neatly telescopes the theoretically separate questions whether D is liable for what he ought to have foreseen or merely for what he foresaw, and whether what he foresaw or ought to have foreseen is to be taken on the basis of certainty, likelihood, or possibility.

As to the first, according to *Ferrier* v. *Wilson* the ground of criminal responsibility should be what D ought to have foreseen. This being so, the second question is automatically answered, for it would clearly be reasonable to expect him to foresee that which is certain but unreasonable to expect him necessarily to foresee that which is merely possible. Thus in *Ferrier* v. *Wilson* the capsizing of the lighter had to be taken on the basis of accident, because there was no evidence of the cause. The accident, since it happened, came into the class of possible occurrences, but could not be given any higher degree of probability. Since it was merely possible, and there was no particular reason why D ought to have foreseen it, no criminal responsibility attached to him.

It is submitted that such an approach to the problem of determining the proper scope of a regulatory offence is always to be welcomed. There can be no doubt that an ordinary regulation of the kind in issue in *Ferrier* v. *Wilson* is aimed as much at preventing the careless distribution of rubbish as at intentional distribution. If the court puts itself in the position of having to choose between full knowledge by D or no knowledge by D of the facts material to the offence, merely because the word "allow" or "suffer" or "permit" happens to be used in a criminal statute, it is in much danger of imposing strict responsibility on the ground only that there seems to be no other way of giving the statute reasonable scope. But if the task of the court is seen to be rather the delimiting of a reasonable area of operation for the statute, the result is likely to be much more satisfactory.

The last element in permitting something by one's own act or, more probably omission, is failure to prevent the occurrence which one ought to have foreseen. On no rational view can there be a permission unless there is at least a failure to prevent under circumstances giving

[36] Griffith C.J., Barton and Isaacs JJ.
[37] (1906) 4 C.L.R. 785, 790.

rise to a choice between allowing and preventing. Once again alternative possibilities present themselves, for D may be made responsible for failing to take either all possible precautions, or reasonable precautions, or any precautions at all.

It is submitted that there is nothing about the word "permit" which constrains a court to require anything more or less than a failure to take reasonable precautions to prevent the forbidden result. Of course, this rule would be of importance only if the case were that D actually had foreseen that consequence, for if he had not foreseen it and P was arguing that it was this failure that was unreasonable, by hypothesis there would be no precautions to take into account.

Only one more link is needed in the chain of argument from the word "permit" to the general rule of responsibility for unreasonable behaviour which is being advanced here, and that is in respect of the failure to take precautions, as opposed to the precautions themselves or foresight of the need for them. It should be clear that only if the failure to take precautions is unreasonable should there be criminal responsibility for permitting, so that a man who could do nothing because he accidentally slipped and injured himself when about to take precautions would not be liable to conviction.

It is therefore submitted that there is nothing inconsistent with the meaning of the word "permit", or synonyms therefor such as "allow" and "suffer", in laying down a rule as regards the acts or omissions of D himself that he should not be criminally responsible unless he unreasonably failed to prevent the forbidden result, whether the question in the particular case turns on lack of foresight, failure to take precautions, or inadequate precautions.[38]

(*b*) *The act of another.* Attention may now be turned to the second form of permitting in regulatory offences, where D is criminally responsible, not for permitting something impersonal to happen, such as allowing rubbish to fall into a harbour, but for permitting someone else to do something unlawful, such as allowing an unlicensed driver to drive a motor vehicle on a public road, or suffering a prostitute to frequent licensed premises.

This form of permitting must be distinguished from vicarious

---

[38] Such a rule would also have the merit of forestalling such ingenious arguments as that if the defendant is charged with permitting, he ought to be acquitted if the evidence discloses, not that he permitted anything, but that he actually did it. For a parallel case with attempts, namely, an acquittal of attempt on the ground that the evidence disclosed the completed offence, see *Rogers* v. *Arnott* [1960] 2 Q.B. 244. Such rules are discreditable to the law.

responsibility. It not infrequently happens that an employer is charged with permitting some unlawful occurrence when the person who actually permitted was an employee. In such a case, it is clear that the liability to conviction of the employer should turn on the rules of vicarious responsibility, which have no necessary connection with permitting, and that neither employer nor employee should be liable unless the latter has permitted within the meaning of the rules suggested herein. The same applies to any relationship other than employer and employee which gives rise to vicarious responsibility.[39]

Responsibility for permitting another to do something normally turns on knowledge by D of some status held by that other person. Thus the offence of permitting an unlicensed person to drive a motor vehicle on a public road usually raises questions, not of driving on roads, but of knowledge in D that the driver was unlicensed.[40] As elsewhere, this basis of responsibility can be approached as a problem either of *mens rea* or of negligence: D may be convicted either only if he actually knew or if he ought to have known that the driver was unlicensed. The choice between *mens rea* and negligence here is linked with another problem, which arises under this form of permitting although it did not where only D's own actions were concerned, and that is the question whether he should be liable only for actively authorising or also, as in the previous situation, for merely failing to prevent when he had the power to prevent.

It should be observed that the form of offences of permitting of this kind by no means prevents strict responsibility. If D is charged with permitting an unlicensed person to drive or with suffering prostitutes to foregather, it is arguable as a matter of literal interpretation that he is responsible once it is proved that he permitted a person or persons of the relevant status to perform the forbidden act. As with the status offences themselves, it can be said that there is no necessary connection between the status of a person and knowledge by D of that status. If this line is taken by the court the result is strict responsibility so far as the state of affairs struck at by the offence in question is concerned.

This distinction between the activity and the status of the person

[39] As in *Quality Dairies* v. *Pedley* [1952] 1 All E.R. 380, where vicarious responsibility arose from a contract which was not in the usual sense a contract of employment, but for the supply of services by an independent contractor.
[40] Other common examples are suffering gaming and permitting drunkenness. At first sight suffering gaming seems to be *sui generis*, no question of status arising. There is, however, room for a mistake as to the nature of the pastime being permitted. The players may conceal the fact that they are betting on the result.

engaged in that activity may have other consequences, however. One possibility is that full *mens rea* may be retained for all the elements of the offence except the status, and some rule other than strict responsibility laid down for that element alone. This possibility emerges from *Proudman* v. *Dayman*,[41] the most influential decision on this part of the law ever handed down by the High Court of Australia.

D was charged with an offence against the Road Traffic Act, 1934–1939 (S.A.), s. 30: "Any person who ... permits any person not being the holder of ... a licence to drive a motor vehicle on any road shall be guilty of an offence." The conviction appealed from was affirmed on the facts, but a number of points of statutory interpretation were canvassed in the judgments. All three judges[42] approached the construction of the offence on the basis that the concept of permission extended only to the driving of a motor vehicle on a road, the absence of a licence in the driver being no more than a description of class of drivers. This part of the reasoning was described with meticulous clarity by Dixon C.J.:

"The [appellant][43] contended ... that upon a charge under s. 30 ... it must be shown, not merely that the driver was unlicensed, but also that the defendant knew it or at all events was indifferent to the question whether he was licensed or not.

"This contention was based upon the ground that the very idea of permission connotes knowledge of or advertence to the act or thing permitted. In other words, you cannot permit without consenting and consent involves a consciousness or understanding of the act or conduct to which it is directed. Be it so. Nevertheless the contention fails in its application to the actual terms of the provision. ... It may be conceded that unless a defendant meant to consent to the three conditions involved in the words (1) drive, (2) a motor vehicle, (3) on a road, he could not be said to have permitted the doing of that thing. But it is to that act that the permission must be directed, not to the absence of a licence. The words 'not being the holder of ... a licence' do not form part of the act permitted. They are a negative qualification upon the word 'person', and operate to exclude persons so licensed from the class who may not be permitted to

---

[41] (1941) 67 C.L.R. 536.
[42] Rich A.C.J. by implication, Dixon and McTiernan JJ. expressly.
[43] The word in the report is "applicant" as this was technically an application for special leave to appeal which was refused.

drive. . . . It is the driving which must not be permitted, that is, unless the driver holds a licence."[44]

The position reached at this point therefore is to bring offences of permitting others to perform unlawful acts into line with offences couched in neutral or impersonal language, for although *mens rea* has been retained for relatively unimportant elements,[45] the relevance of D's state of mind on the main point is left at large. This being so, all the arguments advanced previously against strict responsibility and in favour of a general defence of reasonable behaviour come into play. The decision on this point in *Proudman* v. *Dayman* itself was inconclusive, Dixon C.J. favouring the application of a rule that reasonable mistake as to the status of the driver should be a defence, McTiernan J. favouring strict responsibility for this element, and Rich A.C.J. coming to no clear conclusion but seeming to lean towards the view of Dixon J.[46] It is submitted, however, that for the reasons previously advanced a general rule of criminal responsibility for unreasonable behaviour would be appropriate here as elsewhere.[47]

On this second type of permitting there remains only the question whether D should expressly authorise or merely fail to prevent. The answer is supplied by reference to the conclusions already reached. If the question whether ignorance of the driver's status should be a defence is to be tested by asking whether in the circumstances D ought to have known, on the basis that laws such as these are aimed as much at negligent as at wilfully wrong behaviour, it follows naturally that there should be liability for an unreasonable failure to prevent.

Assuming that D knows all the things relevant to the offence except

[44] (1941) 67 C.L.R. 536, 541–542. See also McTiernan J. at 542–543.
[45] The driving, the motor vehicle and the road are, of course, only relatively unimportant. It is unlikely that an issue would arise in the vast majority of cases on any of these points, but a mistake in relation to any one of them is conceivable. In such a case it might be arguable that the test of reasonableness, instead of full *mens rea*, would be appropriate to this part of the offence also; but the point does not seem to be sufficiently important to be worth labouring.
[46] See *per* Rich A.C.J. at 538–539, Dixon J. at 540–541, and McTiernan J. at 542–543.
[47] It is significant that of the three judgments delivered in *Proudman* v. *Dayman*, that of Dixon J. has been by far the most influential. See particularly *McCrae* v. *Downey* [1947] V.L.R. 194; *Gepp* v. *Anderson* [1949] S.A.S.R. 135; *Lipshut* v. *McKay* [1950] V.L.R. 57; *Belling* v. *O'Sullivan* [1950] S.A.S.R. 43; *Peterson* v. *Curran* [1950] Tas. S.R. 9; *Foster* v. *Aloni* [1951] V.L.R. 481; *Green* v. *Sergeant* [1951] V.L.R. 500; *Bergin* v. *Stack* [1952] A.L.R. 810; (in the High Court) (1953) 88 C.L.R. 248; *Dowling* v. *Bowie* (1952) 86 C.L.R. 136; *Hawthorn* v. *Bartholomew* [1954] V.L.R. 28; *Georgeff* v. *Ryan* [1954] S.A.S.R. 234; *O'Sullivan* v. *Harford* [1956] S.A.S.R. 109; *Thompson* v. *Ewens* [1958] S.A.S.R. 193; *Gherashe* v. *Boase* [1959] V.R. 1; *Coysh* v. *Elliott* [1963] V.R. 114. *Proudman* v. *Dayman* has also been cited in the civil jurisdiction: *O'Brien* v. *Skinner* [1962] N.S.W.R. 575.

the status of the unlicensed driver, there are two possible situations: either he knows that the driver is unlicensed or he does not. If he knows that the driver is unlicensed, then it is reasonable to extend the scope of the offence of permitting unlicensed driving to the case where D having authority and power to prevent that occurrence, nevertheless fails to prevent it, either voluntarily or else under circumstances when he might reasonably be expected to have taken steps to prevent it or else because he takes unreasonably inadequate steps to prevent it.

Alternatively, D may not know that the driver is unlicensed. Here the situation differs according as D's ignorance is reasonable or not, for if his ignorance is reasonable he cannot be convicted but if it is not reasonable he may be convicted. The latter situation is the one relevant to the present argument, but it gives rise to difficulty over express authorisation and mere failure to prevent, for D cannot be said under any circumstances to have expressly authorised that of which he is, by hypothesis in the present case, ignorant. Once unreasonable ignorance is found, conviction follows if the other primary facts are proved.

The conclusion is that there is no convincing objection to extending the general defence of reasonable behaviour advanced above to regulatory offences expressed in terms of permitting, suffering, or allowing, or any synonym for these words.

(iii) *Knowingly*

The last of the three statutory words chosen for detailed examination to see if it would be practicable to extend a general rule for the interpretation of regulatory offences even to statutes employing particular words connoting some degree of *mens rea*, was "knowingly", with which "wilfully" may be classed for present purposes.[48]

Because it may seem at first sight that the word itself implies *mens rea*, "knowingly" presents an obstacle to the general rule contended for here. In the cases "knowingly" has also acquired two other remarkable characteristics. The first is that it has more usually been influential by its absence rather than by its presence, and the second

---

[48] Edwards, *op. cit.*, deals with wilfulness and knowledge separately in Chapters II and III of his book, but this is in accordance with his general scheme of arrangement. It is clear from his discussion that the better view is that both words require *mens rea*. They were unconvincingly distinguished in *O'Sullivan* v. *Harford* [1956] S.A.S.R. 109, on the ground that "wilfully" included wilful ignorance through failure to make an obvious inquiry. But it is hard to believe that the same would not apply to "knowingly".

has been an intermittent and apparently arbitrary association with burden of proof. Before indicating how the word may be interpreted in conformity with the theme of the present chapter, these two characteristics may be dealt with.

(*a*) *Absence.* Absence rather than presence of the word "knowingly" has come to be important[49] by reason of the judicial custom of arriving at a decision upon the proper interpretation of a regulatory offence through a detailed comparison of the section of the statute creating the offence with other sections of the same statute which also create offences. In scores, and possibly hundreds, of cases it has been decided that some offence does not include *mens rea* because a similar offence in a nearby section includes in its definition the word "knowingly", whereas the one under consideration does not.[50]

This myopic mode of statutory construction purports to be a method of discovering the intention of the legislature, which is thereby credited with an ineradicable passion for creating intellectual puzzles entitled to about the same measure of respect as a parlour game. No one who has perused, as the courts do every day, the apparently haphazard arrangement and choice of epithets in the average regulatory statute can possibly be impressed with an argument which makes criminal responsibility turn on so narrow a ground. The mere presence or absence of the word "knowingly" in adjoining statutory offences can rarely, if ever, have anything at all to do with the activity aimed at by those offences. It is incredible that any legislature should choose to express itself on such an important question as *mens rea* with such minute obscurity.

It is submitted that if the word "knowingly" does not appear in the definition of a regulatory offence, it should, like any other particular word which does not appear, be ignored for all purposes in the interpretation of that offence.[51] Its presence in adjoining offences or earlier or later statutes should be regarded as irrelevant.

(*b*) *Burden of proof.* The second acquired oddity of the word

---

[49] Almost the whole of Edwards's discussion of this word, *op. cit.*, Ch. III, is concerned with situations where it does not appear in the relevant section of the statute before the court. For a strong statement of the kind referred to in the text see *Ewart* (1905) 25 N.Z.L.R. 709, 736, *per* Edwards J.

[50] Or because a section in a consolidating statute omits "knowingly" when the corresponding section in previous legislation included it. But see *Bond* v. *Foran*, n. 21, above.

[51] This statement is not intended to contradict the main argument in this chapter and the preceding one that states of mind and defences may be implied in the absence of special mention, but merely to make the point that significance should not be attached to the absence of any one word.

"knowingly" is its periodic association with the burden of proof. It has been said[52] that the effect of omitting "knowingly" from the definition of a regulatory offence is to put upon D the burden of proving that he acted without guilty knowledge, whereas if "knowingly" is included in the definition that burden of proof remains on P in accordance with the usual rule.

It is submitted that this view is not, and never was, intended to be demonstrable as a matter of logic from some inherent quality in the word "knowingly" or some general principle of the interpretation of statutes. The only purpose served by an otherwise quite arbitrary suggestion was that it furnished an escape from the previous argument based on comparison of sections, some of which included "knowingly" and some of which did not. This appears clearly from the best-known of the various dicta on this subject, that of Day J., in *Sherras* v. *De Rutzen*:[53] "An argument has been based on the appearance of the word 'knowingly' in subsection 1 of section 16 and its omission in subsection 2. In my opinion the only effect of this is to shift the burden of proof. In cases under subsection 1 it is for the prosecution to prove the knowledge, while in cases under subsection 2 the defendant has to prove that he did not know. That is the only inference I draw from the insertion of the word 'knowingly' in the one subsection and its omission in the other."

If the learned judge had not felt impelled by the argument from comparison of the subsections to attach some meaning to the omission of "knowingly" it may fairly be suspected that it would never have occurred to him to have resort to the burden of proof. The view taken in this book also is that in regulatory offences it is reasonable to put a burden of proof on D, but this has nothing to do with the chance inclusion or omission of any particular word. That such an improbable escape route had to be invented by judges who did not approve of strict responsibility is another reflection on the practical utility of the doctrine.

[52] *Prince* (1875) 2 C.C.R. 154, 161, *per* Brett J.; *Sherras* v. *De Rutzen* [1895] 1 Q.B. 918, 920, *per* Day J; *Maher* v. *Musson* (1934) 52 C.L.R. 100, 105, *per* Dixon J., at 108 *per* McTiernan and Evatt JJ.; *Gaumont British Distributors Ltd.* v. *Henry* [1939] 2 K.B. 711, 721, *per* Humphreys J.; *Harding* v. *Price* [1948] 1 K.B. 695, 700, *per* Lord Goddard C.J., and at 704 *per* Singleton J.; *Reynolds* v. *G. H. Austin & Sons Ltd.* [1951] 2 K.B. 135, 145, *per* Lord Goddard C.J. For a contrary view see *Roper* v. *Taylor's Central Garages Ltd.* [1951] 2 T.L.R. 284, 287–288, *per* Devlin J. For New Zealand, *Ewart* (1905) 25 N.Z.L.R. 709.
[53] [1895] 1 Q.B. 918, 920.

(c) *Construction.* These aberrations of statutory construction may be ignored in approaching the word "knowingly" *ab initio.* There can be no doubt that of all words, this is the one most apt to create a requirement of *mens rea* if it is to be given any separate weight. In a jurisdiction where strict responsibility has a firm hold, no doubt it should be understood in that sense as a means of mitigating the evil. The purpose in the present chapter, however, is the rather different one of trying to fashion an acceptable general rule for regulatory offences which will be sturdy enough to withstand the varying pressures of individual statutory words, and thereby to prevent the creation of anomalous differences in standards of liability for substantially similar offences. It is thought that this general aim justifies the cutting-down of the prima facie meaning of some statutory words, just as it justifies extending the literal meaning of others. This view in turn, it will be recalled, rests on the opinion that the doctrine of *mens rea* in the form in which it is most favourable to the defendant is not necessarily appropriate to the administration of many minor offences.

On this basis it is submitted that an acceptable attitude to take to the word "knowingly" is to adopt the view expressed by Devlin J., in *Roper* v. *Taylor's Central Garages Ltd.,*[54] which has already been referred to,[55] and regard it as doing no more than "say expressly what is normally implied". In the present context this may be taken as meaning that it is normally implied that a man must know what he is doing in the sense that there must be a voluntary, conscious *actus reus*; but it is not normally implied in regulatory offences that he must know all the facts relevant to the offence, for if this is taken to be normally implied there is no basis for responsibility for negligent acts or omissions, where it may be proper to convict a man because, although he did not know, he ought to have known.

This process of reasoning brings "knowingly" into line with permitting, where, it will be recalled, it was found both possible and desirable to restrict the ambit of the word "permits" to the immediate outward circumstances of the offence, leaving the central element, in that case usually a matter of status, at large for interpretation under the general rule. If in such an offence as "knowingly selling adulterated milk" the word "knowingly" is regarded as adding nothing to the words "selling milk", then knowledge of the adulteration of the milk,

---

[54] [1951] 2 T.L.R. 284, 288.
[55] Above, p. 53, n. 28.

which is what is really being struck at by the offence, is left open for interpretation as a rule of negligence.

The same result follows if "knowingly" is found, as it often is, in conjunction with some such word as "suffering" in an offence like "knowingly suffering a girl under 18 years of age to be in a brothel".[56] If it is accepted that "knowingly" adds nothing to "suffers", there is no difficulty on the foregoing reasoning in requiring *mens rea* for every element of the offence except the age of the girl and applying negligence to that requirement alone.

Conclusion

The conclusion is that neither status offences nor particular statutory words need be allowed to stand in the way of the development of a rational general rule of negligence, in the form of a general defence of reasonable behaviour as that concept has been explained above, for regulatory offences. It is not being argued that the courts should treat regulatory statutes with a cavalier disregard of what the statutes actually say. The much more limited proposition is being advanced that in construing regulatory offences the courts should not abdicate their constitutional function of interpreting the law in favour of an intellectually unimpressive preoccupation with grammatical minutiae. The strength of the law, particularly of the criminal law, lies in its adherence to a comparatively few just but humane general principles.

The clear definition of these principles is of as much benefit to the legislature as to the individual defendant. The amount of parliamentary drafting time which must now go into the devising of statutory defences to regulatory offences in order to spoon-feed the courts the very principles which the courts themselves ought to be developing, must be enormous, and certainly out of all proportion to the whole statutory scheme of which it forms a part.

Here, as elsewhere,[57] the courts have tended to become too sub-

[56] As for example in *Turnbull* (1943) 44 S.R. (N.S.W.) 108 and *Rees* (1956) 115 C.C.C. 1, where the mode of argument adopted in the text was rejected by the New South Wales Court of Criminal Appeal and the Supreme Court of Canada. But in those cases, as in so many others, the court was evidently under the impression that the only alternative to *mens rea* was strict responsibility. If a less drastic choice had been seen to be open, another view might have been taken. In the English case of *Lomas* v. *Peek* [1947] 2 All E.R. 574, the word "knowingly" was regarded as adding nothing to "permitting" when used in conjunction.

[57] In relation to the prerogative writs and the supervision of administrative tribunals, for example.

servient to the legislature. The process has been almost entirely voluntary. Very rarely indeed has a legislature in the common law countries clearly created strict responsibility.[58] The doctrine has been the work of the courts themselves, and it ill becomes them to shelter from the consequences of busying themselves with improbable inferences from otherwise unremarkable words merely because those words happen to appear in a statute.

[58] An example is to be found in the regulations made under the Melbourne Harbour Trust Act, 1928 (Vic.), reg. 122 (*d*) (ii): "If any such permit delivered as aforesaid does not contain a complete and accurate record of all such goods then in or on any such vehicle the person so delivering such permit shall, whether the omission or inaccuracy therein was caused intentionally, by mistake, inadvertently, or however otherwise, be guilty of an offence against these regulations." Not surprisingly this wording was held to create strict responsibility: *Smith* v. *O'Grady* [1953] V.L.R. 303. Another example is the general statutory rule that knowledge of age of the victim in certain sexual offences is irrelevant.

CHAPTER 4

THE MACHINERY OF CHANGE

Introduction

It is one thing to work out rational principles of criminal responsibility for regulatory offences, but quite another to find ways in which they might be satisfactorily introduced into any particular jurisdiction. There is a choice between three alternative methods: the law may be changed either by statute, or by the courts themselves, or by a mixture of the two. It will be argued in this chapter that the effective choice is between the first two of these alternatives, the third being merely an unsatisfactory compromise which has most of the disadvantages and few of the advantages of the other two. It will also be argued that the choice between statute and case-law is not absolute, or to be decided in the abstract, but depends upon the circumstances prevailing in the particular jurisdiction under consideration.

The assumption in this chapter, and as applied to the common law world it appears to be a correct assumption, is that nowhere is the law relating to regulatory offences identical with the law proposed in the two preceding chapters; although, as will be seen, not all jurisdictions are as far from it as is generally supposed. In accordance with the view that the nearer the law approaches to the rules laid down in chapters two and three the better it becomes, the relative merits of statute and case-law as means of effectuating this improvement will be discussed.

Statute

At the outset one has to distinguish two different kinds of statute, the general and the particular. By a general statute is meant a code, in the present context a criminal code. A particular statute is a statute of less generality in scope than a code. By a code is meant a statute covering the whole of one area of law, in this case the criminal law, to the exclusion of all other sources except for cases decided subsequently to the enactment of the code on the interpretation of the code. The main distinguishing mark of a code in the sense used here is that it lays down, not merely particular rules and definitions of limited application, but also general principles in relatively simple language (which does not mean in relatively easy language) which govern the specific interpretation of any particular offence.

(i) *Codes*

(*a*) *Introduction.* A regulatory offence normally forms part of an administrative scheme which has no other connection with the criminal law. If a criminal code is enacted, one of the distinguishing marks of a regulatory offence will therefore be that it appears in a statute other than the code. It would be possible to ensure that every single offence known to the criminal law formed part of the criminal code, but this possibility can be discarded as unwieldy because it would entail constant amendment of the code.

The mere fact that a regulatory offence does not form part of the text of the code does not mean that it is unaffected by the code. If the code is expressed in terms which extend the general principles to all other statutory offences unless expressly excluded, then regulatory offences will be on the same footing as other crimes. Alternatively, the principles in the code might be limited to offences included in the text of the code, in which case, if nothing further were said on the subject, regulatory offences would be left to the common law by virtue, not of the fact that they were defined as a separate class of offences, but of the fact that they were in a different statute. Alternatively again, the code might specifically envisage regulatory offences and include special rules of interpretation and responsibility applicable only to that type of offence. This last course would entail marking regulatory offences off as a separate class by a definition.

The second of these three alternatives, the leaving of regulatory offences to the common law, other crimes being governed by the general principles in the code, may be discarded in a discussion of legislative remedies because as far as regulatory offences are concerned it leaves the problems in the hands of the courts. The first, the enactment of general principles applicable as much to regulatory as to any other offences, is exemplified by the criminal codes of Queensland and Western Australia, the effect of which will be discussed in detail in a later chapter.[1] The third alternative, the enactment of special principles of responsibility applicable only

[1] Ch. 7, below.

to regulatory offences defined as a separate class of offences, is
exemplified by the Model Penal Code of the American Law Institute,
which is also the subject of detailed study below.[2] However, some
general observations are relevant at this point.

The choice between these two alternatives is not merely a matter
of convenience in drafting. There is an important issue of principle
at stake. This issue is whether regulatory offences ought to be
regarded as part of the general criminal law or not. The importance
of the question is that if regulatory offences are not to be regarded as
part of the criminal law, arguments based on the assumption that
they are can be plausibly attacked as irrelevant.

An example is furnished by the argument in favour of strict
responsibility that punishments for regulatory offences are too small
to be worth worrying about.[3] This argument was rebutted by evidence
to the contrary, but it was also pointed out that the punitive effects
of conviction of a regulatory offence did not end with the formal
sanction. Loss of reputation and the general unpleasantness of trial
and conviction for a criminal offence also had to be taken into
account. It can be argued that if regulatory offences are removed
from the criminal law, so that conviction of such an offence no longer
involves the stigma of conviction of a crime, the chief harm caused
by strict responsibility is removed. The change is not confined merely
to intangibles like reputation, for other consequences attaching to
conviction of a criminal offence, such as ineligibility for certain
offices, would similarly cease to attach to conviction of a mere
regulatory offence.

(*b*) *The Model Penal Code.* This line of argument has found
adherents in America and is adopted in the Model Penal Code. The
scheme, as tentatively drafted, is to divide the standard criminal
offences into felonies, misdemeanours and petty misdemeanours and
then create a further category of lesser infractions called "violations".
Violations are defined in part[4] by section 1.04 (5) as follows:

> An offense defined by this Code or by any other statute of this State
> constitutes a violation if it is so designated in this Code or in the law
> defining the offense or if no other sentence than a fine, or fine and

[2] Ch. 7, below.
[3] Above, pp. 18, 20–21.
[4] This is apparently intended by the draftsmen of the Code to be a complete definition,
but in fact it has to be read together with s. 2.05 (2) (a). See the discussion under
The Definition of Violation, Ch. 8, below. The definition in the text serves for the
present purpose.

forfeiture or other civil penalty is authorized upon conviction or if it is defined by a statute other than this Code which now provides that the offense shall not constitute a crime. A violation does not constitute a crime and conviction of a violation shall not give rise to any disability or legal disadvantage based on conviction of a criminal offense.

This definition is supplemented by sections limiting the punishment which may be imposed upon conviction of a violation to a fine.[5] It is also supplemented by sections laying down the rule, in effect, that *prima facie* there is strict responsibility for violations,[6] although the scope of strict responsibility in terms of punishment is reduced as much as possible by the further rule that where strict responsibility is imposed with respect to any material element of an offence, that offence shall be classed as a violation.[7]

This scheme is described by the reporter of the Code as a "frontal attack" on strict responsibility,[8] but it has to be remembered that the scope of the attack is limited to crimes punishable with imprisonment. In seeking the reasons for this limitation one has to remember that the framers of the Model Penal Code are creating a model, not an ideal. The object of the Code is to furnish future legislators with a framework of penal law which they can adopt wholly, or in part, or not at all, according to their needs.[9] It is no doubt true that in devising the violations scheme the draftsmen have reduced the effect of strict responsibility in the criminal law to the greatest extent likely to command legislative acceptance in America at the present day. This consideration does not preclude comment on the intrinsic merits of the scheme.

The observation which immediately suggests itself is that the Model Penal Code scheme is an evasion of the main issue: whether strict criminal responsibility is ever necessary as an instrument of social regulation. Certainly much of the sting is taken from the doctrine if the grosser forms of injustice in terms of punishment are done away with; but this is only a reduction, not a removal, of the evil. Something more than merely taking regulatory offences and putting them in a separate category must be done if a criminal code is to furnish an effective means of changing the law in the manner advocated herein.

[5] Ss. 6.02 (4); 6.03 (4); 6.03 (5); 6.03 (6). [7] S. 2.05 (2) (*a*).
[6] Ss. 2.05 (1), 2.05 (2). [8] Tentative Draft No. 4, Comment 140.
[9] Wechsler, "The Challenge of a Model Penal Code", (1952), 65 *Harvard Law Review*, 1097, 1131.

The Model Penal Code was cited as an example of a code which enacted special principles of responsibility applicable only to regulatory offences defined as a separate class of offences. The foregoing criticism does not detract from the utility of the example. It merely makes the point that in this particular instance the special principles are not satisfactory. The device of marking regulatory offences off as a separate class still remains, the virtue claimed for this course being that such offences should not be confused with the criminal law properly so-called because criminal responsibility so-called is not in issue in such prosecutions. It is this contention, which has clearly influenced the drafting of the Model Penal Code, which has to be either denied or accepted.

It is submitted that regulatory offences ought to be regarded as part of the general criminal law because to treat them in any other way, however benevolently meant, is an evasion of the moral duty upon society to use its collective power reasonably when directed against individual members of the community. This applies no matter how powerful, as in the case of great corporations, those individuals may sometimes be.

Once regulatory offences are removed from the criminal law it becomes easy to forget, or even deliberately to reject, the idea that the forcible imposition of a fine is a punishment. The main aim of the framers of the Model Penal Code was undoubtedly the removal of strict responsibility from the criminal law. Because it was thought impracticable to remove the doctrine from regulatory offences the decision was taken to remove regulatory offences from the criminal law also, rather like the amputation of an incurably diseased limb from an otherwise healthy body. Unfortunately, this course tends to strengthen the hold of strict responsibility in that part of penal law where it is left intact.

It is true that logically the retention of the doctrine for regulatory offences does not imply approval of that retention. In the case of the Model Penal Code it is quite clear that the opposite is true: that if the framers had thought it practicable in terms of politics to dispense with strict responsibility altogether, they would have done so. Nevertheless, once it is said that regulatory offences are not part of the criminal law, much of the emotive force of the arguments against the doctrine is lost, and the chances of its being retained indefinitely for regulatory offences are correspondingly increased.

The whole of this part of the law has hitherto been a striking testimony to the indifference even of highly trained lawyers to considerations of evidence and logic. It is difficult to believe that a code which put regulatory offences into a category of infractions of penal law not classified as criminal would not ultimately have the effect of weakening the protection of the individual against the power of the state because the true nature of a regulatory offence prosecution would henceforth be disguised. The fact that the defendant was being exposed to punishment, by whatever name called, would tend to be forgotten. The safeguards to which any individual ought to be entitled when threatened with punishment by the state would not be treated with the same respect as they are in the criminal law. Ultimately it is not too fanciful to foresee the danger of a new class of administrative offences arising which might go far beyond the present confines of regulatory offences, but not carry with them the safeguards of the criminal law because they would not be part of the criminal law.[10]

It is one thing to put infractions of penal law into a separate and safely defined class; it is quite another to keep them there under political and administrative pressure. The courts have not always shown themselves alert to developments in society and the law of this kind, partly no doubt because such changes tend to be inconspicuous, even innocuous, in origin.[11]

It is therefore submitted that if an alternative course is open the expedient should not be adopted of drafting a criminal code which

[10] *Cf.* Schwenk, "The Administrative Crime, Its Creation and Punishment by Administrative Agencies", (1943) 42 *Michigan Law Review*, 51, 86: "Only in those cases in which neither direct compulsion nor substituted action is possible, should the concept of the 'administrative crime' be used, not as a means of punishment, but as a means of indirect compulsion. This punishment is not to vindicate past conduct, but to enforce future conduct. Consequently, it has nothing to do with the ordinary concept of crime. Therefore, a penalty can be imposed as often as necessary to make the individual comply with the administrative order, and the prohibition of double jeopardy does not apply." If one might be permitted the expression, this is simply double-talk. The plain fact of the matter is that the defendant is being punished without the normal safeguards of the criminal law. The reason why he is put in this position is immaterial to him.

[11] Another illustration of the sort of argument thrown up by the idea that regulatory offences are not true crimes is furnished by the American writer Perkins: *Criminal Law*, 692–710; 100 *University of Pennsylvania Law Review*, 832. He first weaves strict responsibility into the historical tradition of the criminal law by identifying it with offences *mala prohibita*, as opposed to offences *mala in se*, and then proceeds to argue that offences *mala prohibita* never have been regarded as true crimes. Since modern regulatory offences are *mala prohibita* only, it follows that strict responsibility is, and always has been, appropriate thereto. The objection to this argument is that the *malum in se*, *malum prohibitum* distinction referred to different categories of crimes, not to crimes and non-crimes, and therefore cannot be cited to support the argument that strict responsibility is appropriate outside the criminal law. The term "civil offense" used by Perkins is tendentious and self-contradictory. *Cf.* Ewart (1905) 25 N.Z.L.R. 709, 729, *per* Williams J.

fails to include regulatory offences as part of the general criminal law. This reservation is not to be confused with the quite different point that within the framework of the criminal law particular rules, as for example those relating to burden of proof, may properly be modified in relation to particular types of crimes. The scheme which it is submitted ought to be adopted here has already been described.[12]

(c) *Other codes.* The other statutory scheme possible within the framework of a criminal code is the enactment of general principles applicable as much to regulatory as to any other offences. This is the scheme of the Queensland and Western Australian Criminal Codes, which may therefore be taken as exemplifying the opposite philosophy from the separatist ideas embodied in the Model Penal Code.

It is true, first, that the explicit rejection of regulatory offences as part of the criminal law had not been formulated as an exact concept at the time when these codes were enacted;[13] and secondly, that the sections laying down the relevant general principles have not in all respects been drafted with the clarity one could wish. This second fact is in large measure owing to developments in the criminal law which have revealed problems not present to the minds of the draftsmen. Nevertheless, there is much to be learnt from the Australian codes.

The scheme of the Queensland Code, to which reference will be confined in this chapter, is to lay down general principles which are both exclusive, in that they constitute the whole law on the subjects with which they deal, and general, in that they apply not merely to the Code itself but also to the whole statute law of Queensland.[14] The operation of the general principles of the criminal law is therefore limited only by the rules governing the express and implied repeal of statutes.

---

[12] Above, Ch. 2.

[13] The first Australian criminal code was enacted in Queensland in 1899, the second in Western Australia in 1902 (repealed and re-enacted in 1913), and the third in Tasmania in 1924. The Queensland and Western Australian Codes are almost identical. All three codes have been amended from time to time. For the present purpose the Tasmanian Code is fundamentally different from the other two: see n. 19 below.

[14] By the Criminal Code Act, 1899 (Qld.), s. 2, the Code "shall be the law of Queensland with respect to the several matters therein dealt with." By s. 36 of the Code itself (which is in form the first schedule to the Act), the rules in Chapter V of the Code, which contains the general principles of criminal responsibility, "apply to all persons charged with any offence against the Statute Law of Queensland".

The fundamental rule is set out in section 23:

> Subject to the express provisions of this Code relating to negligent acts and omissions, a person is not criminally responsible for an act or omission which occurs independently of the exercise of his will, or for an event which occurs by accident.

A second rule for the particular case of positive mistake is in section 24:

> A person who does or omits to do an act under an honest and reasonable, but mistaken, belief in the existence of any state of things is not criminally responsible for the act or omission to any greater extent than if the real state of things had been such as he believed to exist.
>
> The operation of this rule may be excluded by the express or implied provisions of the law relating to the subject.

These two rules between them cover the ground affected by the doctrine of strict responsibility at common law and appear to have the effect of laying down a general rule that there cannot be criminal responsibility unless at least negligence is proved against the defendant. The case for reading them in this way will be argued in detail at a later stage,[15] but briefly the two main reasons are the following.

First, section 23 clearly envisages a general rule more favourable to the defendant than responsibility for negligence, but in making an exception to that general rule in the opening words does not envisage any exception less favourable than responsibility for negligence. Secondly, the mistake defence in section 24 is expressly limited to such mistakes as are reasonable, *i.e.*, non-negligent, except where this limitation is expressly or impliedly excluded.

The overall effect is to create a prima facie rule similar to what at common law would be called *mens rea*[16] capable of extension to cover negligence in appropriate cases. This is very similar to what has been advocated above as the appropriate criminal law structure into which to fit regulatory offences.

(*d*) *Conclusion on codes.* It is submitted that even if the actual wording of the relevant sections were materially altered for the purposes of any code, the older Queensland scheme is basically much superior to the newer Model Penal Code scheme because it ties

---

[15] Ch. 7, below.
[16] The terms *mens rea* and *actus reus* are not used in the Code. Whether the result of the statutory rules is the same as the common law is open to argument.

regulatory offences in with the rest of the criminal law and thereby emphasises that a defendant put in danger of penal punishment is entitled to the equal protection of the law however minor the degree of his misbehaviour.

It is therefore further submitted that if reform of the criminal law through the enactment of a criminal code is being contemplated, the problem presented by the proposed abolition of strict responsibility for regulatory offences should be solved in this way in preference to the course adopted by the framers of the Model Penal Code.

(ii) *Particular statutes*

The alternative to a code is a series of particular statutes. More precisely, if the problem of abolishing strict responsibility for regulatory offences is not dealt with as an incident of a wider scheme for the ordering of the criminal law, the only other legislative course open is to ensure that every statute creating new regulatory offences also enacts the principles of responsibility to be applied. This course involves, in effect, the adoption as a norm of legislative draftsmanship in this area the inclusion of statutory defences to statutory crimes. Although this course has been increasingly taken by legislatures in the twentieth century,[17] there are a number of objections to it.

In the first place, reliance on the continual watchfulness of the legislature can never be as satisfactory as reliance on a general principle applicable regardless of other statutory activity. It would be remarkable indeed if parliamentary drafting were ever to become as reliable as this course would require if anomalies were to be avoided. Oversights are inevitable. Also, it is not merely the oversight which has to be guarded against. There is also the greater danger of small differences in wording as between one statute and the next. If there is no general principle to guide the courts, such small differences are apt to assume disproportionate importance in the process of comparative interpretation.

Secondly, the adoption of this course does not really amount to a legislative solution even if the legislature is unnaturally alert to play its part without oversight or inconsistency, for the effect of a statutory defence still remains with the courts as a matter of interpretation. For example, if an express statutory defence is included in a section creating a regulatory offence, are all common law defences thereby

[17] Above, p. 19 n. 58.

excluded by implication, or only those which may be regarded as inconsistent with the statutory defence, or are they not to be excluded at all? If inconsistency is the criterion of exclusion, what is to be the criterion of inconsistency? These and many other questions, such as the precise meaning of the defence without regard to its effect on the common law, will remain to be decided by the courts. If the past is any guide to the future, their decisions will not be uniform.

Admittedly there is scope for the same kind of difficulties to arise in the interpretation of a general principle in a code as arise with all statutory words. The argument is that far fewer such problems arise with a general principle than with a particular defence, if only because its meaning is likely to be authoritatively established by a high court of appeal fairly soon in its history, whereas the number of cases on minor statutory defences to regulatory crimes which will be taken to a high court of appeal is likely to be small, even if an appeal to a court of high authority is available on such a comparatively small matter.

Thirdly, it has been the very lack of a unifying general principle, whether statutory or common law, which has led to the present situation of almost universal doubt and confusion in this part of the law. Perhaps the most conspicuous result of the absence of general judicial agreement on the correct basis upon which to approach new minor statutory offences has been the unrealistic preoccupation with minute verbal oddities which characterises much modern interpretation of regulatory statutes. Once this degree of particularisation is reached, obscurity and inconsistency is inevitable. There is no reason to think that the proliferation of statutory defences would do anything to alter this process, and good reason to think that it would even make matters worse.

It is submitted that for the foregoing reasons the course of trying to replace strict responsibility for regulatory offences with statutory defences less draconic in their operation is unlikely to be successful and should therefore not be adopted.

Conclusion on statutes

So far as the possibility of statutory reform of the law is concerned, it is submitted that the only method likely to be satisfactory in practice is the enactment of a general criminal code which includes a detailed statement of the basic principles of criminal responsibility and applies those principles as much to regulatory as to any other offences, without differentiating regulatory offences from the rest of the criminal law except within the structure of the criminal law as a whole.

Case-law

In most common law jurisdictions nowadays it is not realistic to expect reform of the criminal law through the enactment of a criminal code.

It is true that in the U.S.A. the State of Louisiana revised its substantive statutory criminal law in 1942, Wisconsin in 1956, and Illinois in 1961, whilst similar major revisions are currently in progress in Maryland, Minnesota and New Mexico.[18] It is also true that in such countries as Canada and New Zealand periodical revisions of the criminal codes are made.[19] But these jurisdictions are a small minority. The more usual pattern of legislative activity in the criminal law field is occasional minor amendment in response to some particular pressure.[20]

It requires most unusual pressure to arouse legislative interest in the enactment of a criminal code. There is no reason to suppose that that pressure is likely in the foreseeable future to build up in those parts of the common law world where regulatory offences present a daily problem. There is, however, good reason to suppose that the courts of many jurisdictions would not be averse to bringing into the law through their own decisions a greater degree of order and

[18] [1960] *University of Illinois Law Forum*, 481, 484.
[19] These codes are not codes in the strict sense used herein and applicable to the Queensland and Western Australian Codes because they are not exclusive sources of the general principles. By Canadian Criminal Code, s. 7 (2), "Every rule and principle of the common law that renders any circumstance a justification or excuse for an act or a defence to a charge continues in force and applies in respect of proceedings for an offence under this Act or any other Act of the Parliament of Canada, except in so far as they are altered by or are inconsistent with this Act or any other Act of the Parliament of Canada." By Crimes Act, 1961 (N.Z.), s. 20 (1), "All rules and principles of the common law which render any circumstances a justification or excuse for any act or omission, or a defence to any charge, shall remain in force and apply to any defence to a charge under this Act or under any other enactment, except so far as they are altered by or are inconsistent with this Act or any other enactment." The Criminal Code Act, 1924 (Tas.), s. 8, is similar to the New Zealand section but limited to charges on indictment.
[20] The outstanding recent instance of this is the English Homicide Act, 1957, introducing degrees of murder into English law as a compromise concession to strong pressure for the abolition of the death penalty. Only "capital murder" as defined by the Act is now subject to the death penalty. Other murders are non-capital. There is general agreement that this compromise, like most such piecemeal amendments to the criminal law, is unsatisfactory from all points of view.

rationality than is now apparent. It is to the problems of reform through case-law that the remainder of this chapter will be devoted.

It is possible to regard the reform of the present law as largely a problem in precedent. England may be taken as an example. Until recently there was no possibility of taking an appeal from the determination by a magistrate in summary jurisdiction of a regulatory prosecution further than a divisional court. Since the vast majority[21] of regulatory prosecutions were limited to summary trial, the consequence was that however carefully the judges addressed themselves to the problem, no coherent body of principles could be evolved because there was no available court of sufficient authority to impose those principles on the judiciary as a whole.

In the well-known case of *Reynolds* v. *G. H. Austin & Sons Ltd.*,[22] for example, three concurring judgments were delivered by judges particularly noted for their interest in and knowledge of the criminal law.[23] At least one of these judgments, that of Devlin J., contains some interesting indications[24] that at that date the time might have been ripe for the introduction of a modification to the English law of strict responsibility by way of negligence. Had the court been sitting, as no doubt it was either earlier or later on the same day, as the Court of Criminal Appeal instead of as a Divisional Court of the King's Bench, the influence exercised by the judgments delivered might have been considerable owing to their binding force. As things were, notwithstanding the eminence of the judges concerned, *Reynolds* v. *G. H. Austin & Sons Ltd.* was, and is, no more than another divisional court decision among hundreds, and one moreover

---

[21] Not all. See *Erson* [1914] V.L.R. 144, and *R.* v. *St. Margarets Trust Ltd.* [1958] 1 W.L.R. 522, for prosecutions of regulatory offences on indictment.
[22] [1951] 2 K.B. 135.
[23] Lord Goddard C.J., Humphreys and Devlin JJ.
[24] [1951] 2 K.B. 135, 149: "[I]f a man is punished because of an act done by another, whom he cannot *reasonably be expected to influence or control*, the law is engaged, not in punishing thoughtlessness or inefficiency, and thereby promoting the welfare of the community, but in pouncing on the most convenient victim." At 150: "In the present case there is nothing which the owner of the vehicle could be *reasonably expected to have done* to see that the offence was not committed." "I think it a safe general principle to follow . . . that where the punishment of an individual will not promote the observance of the law either by that individual or by others whose conduct he may *reasonably be expected to influence*, then, in the absence of clear and express words, such punishment is not intended." At 153 Devlin J. concludes his judgment by citing the dictum in *Bank of New South Wales* v. *Piper* [1897] A.C. 383, 389–390, so often cited in Australia as a basis for the reasonable mistake rule, that "the absence of *mens rea* really consists in an honest and reasonable belief entertained by the accused in the existence of facts which, if true, would make the act charged against him innocent". (Italics added.)

which has exercised disappointingly little influence over the subsequent course of events.[24a]

By contrast, the influence exerted by the rare case in which the Court of Appeal has passed upon a strict responsibility question arising in a civil action has been out of all proportion to the importance of the decision. An outstanding example is *Hobbs* v. *Winchester Corporation*[25] which, although a civil claim for compensation, did much to establish strict responsibility for regulatory offences because of the high place in the hierarchy of the English courts occupied by the Court of Appeal.

A butcher had been unsuccessfully prosecuted by a local authority for supplying meat unfit for human consumption. He was acquitted and then sued the authority under a statutory power for compensation for loss occasioned by the prosecution. The meat had in fact been diseased as to a small part, but it was found on the claim for compensation that neither the butcher nor his assistants could have discovered this on reasonable inspection. One of the statutory conditions for the recovery of compensation was that the claimant should not himself have been in default. The Court of Appeal held that the claim failed because, applying strict responsibility, the claimant could not be heard to say that he was not at fault as the meat was in fact diseased.

There seems to be no reason why the claim could not have been dismissed on the simple ground that since the meat was diseased and had to be destroyed, and since under those circumstances it was reasonable for the local authority to prosecute, even if unsuccessfully, the claimant had suffered no recoverable loss. To regard the decision as an authority on strict responsibility is almost entirely without warrant and merely illustrates the disadvantage of cutting off appeals from minor statutory convictions too low in the hierarchy of courts.

The situation in England has recently been remedied by legislation enabling appeals to be taken, by leave, from a Divisional Court of the Queen's Bench Division to the House of Lords in a criminal cause or matter.[26] Unless the American theory that a regulatory offence

---

[24a] See next chapter, n. 86b, and for a recent case illustrating well the reluctance of the English courts to adopt negligence as a basis of responsibility even when this course is properly open to them, *G. Newton Ltd.* v. *Smith* [1962] 2 Q.B. 278.

[25] [1910] 2 K.B. 471. This case is constantly cited on strict responsibility and was followed by the English Court of Criminal Appeal as recently as the *St. Margarets Trust* case, n. 21 above, in 1958. In the Canadian case of *Beaver* v. *The Queen* 118 C.C.C. 129, decided in 1957, it was much discussed: see at 136–139.

[26] Administration of Justice Act, 1960, s. 1 (1) (*a*).

prosecution is not a criminal cause or matter takes hold in England, this change should furnish this part of the law with the high court of appeal which it so badly needs.[27]

The importance of a court of high authority for the laying down of general principles may be illustrated from the opposite point of view through the Australian law.[28] Whereas in England the law of strict responsibility for regulatory offences has descended into and remains in a disgraceful state, the picture in Australia, although far from perfect, is very different and much better. This situation has been the work of the High Court of Australia and could not have occurred without the possibility of appeal to that court, by leave, in regulatory offence cases.

Over a period of nearly sixty years since its inception the High Court of Australia, acting as the highest available court of appeal in regulatory offence cases, has adhered with almost unbroken consistency to the principle that there should be no criminal responsibility without fault. It has laid down the general rule that in a case of this kind, although it is not normally incumbent upon the prosecution to prove *mens rea* or negligence in the defendant, it is always open to the defendant to exculpate himself by proving affirmatively that he acted under a reasonable mistake of fact such that if the facts had been as he reasonably supposed them to be, no offence would have been committed.

The unifying value of such a principle in this part of the law is not easily overstated. When one recalls that the High Court of Australia is on most matters[29] the highest court of appeal from no less than six distinct state court systems, all exercising both federal and state jurisdiction, as well as from a variety of other tribunals, it becomes apparent that the confusion into which this part of the law might have fallen without that guiding hand could have been spectacular. First among the necessary conditions for the development of a general principle through case-law must be put a single final court of appeal of high authority.

Perhaps the next most important requirement, paradoxical as it may seem at first sight, is a flexible system of precedent. The English courts are governed by a system of precedents notably more rigid in

---

[27] On the term "criminal cause or matter" see [1961] *Annual Practice* 3170.
[28] For a detailed discussion see Ch. 5 and Ch. 6, below.
[29] There is a limited class of cases, not relevant here, which may be taken on appeal to the Privy Council.

its operation than has been found acceptable elsewhere. The consequence has been that the English judiciary have developed a skill in the distinguishing of cases they do not desire to follow which is probably also without parallel in other jurisdictions. It is submitted that the introduction of a new general principle into the law, or the adaptation to new uses of a familiar principle, is likely to be less successful if the legal system in which it is to operate purports to give the innovation the status of immutability.

Any innovation ought if possible to establish itself on its own merits. This is not to say that all the power of a system of precedent should be done away with. To a large extent such a course would be impossible in the nature of things, for all courts normally follow the spirit, if not the letter, of previous decisions both out of respect and because of the universal tendency to adhere to what has already been decided. What is suggested is that the courts are more likely to accept innovation if they are not supposed to be thereby committing themselves to the new view for ever than if the theory is that they are.

If a comparison is made between the House of Lords on the one hand and the Supreme Court of the United States and the High Court of Australia on the other, the effect of an over-rigid system of precedent is immediately apparent. By comparison with the other two courts the House of Lords wears an appearance of ultra-conservatism. It is true that the English court has from time to time made breaks with the past and set the law on a radically different course for the future.[30] Such occasions, however, are rare indeed in the twentieth century, and not to be compared in frequency, or often even in scope, with the major changes brought about by the American and Australian courts.[31] It is reasonable to see a connection between this contrast and the fact that whereas the House of Lords holds itself strictly bound by its own decisions, the Supreme Court of the United States and the High Court of Australia do not accord the same status to their own mistakes. If there is no possibility of rectifying error,

---

[30] Notably in *Woolmington* v. *D.P.P.* [1935] A.C. 462. For an historical appreciation of this decision, showing just how great a break with the past it represented, see Dixon, "The Development of the Law of Homicide" (1935) 9 *Australian Law Journal* (Supplement), 64.

[31] Two of the best-known instances of the Supreme Court of the United States reversing itself occurred in *West Coast Hotel Co.* v. *Parrish* (1937) 300 U.S. 379, which signalised the end of the court's opposition to Roosevelt's New Deal legislation; and in *Brown* v. *Board of Education* (1954) 347 U.S. 483, which departed from the "separate but equal" doctrine of racial segregation laid down in *Plessy* v. *Ferguson* (1896) 163 U.S. 537. For an Australian example see the *Engineers' Case* (1920) 28 C.L.R. 129.

there is almost inevitably a tendency to excessive caution in introducing innovation.

It therefore seems probable that the introduction by the courts themselves of a new principle to govern the trial of regulatory offences requires not only a high court of appeal to effect the change, but also a reasonably flexible system of precedent to encourage it.

A flexible system of precedent is not confined in importance to the mere introduction of a new principle. Unless the system is sufficiently adaptable, not wedded to an over-rigid theory of precedent, with the concomitant characteristic of excessive distinguishing of previous cases, there is a danger that the irreversibility even of small errors may destroy the generality of a new rule. It is quite possible that the initial enunciation of a new rule may prove in the light of experience to be faulty and in need of amendment. If the hold of *stare decisis* is too strong, the only available method of effecting the amendment may be to embark once more on the course of restrictive distinguishing instead of straightforward overruling.

It is sometimes urged that a disadvantage of case-law as against statute is its uncertainty. Judicial statements of the law lack the precision attainable in a statute, especially in a carefully drafted code. This observation merely focuses attention on the converse aspect of the virtue of flexibility. If a need for flexibility is to be put forward, it must at the same time be conceded that something is likely to be lost by way of certainty. The amount so lost, however, is easily capable of exaggeration.

The law relating to regulatory offences shows beyond argument that statute law is not at all synonymous with certainty of law; indeed, that unless a statute is drafted with quite exceptional care and generality, it is likely to give rise to more uncertainty than case-law. Unless one has in mind a statement of governing principle of the order quoted above from the Queensland Criminal Code, it is highly unlikely that a ruling principle enunciated in cases of sufficient authority to be generally followed will lack certainty to any greater extent than the law is by its very nature uncertain.

Conclusion on case-law

As a matter of practical politics, in those jurisdictions which do not have criminal codes already it is unrealistic to expect reform of the law relating to regulatory offences otherwise than through the introduction of new principles of criminal responsibility in this area by the courts themselves. The best possible combination of circumstances for the success of such a development is the existence of a high court of appeal to exercise a guiding influence over the inferior courts which will necessarily handle the vast majority of cases, together with a flexible system of precedent which will permit that court of appeal to overrule its own previous decisions if necessary. If either or both of these conditions is absent the chances of the successful introduction of a change in the case-law of general importance will be materially reduced.

Statute and case-law combined

As will now be apparent from the foregoing discussion, this remaining theoretical alternative is merely the case of reform by the particular statute, an expedient which has already been rejected. Unless a criminal code is to be enacted, reliance on legislative intervention does not seem to be advisable.

Administrative courts

One other possibility which has been canvassed[32] should perhaps be mentioned here, and that is the device of taking the trial of regulatory offences out of the jurisdiction of the criminal courts altogether and creating a hierarchy of administrative tribunals to deal with them instead.

As might be expected from the views previously expressed on the undesirability of severing the connection between the criminal law and minor penal laws, this suggestion is not thought to be a good one. At first sight it might seem attractive to turn over the trial of an income tax offence to a court more concerned with income tax than with crime. Further reflection leads to the conclusion, however, that in such a case the court has to do with a problem, not of income tax at all, but of criminal law. If a man is charged with conspiracy to defraud the revenue he is tried on indictment as for a criminal offence. It is difficult to see the justification for trying him before a civil or quasi-civil court merely because the infraction with which he is charged is less serious than an indictable crime.

[32] Schwenk, "The Administrative Crime, Its Creation and Punishment by Administrative Agencies" (1943) 42 *Michigan Law Review*, 51; Remington, "Is Criminal or Civil Procedure Proper for Enforcement of Traffic Laws?" [1959] *Wisconsin Law Review*, 418, [1960] *ibid.*, 3; Kadish, "Some Observations on the Use of Criminal Sanctions in Enforcing Economic Regulations", (1963) 30 *University of Chicago Law Review* 423.

CHAPTER 5

REASONABLE MISTAKE OF FACT

Introduction

The closest approach to a law for regulatory offences of the kind advocated in preceding chapters has been made by the High Court of Australia. This law is still in the process of development but the following is believed to be an accurate statement of its present effect: if D is charged with a regulatory offence, although P does not have to prove *mens rea* or negligence as a prerequisite for conviction, it is nevertheless open to D in most or all cases to defend himself by proving affirmatively that he committed the culpable act or omission owing to a reasonable mistake of fact of such a nature that, had the facts been as he believed, he would be innocent.

There is room for further development of this rule in several directions. In the first place, as the reservation in the foregoing statement implies, it is not clear whether this defence should apply to all regulatory offences or only to most of them. On this point the attitude of the High Court itself seems to be fairly clear, for, except on three occasions when the abnormal stresses of wartime conditions caused a departure from the usual rule,[1] there is no case in which strict responsibility has been imposed in that court.[2] The doubt occurs at the State Supreme Court level, where the rule supported by the High Court has had a mixed reception.

Needless to say, on the rare occasions when a High Court decision is directly in point, there is and can be no argument. In the majority of cases, however, the question is not so easily settled. Where the question before the court is whether the High Court doctrine should be extended by analogy to a similar, or perhaps not very similar, regulatory offence, there is often a difference of opinion. Sometimes the reasonable mistake of fact defence is accepted as having a high

---

[1] *Duncan* v. *Ellis* (1916) 21 C.L.R. 379; *Myerson* v. *Collard* (1918) 25 C.L.R. 154; *Francis* v. *Rowan* (1941) 64 C.L.R. 196. Of these three cases, the first two are much stronger instances than the third. All three are discussed critically in Ch. 6, below.
[2] The High Court of Australia was created by s. 71 of the Constitution, which came into force on January 1, 1901. The formal opening of the High Court took place on October 6, 1903, in Melbourne, and the first case was heard on October 15, 1903. The first judges to be appointed were Griffith C.J. and Barton and O'Connor JJ.

degree of generality, but sometimes it is rejected in favour of strict responsibility because the effect of the High Court decisions is not found to be sufficiently clearly established.

This situation is prolonged by the fact that the reasonable mistake rule in the present context is largely the work, not of the whole number of High Court Justices, but of two Chief Justices, Sir Samuel Griffith and Sir Owen Dixon. It has not infrequently happened that a statement of the rule made by one of these two judges has been either dissented from in relation to the particular case by his brethren, or at least not commented on. This has left it open for other judges in later cases in effect to choose between the different views. A prominent instance was the most important of all the High Court decisions on regulatory offences, *Proudman* v. *Dayman*.[3] In that case Sir Owen Dixon (not at that date Chief Justice) gave a long and careful statement[4] of his understanding of the present rule. Of his two brethren, McTiernan J. dissented from Sir Owen Dixon's view in its application to the offence before the court and Rich A.C.J. gave no clear indication what he thought about the matter. This divergence of opinion has not passed unnoticed in later cases.

The present status of the reasonable mistake rule, however, is a good deal higher than the preceding two paragraphs would suggest. It is a mistake to try to interpret the law without regard to matters of time and individual personality, for, whatever the theory may be, in reality the law is only to the smallest extent a matter of binding precedents and immutable rules. In this chapter and the next it will be seen that the nearer one approaches to the present day, the higher becomes the proportion and the wider the range of both High Court and State Supreme Court decisions and expressions of opinion in favour of the reasonable mistake rule and against strict responsibility. It seems reasonably clear that this is because the intrinsic desirability of the rule as a way out of the confusion caused by the doctrine of strict responsibility is becoming steadily more widely recognised. The working of an idea in this way cannot be easily reconciled with an inflexible doctrine of precedent, although, of course, the higher the court which initiates the idea, the more chance does it have of acceptance.

Another factor which must be taken into account is the standing in the eyes of their brethren of the judges who initiate new ideas.

---

[3] (1941) 67 C.L.R. 536.
[4] *Ibid.*, 540–541.

Without drawing invidious distinctions it may fairly be said that in the history of the Australian judiciary no judges have carried greater personal prestige, certainly in the context of the criminal law, than Sir Samuel Griffth and Sir Owen Dixon. Moreover, where differences of opinion are expressed, the respect naturally accorded to the office of Chief Justice of the High Court also weighs in the balance against a mere counting of heads.

For these reasons it is safe to say that the reasonable mistake rule is now well established in the common law[5] of Australia, the only problem remaining being its further definition and refinement. The question of the range of offences to which it applies has already been referred to. Another area of future development, in which the courts have much work to do, is the relationship of the rule with particular statutory words and phrases. Here two courses are open.

Since the reasonable mistake rule has been developed in opposition to strict responsibility, it follows logically that the only forms of words with which it may appear to be inconsistent are those which are understood as imposing upon P the need to prove *mens rea*. Examples are "knowingly" and "permit". Now, if the reasonable mistake rule were simply the first step away from strict responsibility towards the universal re-establishment of *mens rea* in the criminal law, one would not expect to see any tendency to cut down the prima facie meaning of such words; but if the reasonable mistake rule were intended to be, not so much a stepping stone to *mens rea* as a permanent compromise between *mens rea* at one extreme and strict responsibility at the other, then one would expect to see a tendency to cut down the prima facie meaning of such words in order to bring them into line with the emerging general rule. The indications are as yet too few to pronounce with confidence on which course the law is likely to follow; but nevertheless there are some interesting signs that it is a permanent general rule which is being aimed at.[6]

The remainder of this chapter will be devoted to a detailed discussion of the characteristics of the reasonable mistake rule as it has so far emerged in the case-law, and will end with a reference to such signs of a similar rule as have appeared in other common law

[5] This chapter and the one following are concerned only with the common law jurisdictions of Australia, namely, the Federal Territories within Australia and the States of New South Wales, Victoria and South Australia. Cases from other jurisdictions are cited only where they throw light on a question relevant to the Australian common law.

[6] See particularly the discussion of Dixon J.'s approach to the construction of the word "permit", above, pp. 60–62, and below, pp. 137–140.

jurisdictions. Chapter 6 will continue the discussion with reference to particular forms of statutory words.

Characteristics of the reasonable mistake rule

(i) *There must be a mistake*

It is said that for D to set up this defence it is not enough for him to prove that he was at the material time ignorant of some fact essential to the commission of the offence with which he is charged, for he could be ignorant through failing to apply his mind to the question at all. D must prove that he actually directed his mind to the fact in question and on reasonable grounds came to a wrong conclusion as to the true state of affairs. Exactly what this limitation on the main rule means is not clear. The available judicial comment is to be found in *Proudman* v. *Dayman*[7] and in four other cases.

It will be recalled that in *Proudman* v. *Dayman* D was charged with permitting an unlicensed person to drive a car on a road.[8] Her application to the High Court for special leave to appeal against conviction was dismissed[9] on the ground, as to Rich A.C.J. and Dixon J., that there was no evidence that she had made a reasonable mistake, and as to McTiernan J., that the offence charged imposed strict responsibility for the fact as to which she said she was mistaken. McTiernan J.'s view on this point can now be disregarded because the law is clear that the word "permit" does not impose strict responsibility for any element of the offence.[10]

The mistake alleged by D was that she thought that the person she allowed to drive was licensed. Dixon J.'s comment[11] was, "the applicant assigned reasons for her alleged belief which neither the magistrate nor the Full Court found convincing or sufficient. Indeed, it may be doubted if she thought at all upon the question whether the person she permitted to drive her car did or did not hold a subsisting licence." Rich A.C.J. expressed himself in stronger terms:[12] "It is not a case of mistake upon reasonable grounds. If she did not know she

---

[7] (1941) 67 C.L.R. 536.

[8] Road Traffic Act, 1934–1939 (S.A.), s. 30.

[9] D had been convicted on summary trial. Her appeal to the Supreme Court of South Australia was allowed by Cleland J. on the ground that she had made a reasonable mistake of fact. P's appeal to the Full Court was allowed on the ground that the evidence did not support the view of Cleland J., Murray C.J. further holding that the offence in any event imposed strict responsibility for the licence.

[10] The same rule applies in England. For a full discussion see Edwards, *Mens Rea in Statutory Offences*, Ch. IV.

[11] (1941) 67 C.L.R. 536, 541.

[12] *Ibid.*, 538–539.

did not inquire, and a fair inference is that she did not care. . . . It is simply a case where a person showing complete indifference to the fulfilment of a duty laid on her by the legislature says: 'I didn't know.' "

The next reference to this distinction between ignorance and mistake occurs in *Pelham* v. *Harris*.[13] D appealed to the Supreme Court of South Australia from summary conviction under the Landlord and Tenant (Control of Rents) Act, 1942 (S.A.), s. 33, for refusing to answer questions put to him by an authorised officer of the South Australian Housing Trust about certain premises. One of the grounds of appeal was that P had not shown that D was aware that the officer who put the questions was authorised to do so. In dismissing the appeal, Richards J. made the following comment on this contention.[14] "It may be pointed out that the question much discussed in *Dayman* v. *Proudman*, and on the application for leave to appeal (*Proudman* v. *Dayman*), i.e., namely, whether mistake or reasonable grounds would be a good defence, does not arise in the present case, for the appellant does not appear to have applied his mind to the question whether his questioner was an authorized person; on the contrary there is nothing in the evidence to lead one to think he had any doubt about it."

A more intriguing situation arose for discussion in *Foster* v. *Aloni*.[15] D was charged with offending against regulations for the control of electrical appliances[16] in that he had made an improper use of electricity by not complying with restrictions advertised in the daily press pursuant to the regulations. The information was dismissed by the magistrate on the ground that,[17] "the defendant was asleep at the relevant time and had no knowledge that the appliance[18] was in operation and no idea of guilt in the matter".

P's appeal from the dismissal of the information was in turn dismissed by the Victorian Full Court[19] on the ground that the advertisement in the daily press relied on was ineffective for uncertainty and lack of definition, but the view taken by the magistrate was also dealt with in the judgment. The court indicated[20] that, accepting Dixon J.

---

[13] [1944] S.A.S.R. 224.
[14] *Ibid.*, 229.
[15] [1951] V.L.R. 481.
[16] Protection of Electrical Operations Regulations, reg. 4 (*b*), made under the State Electricity Commission Act, 1928 (Vic.).
[17] [1951] V.L.R. 481, 482.
[18] The appliance was a water heater.
[19] Lowe A.C.J., Barry and Sholl JJ.
[20] [1951] V.L.R. 481, 488.

in *Proudman* v. *Dayman* as correctly stating the modern reasonable mistake rule, yet for D merely to prove that he was asleep at the relevant time did not amount to "evidence of the facts necessary to apply that rule in his favour". In other words, even if it were arguable that D must have been ignorant of the material facts because he was asleep, on no view could it be said that the mere fact of unconsciousness was evidence of a positively mistaken belief. Indeed, the contrary was more likely.

The point arose again clearly in *Green* v. *Sergeant*,[21] decided a few days after *Foster* v. *Aloni*. D had been summarily convicted of killing native game, in the form of two wild ducks, in an area proclaimed as a wild life sanctuary.[22] At his trial D gave evidence that he did not know that the land over which he was shooting was a sanctuary, and that therefore he was entitled to be acquitted on the basis that he had made a reasonable mistake of fact, the fact being the status of the land.[23] The magistrates accepted D's evidence on the point but declined to agree that he had therefore established a reasonable mistake of fact. This decision was upheld by Martin J. on appeal to the Victorian Supreme Court.[24]

"[H]is ignorance of the nature of the area in which he was engaged does not necessarily mean that he had an honest belief in a state of facts which, if they existed, would make his action innocent. There is no doubt he knew he was shooting duck at Werribee[25] and he never bothered to enquire whether he was on prohibited land or not. He really had no belief on the subject, for it never entered his head what was the nature of the property where he was. As was said by Rich A.C.J. in *Proudman* v. *Dayman* . . . 'It is simply a case where a person showing complete indifference to the fulfilment of the duty laid on her by the legislature says: "I didn't know." ' "

The latest case, *Gherashe* v. *Boase*,[26] was similar to *Green* v. *Sergeant*, the only material difference being that D was charged with cutting firewood in a state forest without a permit[27] instead of shooting wild life in a sanctuary. D maintained that he had not realised that he had passed from his own land, which was contiguous, over the border into the state forest. Dean J. of the Victorian Supreme Court,

[21] [1951] V.L.R. 500.
[22] Game Act, 1928 (Vic.), s. 5 (2).
[23] It is clear that status is a question of fact. See below, pp. 96–98.
[24] [1951] V.L.R. 500, 504–505.
[25] The name of the sanctuary.
[26] [1959] V.R. 1.
[27] Forests Act, 1957 (Vic.), s. 95 (*h*).

allowing P's appeal from dismissal of the information, followed *Proudman* v. *Dayman* and *Green* v. *Sergeant* in holding that since on the evidence D had not established that he had directed his mind to the question of precisely where he was at all, he could not rely on having made a positive mistake.

The nature of the distinction between simple ignorance and mistake in the criminal law has been well put by Glanville Williams.[28] "Now mistake is a kind of ignorance. Every mistake involves ignorance, but not *vice versa*. Ignorance is lack of true knowledge, either because the mind is a complete blank or because it is filled with untrue (mistaken) [belief] on a particular subject. The first variety, lack of knowledge without mistaken [belief], may be called simple ignorance. The second variety, lack of true knowledge coupled with mistaken [belief], is mistake. Ignorance is the genus of which simple ignorance and mistake are the species."

The effect of the foregoing cases appears to be that for the purposes of the reasonable mistake rule D must prove mistake in the sense arrived at by Glanville Williams, and not merely simple ignorance. However, there is another question to be taken into account before accepting this conclusion which is aptly introduced by a further quotation from the same source. Immediately after the foregoing passage the learned author continues, "either simple ignorance or mistake is sufficient to destroy the intentional nature of an act as to the unknown circumstance. Mistake will displace recklessness also. Whether simple ignorance will displace recklessness is a matter that we have now to consider."

This passage refers to crime of *mens rea*, but a parallel problem arises with regulatory offences under the reasonable mistake rule. In this context it is irrelevant to inquire whether simple ignorance or mistake will "destroy the intentional nature of an act as to the unknown circumstance" because regulatory offences do not require intention (*mens rea*) as to material circumstances. The same applies to recklessness, for D can be convicted of a regulatory offence under the reasonable mistake rule if, in effect, he fails to rebut a presumption of culpable negligence raised by the proof by P of facts showing a prima facie breach of the law. One has to start lower down in the scale of culpability than either intention or recklessness. What one

[28] *Criminal Law: The General Part* (2nd ed.), 151–152. In the quotation in the text the word "belief" where it appears in square brackets has been substituted for the word "knowledge" used by Williams because to talk of "mistaken knowledge" seems misleading.

can say is that reasonable mistake will rebut the presumption of negligence and unreasonable mistake and unreasonable simple ignorance will not. But what remains to be decided is whether reasonable simple ignorance rebuts the presumption. The uncertainty of the answer to this question is shown by four of the preceding five cases.

In each case except *Foster* v. *Aloni*, where the problem of mistaken belief arose because D was asleep at the relevant time, the court evidently regarded D's ignorance as culpable. In each of these four cases D's ignorance was not regarded as sufficient excuse, not so much, it may be suggested, because it did not amount to a positive mistake, as because it was unjustifiable. It is perfectly reasonable to require D in *Proudman* v. *Dayman* to inquire whether the person being allowed to drive the car is licensed; in *Pelham* v. *Harris* to ask the housing officer to produce his authority; and in *Green* v. *Sergeant* and *Gherashe* v. *Boase* to take some trouble to find out whose land he is on before shooting ducks or cutting firewood. From this point of view it is possible to argue that the courts have unduly refined the reasonable mistake rule by isolating a separate requirement of positive mistake as opposed to simple ignorance. In each of these four cases it can be said that D could not set up the reasonable mistake defence because, whatever the nature of his misapprehension, it was unreasonable. The difference between positive mistake and simple ignorance was therefore irrelevant.

Foster v. *Aloni*, the fifth case, is a little more complex. The problem posed there was as to the application of a defence requiring a particular state of mind to the situation where D has no legally relevant state of mind because he is unconscious through sleep. At first sight it seems easy to say that since D was asleep the defence of reasonable mistake cannot be available, and that therefore, if no other defence is available, it is right that he should be convicted. This is too superficial a view. It leads to the conclusion that a person who has no chance of complying with the law because he is asleep may be convicted where someone who had a chance to comply may be acquitted because he was awake enough to make a reasonable mistake. One ought not to be exposed to criminal responsibility merely by virtue of going to sleep. Conversely, it should not be possible to evade criminal responsibility, if one has the ability to do so, by falling asleep at a convenient moment.

This analysis shows that in truth it is neither the reasonable mistake rule nor sleep which causes difficulty, but the general rule that states of mind are relevant in the criminal law only if they are contemporaneous with the forbidden conduct. Suppose that in *Foster* v. *Aloni* the regulation had said that water heaters of the kind in question should not be used after 9 p.m. and D had gone to sleep at 8.30. At the time when the forbidden event occurs, 9 p.m. or later, D is unconscious and therefore incapable of a legally relevant state of mind. One's natural reaction is not to be discommoded by this rather technical difficulty but to say that D's criminal responsibility should be determined by the circumstances under which he went to sleep. If he was reasonably under the impression when he went to sleep that the water heater was switched off, he should be allowed to set up this mistake in his own defence. In *Foster* v. *Aloni* itself the attitude which the court would have taken to such an argument was left uncertain,[29] but guidance is furnished by two cases on indictable offences in which similar, although not identical, problems arose.

The first is the Queensland case of *Scarth*.[30] D was driving along a country road late at night when he fell asleep. His car veered out of control and collided with and killed three young men who were repairing an ignition fault on a motor cycle by the side of the road. D was convicted of manslaughter. On appeal to the Court of Criminal Appeal the conviction was set aside and a new trial ordered. It had been argued for D that his being asleep when the accident happened was a complete defence, and against him that it was no defence. The trial judge correctly directed the jury that sleep of itself was not a defence but omitted to give any other direction on its relevance to D's criminal responsibility. It was held that the jury should have been told that the important point was whether the circumstances under which D fell asleep *before* the accident amounted to an answer to the charge.

"When a *prima facie* case of criminal negligence has been proved against the driver of a motor vehicle, evidence which showed that the driver of the motor vehicle was asleep at the relevant time, but showed nothing more than this, would not, in my opinion, destroy or weaken the *prima facie* case against him. On the contrary, it would

---

[29] [1951] V.L.R. 481, 488: "We do not think this regulation admits of a construction which would require the informant ... to prove guilty intent, or that that proof would fail if on the whole of the evidence it appeared that, or it was uncertain whether or not, the defendant intended to switch off the system at or before the prescribed time, but failed by reason of sleep or otherwise to do so. . . ."
[30] [1945] St. R. Qd. 38.

strengthen it. But if a driver of a motor car fell asleep at the wheel without any prior warning of his inability to keep awake, and in circumstances where a reasonably careful driver would not have been aware that he was likely to fall asleep, and as a result of his so falling asleep personal injury or death was caused to some other person, no criminal liability would, in my opinion, attach to the driver of the motor car . . . the summing-up did not deal with the circumstances in which the fact that he fell asleep at the wheel might be available as an excuse to a driver of a vehicle charged with killing another by criminally negligent driving."[31]

The second case is the decision of the House of Lords in *Attorney-General for Northern Ireland* v. *Gallagher*,[32] in which it was held, *inter alia*, that if on a charge of murder the defence of insanity is set up on the basis that a quiescent psychopathic condition developed into actual insanity owing to voluntary intoxication, D being insane at the time when he killed, the relevant point of time for the application of the M'Naghten Rules is when D started to drink and not when he killed.

It is therefore submitted, by analogy with these cases, that in such a case as *Foster* v. *Aloni* the relevant time to inquire whether D was acting under the influence of a reasonable mistake of fact is the time when he fell asleep, and not the time when the forbidden event occurred. Since this approach was not made in that case, *Foster* v. *Aloni* affords no assistance in answering the question whether reasonable simple ignorance is a sufficient misapprehension for the purpose of the reasonable mistake defence.

The form in which the problem is most likely to arise is where D is not under the conscious influence of a positive mistake because he did not direct his mind to the fact in question at all; but he did not so direct his mind because in the circumstances it was reasonable for him not to, or, in other words, because the question would not have occurred to a reasonable man in the circumstances. Suppose that D is charged with driving through traffic lights whilst they were showing red against him and his answer is that he was waved on by a policeman. The fact is that the "policeman" was a practical joker dressed in police uniform. D admits that the question whether the man whose signal he obeyed was really a policeman never entered his head. He naturally and without conscious thought assumed that he was

[31] *Ibid.*, 42, *per* Macrossan S.P.J.
[32] [1963] A.C. 349.

dealing with an authorised official. This is a case of reasonable simple ignorance, but if D actually thought, "That man might be a practical joker, but I believe him to be a policeman because no practical joker could look so much like a policeman", it would be a case of positive mistake. It is difficult to believe that in the former case, in which some might think that D had acted more reasonably than in the latter, D would be convicted whereas in the latter he might be acquitted. Yet this is the consequence of persisting in the distinction between simple ignorance and mistake.

The truth of the matter is that the difference between these two states is a matter of degree of consciousness only. If an unconscious assumption is acted on which turns out to be wrong, this is called simple ignorance, but if the same assumption is brought to the conscious level of thought it is said to be a mistake. In doubtful cases it is submitted that the court will be compelled to fall back on the test whether D's assumptions, conscious or unconscious, were reasonable; and it is further submitted that this is in fact what the courts do now. In nearly all cases where D pleads mere ignorance the true situation will be the one described by Rich A.C.J. in *Proudman* v. *Dayman* in the passage already quoted:[33] "If she did not know she did not inquire, and a fair inference is that she did not care."

It would be going too far to say that this state of mind amounts to wilful blindness. The deliberate refusal to make obvious inquiries may be treated in the criminal law as equivalent to intention, or at least to recklessness. Glanville Williams seems to regard simple ignorance also as amounting to recklessness,[34] but it is not necessary for the present purpose to go so far. If the basis of the law is negligence, which is clearly true of the Australian reasonable mistake rule, it is necessary only to be able to regard a failure to make inquiries as negligent. There is no difficulty about this, and the requisite failure to conform with accepted standards need come nowhere near wilful blindness to ground responsibility for a regulatory offence.

The conclusion therefore is that although the courts at present refer to the necessity for a positive mistake by D as an element of the reasonable mistake of fact defence, and will, no doubt, continue to

[33] (1941) 67 C.L.R. 536, 538.
[34] *Criminal Law: The General Part* (2nd ed.), 151–154. At 155 the author regards this use of the concept of recklessness as "rather forced" and sees it as following from the rule that ignorance of the law is no excuse.

do so, there is no need to regard this in the exceptional case as excluding from the defence one whose action was based on reasonable simple ignorance; for upon analysis the apparently separate requirement of a positive mistake turns out to be only a particular application of the main rule that the misapprehension guiding D's actions be reasonable.

(ii) *The mistake must be of fact, not law*

The reasonable mistake defence does not abrogate the general rule that ignorance of the law is no excuse.[35] This was put beyond doubt in *Bergin* v. *Stack*.[36] D was a steward employed by a club not registered for the sale of liquor. He was charged with selling liquor contrary to the Licensing Act, 1928–1934 (Vic.), s. 161: "(1) Every person who (except as the agent or servant of a licensed person and then only in accordance with such person's licence) sells any liquor without a licence authorising such sale [shall be liable to certain penalties]."

It was agreed that there had been an act of sale by D, but he maintained that he did not know that the club was unregistered, and had taken it for granted, without inquiry, that it was licensed. The sale, however, had taken place outside normal hours at a time when the club, in addition to a normal licence, would have needed also a special permit to sell liquor. As to this, D said he did not know about the law on the point (although he had been twenty-five years in the trade) and had believed throughout that he was acting within the terms of the club's supposed licence. It was held[37] that if D had made a mistake it was as to a point of law (licensing hours), not of fact (the club's possession of a special permit), and that a mistake of law afforded no defence.[38]

It has already been observed in connection with status offences that questions of status are of considerable importance in this part of the law. The question can arise whether status is fact or law, *i.e.*, whether a mistake as to status can be a reasonable mistake for the purposes of this defence. *Thomas* v. *The King*[39] decided in the context

---

[35] *Cf. Wilson* v. *Chambers* (1926) 38 C.L.R. 131; below, p. 142.

[36] (1953) 88 C.L.R. 248.

[37] By Williams A.C.J., Webb, Fullagar and Taylor JJ. Kitto J. regarded the language of the section as "quite decisively" against the reasonable mistake defence in any event (at 273).

[38] Barry J. of the Victorian Supreme Court had allowed the defence of reasonable mistake of fact in the decision appealed from: [1952] A.L.R. 810.

[39] (1937) 59 C.L.R. 279.

of bigamy that a mistake of status in an indictable offence is a mistake of fact and therefore negatives *mens rea* if the status concerned is material to the offence charged. In that case the mistaken belief was that a divorced woman was still married. The same rule seems to apply to regulatory offences, although it has not been expressly passed upon.

In *Dowling* v. *Bowie*[40] D was charged under the Licensing Ordinance, 1939–1952 (Northern Territory), s. 141, with having unlawfully sold liquor to S, a half-caste within the meaning and for the purpose of the Aboriginal Ordinance, 1918–1947 (N.T.), ss. 3 and 3A. The Ordinance contained power[41] for a declaration to be made by the appropriate authority that any particular person should no longer be deemed to be a half-caste within the meaning and for the purpose of the Ordinance. D did not deny that he had sold liquor to S but asserted that he had acted under a reasonable mistake of fact in that he had believed S to be a person in respect of whom a declaration had been made, for he had over a period of years frequently seen S drinking in bars. In fact no declaration affecting S had been made.

At the trial P offered no evidence that S was not a person in respect of whom a declaration had been made. D was convicted and his appeal to the Supreme Court of the Northern Territory was dismissed. He appealed from this decision to the High Court on two grounds: (1) that the status of S was a material element of the offence charged which P had failed to prove; and (2) that he himself had proved a reasonable mistake of fact which was an answer to the charge. The court held unanimously that the appeal succeeded on ground (1). Williams and Taylor JJ. in a joint judgment held that D succeeded on ground (2) also. Dixon C.J., with whom the remaining members of the court, Fullagar and Kitto JJ., agreed *in toto*, was "prepared to concede"[42] that reasonable mistake of fact would have been available defence but held that it had not been made out on the evidence. The question whether a mistake as to the status of S was a mistake of fact or of law was canvassed neither in argument nor in the judgments; but since it was implicit in the acceptance of the defence of reasonable mistake, the point may be taken to have passed *sub silentio*. The same inference can be drawn from *Proudman* v.

[40] (1952) 86 C.L.R. 136. Followed in *Roddy* v. *Perry No. 2* [1958] S.R. (N.S.W.) 41, and *Bergin* v. *Thompson* [1953] V.L.R. 408. *Cf. Steele* v. *Starr* (1912) 29 W.N. (N.S.W.) 82.
[41] S. 3A.
[42] (1952) 86 C.L.R. 136, 141.

Dayman itself, where the question of the status of the driver (*i.e.*, whether licensed or unlicensed) was treated by all three judges, without comment, as an issue of fact.[43]

The actual test of the distinction between law and fact in a borderline case is not less obscure in regulatory offences than elsewhere. *Bergin* v. *Stack* suggests some of the potential difficulties. In such a situation as arose there much may depend on the way in which D's case is presented. Suppose D is charged with selling liquor outside the terms of his employer's licence and he gives evidence that he thought the licence covered the situation in which he sold the liquor. This error may be classified as a mistake of law because the construction of documents is a matter of law. But if D gives evidence that he thought his employer had a licence which covered the situation in which he sold the liquor, the facts being identical with the first case, D's story may be classified as a mistake of fact, namely, whether his employer had a certain document at all. The situation becomes yet more complicated if the rule mentioned above that status is a question of fact is borne in mind, for D could also argue that his true mistake was as to the status of his employer, namely, whether at the relevant time he was a licensed person.

There does not seem to be any ready way of resolving such problems as these, for they depend, not on any peculiarity of the fact situation in which they arise, but on the inherently vague nature of the distinction between law and fact. They can be disposed of only by the radical step of abolishing the rule that ignorance of law does not excuse from criminal responsibility. This is not the place to enter upon a detailed discussion of the desirability or practicality of that reform, which the present writer would certainly advocate, but the observation may be made that precedents for such a step are accumulating to a greater extent than may be generally realised.[44]

It would be good to be able to say that at least errors of mixed law and fact are within the reasonable mistake defence, but *Bergin* v. *Stack* seems to lay down the contrary. The steward's errors in that

[43] See also *Roddy* v. *Perry No. 2* [1958] S.R. (N.S.W.) 41, and *cf. Green* v. *Sergeant*, above, p. 90.
[44] See Mueller, "The German Draft Criminal Code 1960 – An Evaluation in Terms of American Criminal Law" [1961] *University of Illinois Law Forum*, 25, 50–51; *Lambert* v. *California* (1957) 355 U.S. 225; *Smith* v. *California* (1959) 361 U.S. 147. There is also the considerable inroad on the ignorance of law rule made by the exceptions in favour of claim of right in property offences: *Twose* (1879) 14 Cox 327; *Bernhard* [1938] 2 K.B. 264. *Cf.* Model Penal Code, Proposed Official Draft, ss. 2.04 (1) (a), 2.02 (9), and 2.04 (3). *Wilson* v. *Chambers* (1926) 38 C.L.R. 131, below, p. 142.

case were a compound of law and fact, but for the purposes of the reasonable mistake rule the element of law in them was decisive.

(iii) *The mistake must be reasonable*

The central characteristic of the defence under consideration is that if the mistake set up by D is to furnish an answer to the charge, it must in the opinion of the court have been a reasonable one to make in the circumstances. The nature of this requirement appears clearly in the following passages from the judgment of Dixon J. in *Proudman* v. *Dayman*,[45] where, it will be recalled, the offence charged was permitting an unlicensed person to drive a motor vehicle on a road.

"It is one thing to deny that a necessary ingredient of the offence is positive knowledge of the fact that the driver holds no subsisting licence. It is another to say that an honest belief founded on reasonable grounds that he is licensed cannot exculpate a person who permits him to drive. As a general rule an honest and reasonable belief in a state of facts which, if they existed, would make the defendant's act innocent affords an excuse for doing what would otherwise be an offence."

"There may no longer be any presumption that *mens rea*, in the sense that a specific state of mind, whether of motive, intention, knowledge or advertence, is an ingredient in an offence created by a modern statute; but to concede that the weakening of the older understanding of the rule of interpretation has left us with no *prima facie* presumption that some mental element is implied in the definition of any new statutory offence does not mean that the rule that honest and reasonable mistake is *prima facie* admissible as an exculpation has lost its application also."

The true significance of these dicta will not be appreciated unless it is remembered that in relation to reasonableness the effect of mistake of fact in the criminal law is not uniform. Sometimes it is true to say in a literal sense that to constitute a sufficient answer to a criminal charge a mistake of fact must be reasonable, and sometimes not. Thus Glanville Williams says[46] that the "idea that a mistake, to be a defence,[47] must be reasonable, though lurking in some of the cases, is certainly not true as a general proposition", except, of

[45] (1941) 67 C.L.R. 536, 540–541.
[46] *Criminal Law: The General Part* (2nd ed.), 201. See also by the same author, "Homicide and the Supernatural" (1949) 65 *Law Quarterly Review*, 491.
[47] Williams was not here intending to imply that any burden of proof rested on D to establish the kind of mistake he was referring to in the passage quoted.

course, where some statute expressly confines the defence to reasonable mistake. With this may be contrasted the rather different formulation by Perkins:[48] "If no specific intent or other special mental element is required for guilt of the offense charged, a mistake of fact will not be recognized as an excuse unless it was based upon reasonable grounds."

The reason why there should not be a general literal requirement of reasonableness of mistake in the criminal law has been described as follows.[49] "Must the mistake be reasonable? An act is reasonable in law when it is such as a man of ordinary care, skill, and prudence would do under similar circumstances. To require that the mistake be reasonable means that if the defendant is to have a defence, he would have acted up to the standard of an average man, whether the defendant is himself such a man or not. This is the application of an outer standard to the individual. If the defendant, being mistaken as to material facts, is to be punished because his mistake is one which an average man would not make, punishment will sometimes be inflicted when the criminal mind does not exist. Such a result is contrary to fundamental principles and is plainly unjust, for a man should not be held criminal because of lack of intelligence. If the mistake, whether reasonable or unreasonable, as judged by an external standard, does negative the criminal mind, there should be no conviction."

Nevertheless it is undoubtedly true that in many judicial references to mistake of fact the word "reasonable" or some synonym appears. Perhaps the best known is the sweeping declaration of the Privy Council in *Bank of New South Wales* v. *Piper*,[50] often cited in Australian cases, that "the absence of *mens rea* really consists in an honest and reasonable belief entertained by the accused of the existence of facts, which, if true, would make the act charged against him innocent".

Many other examples could be cited,[51] but as applied to offences requiring *mens rea* they are equally unsatisfactory if read literally.

---

[48] *Criminal Law*, 827.
[49] Keedy, "Ignorance and Mistake in the Criminal Law" (1908) 22 *Harvard Law Review*, 75, 84.
[50] [1897] A.C. 383, 389–390.
[51] For a selection see *Prince* (1875) 2 C.C.R. 154, 170, *per* Brett J.; *Tolson* (1889) 23 Q.B.D. 168, 181, *per* Cave J., 188, *per* Stephen J.; *Hardgrave* v. *The King* (1906) 4 C.L.R. 232, 237, *per* Griffith C.J.; *Maher* v. *Musson* (1934) 52 C.L.R. 100, 104, *per* Dixon J. For American examples see Perkins, *Criminal Law*, 826–827, nn. 71–77; *U.S.* v. *Ah Chong* (1910) 15 Philippine 488; *Adams* v. *State* (1928) 110 Tex. Cr. 20, 7 S.W. 2d. 528.

The reason is that to require *mens rea* but to limit the defence of mistake of fact to reasonable mistakes is a contradiction in terms. If the definition of an offence requires a particular state of mind in D and that state of mind is intention or advertence, as is the case with offences of *mens rea*, then if D does not have that state of mind he must be acquitted of that offence.[52] It follows that if P has to prove *mens rea* and D sets up mistake of fact, D is doing no more than deny an essential part of P's case, for he is saying simply that he did not have the requisite state of mind at the relevant time. If D's opportunity to say this is limited to the case where he made a reasonable mistake, a mistake such as a reasonable (*i.e.*, average) man would have made, then the effect is to limit the protection afforded to D by the *mens rea* requirement to the standard of behaviour and understanding of an average man. Instead of asking merely, "Did D have *mens rea* as required by the definition of this crime?" one asks that question first and then, if the answer is, "No, because he acted under a mistake of fact", the further question, "Would a reasonable man have made that mistake?" Only if this second question is answered "Yes" is D on this argument entitled to be acquitted. There is no warrant in the definition of a crime defined to include *mens rea* for this additional liability of D to conviction.

It is therefore not surprising to find that there are also dicta of high authority which do not limit the defence of mistake of fact to reasonable mistake. Thus Lord Atkin in *Thorne* v. *Motor Trade Association*,[53] commenting on a passage in Darling J.'s judgment in *Dymond*,[54] remarked that "language was used in the judgment which seemed to indicate that even if the mistake were as to a fact which would have constituted a reasonable cause such a mistake would be irrelevant; in other words, there must be in fact a cause not merely a genuine belief in a cause. This seems to be incautiously expressed: and I do not think that doubt should exist upon a well established

---

[52] This line of argument leaves out of account the effect of the recent decision of the House of Lords in *D.P.P.* v. *Smith* [1961] A.C. 290, which, whatever it may in the future be interpreted as saying, clearly lays down the rule for English courts that where *mens rea* must be proved in D it is sufficient to prove what a reasonable man would have known or intended in D's situation, and not what D actually knew or intended. It would be outside the scope of the present work to undertake a critique of this decision, which the writer believes to be wrong. For demonstrations of the undesirability and dubious theoretical basis of the *Smith* case see Glanville Williams, "Constructive Malice Revived" (1960) 23 *Modern Law Review*, 605; Travers and Morris, "Imputed Intent in Murder" (1961) 35 *Australian Law Journal*, 154.

[53] [1937] A.C. 797, 809. *Cf. Thomas* v. *The King* (1937) 59 C.L.R. 279, 299–300, *per* Dixon J. And see Perkins, *Criminal Law*, 828, n. 82; *Marshall* (1830) 1 Lew. 76.

[54] [1920] 2 K.B. 260.

proposition in criminal law that normally a genuine belief in the existence of facts as apart from law, which if they existed would constitute a defence, is itself a sufficient defence."

The point is sufficiently important to be further emphasised by another quotation, this time from the judgment of Dixon J. in *Thomas* v. *The King*,[55] a case which was a landmark in the development of the doctrine of mistake of fact in the criminal law. "Whenever a legal standard of liability includes some exercise or expression of the will, some subsidiary rules of law must be adopted with respect to mistake. States of volition are necessarily dependent upon states of fact, and a mistaken belief in the existence of circumstances cannot be separated from the manifestation of the will which it prompts. Whether consent, intention, or motive, is the element which a legal criterion of liability includes, it is undeniable that a misapprehension of fact may produce a state of mind which though apparently of the required description is yet really of an entirely different quality."

There is a clear denial in the two foregoing passages of the apparent requirement of reasonableness as a matter of law which appears in the other dicta referred to. The conflict of view is usually resolved by explaining that the word "reasonable" in this context means only that unless the grounds alleged for the mistake appear to be reasonable, D is not likely to be believed, and does not mean that reasonableness is required as a matter of law. Thus in *Gurney*[56] Cockburn C.J. said that "the reasonableness of belief, though it may be one element of judging of its honesty, is not conclusive", and Lord Bramwell in *Derry* v. *Peek*[57] referred to "a confusion of unreasonableness of belief as evidence of dishonesty, and unreasonableness of belief as of itself a ground of action".

Now, this explanation, although it reconciles many of the dicta satisfactorily, is not adequate in all cases. For instance, it is difficult to say that the court is referring only to an evidentiary caution when it deliberately requires that the mistake be such "as does not arise from a want of proper care",[58] or "not superinduced by fault or negligence",[59] or even more explicitly lays down that if D pleads

---

[55] (1937) 59 C.L.R. 279, 299.
[56] (1869) 11 Cox 414, 467.
[57] (1889) 14 App. Cas. 337, 352. See also *Wilson* v. *Inyang* [1951] 2 K.B. 799, and the note thereon by Glanville Williams, (1951) 14 *Modern Law Review*, 485; *Bonnor* [1951] V.R. 227, 253–254, *per* Barry J.; *Bergin* v. *Stack* [1952] A.L.R. 810, 813, *per* Barry J.
[58] *Hamilton* v. *State* (1930) 115 Tex. Cr. 96, 97; 29 S.W. 2d 777, 778.
[59] *Dotson* v. *State* (1878) 62 Ala. 141, 144.

mistake he "is bound to exercise reasonable diligence to ascertain the facts".[60] There is a further difficulty over offences of negligence.[61] It is a contradiction to say that an offence can be committed on proof of negligence and yet allow a negligent mistake merely because it happened to be genuine. This is the opposite contradiction from saying that an offence cannot be committed by mere negligence and yet requiring a mistake to be reasonable to amount to a defence. It is clear that for a mistake of fact to afford a defence to a charge based on negligence, it must also be reasonable, *i.e.*, such a mistake as a reasonable man would have made in the circumstances; just as it is clear that a mistake of fact cannot be so limited to afford a defence to a charge based on *mens rea*.

The conclusion follows that the difficulties hitherto encountered by attempts to state the effect of mistake of fact in the criminal law in one uniform way have been occasioned by a failure to recognise that the effect of mistake of fact is certain to be different according as *mens rea* or negligence is the basis of liability for the offence in question. If this is borne in mind the significance of the contrast made in *Proudman* v. *Dayman*[62] and other Australian cases in the present context[63] between full *mens rea* and reasonable mistake of fact becomes clear. No antithesis can be drawn between *mens rea* and mistake of fact *simpliciter* because if an offence does not require *mens rea*, it follows that mere mistake of fact is irrelevant. The antithesis which can be and is drawn is between *mens rea* and *reasonable* mistake of fact, for an offence which does not require *mens rea* may yet require negligence for conviction, and to talk of unreasonable mistakes is only another way of referring to a culpability based on negligence. Unless the contrast made in the cases between *mens rea* and reasonable mistake of fact is interpreted in this way it is unintelligible, and it cannot be unintelligible because the courts have for some years now applied it perfectly intelligibly.

Although the requirement of reasonableness is so basic that it pervades every case on this defence, it is not easy to find examples

---

[60] *Gordon* v. *State* (1875) 52 Ala. 308, 315.

[61] The term "negligence" is used here as meaning "a non-intentional failure to conform to the conduct of the reasonable man in respect of the consequence in question". (Williams, *Criminal Law: The General Part* (2nd ed.), 102.) The antithesis sometimes drawn between negligence as conduct and negligence as a state of mind is thought to serve no useful purpose (see *ibid.*, 102–103).

[62] (1941) 67 C.L.R. 536.

[63] For a list of cases since *Proudman* v. *Dayman* see p. 61 n. 47, above. See also *Maher* v. *Musson* (1934) 52 C.L.R. 100.

where D has failed to establish the defence expressly on this ground.[64] By way of one illustration, it has already been observed that the supposed necessity for a positive mistake, as opposed to simple ignorance, proves on analysis to be merely a particular aspect of reasonableness. The same might also be rather artificially said of the exclusion from this defence of mistakes of law, for it might be said that in the eye of the law a mistake of law can never be reasonable. But these are not instances of the express disallowance of the defence for unreasonableness. What the courts usually mean by the term "reasonable mistake" in practice is "reasonable grounds for making the mistake", and although in a number of cases this would evidently have afforded a ground for the decision if necessary, more often than not some other ground, such as error of law or absence of positive mistake, has presented itself and been relied on. An instance of the former is *Bergin* v. *Stack*,[65] and of the latter, *Proudman* v. *Dayman*.[66]

However, in the South Australian case of *Belling* v. *O'Sullivan*[67] the absence of reasonable grounds for making the mistake relied on was assigned as a distinct ground for dismissing appeals from conviction. D had been convicted of offences against the Licensing Act, 1932–1945 (S.A.), s. 170, which said that if a child under sixteen, other than his son, daughter or servant, was on licensed premises, the person in charge of the premises should forthwith remove him, under pain of a penalty if he failed to do so. On D's appeals from conviction Ligertwood J. first held that the reasonable mistake of fact defence as stated in *Maher* v. *Musson*[68] and *Proudman* v. *Dayman*[69] applied, and then turned to D's argument that he had been reasonably mistaken as to the ages of the children because he had asked them their ages and been misinformed.[70]

"In each of the present cases, there was ample evidence to raise a *prima facie* case against the defendant. He himself thought in the first instance that each boy was under the age of sixteen years. He was thus put on inquiry. He was content in each case with the boy's assurance that he was over sixteen. The Magistrate did not regard the defendant's questioning of the boys as affording reasonable grounds for an honest belief that they were over sixteen. His finding is not one with which an appellate court ought to interfere. He had

---

[64] But see the early case of *Spooner* v. *Alexander* (1912) 13 C.L.R. 704, p. 116.
[65] (1953) 88 C.L.R. 248, above, p. 96.   [68] (1934) 52 C.L.R. 100.
[66] (1941) 67 C.L.R. 536, above, p. 88.   [69] (1941) 67 C.L.R. 536.
[67] [1950] S.A.S.R. 43.   [70] [1950] S.A.S.R. 43, 47.

the advantage of seeing each boy when he gave his evidence, and he said, in effect, that no reasonable person would be satisfied with the boy's word that he was over sixteen."

It is quite clear from this passage that Ligertwood J. was not treating reasonableness as a matter of evidence only. There is no suggestion that either he or the magistrate disbelieved D; only that D was being unreasonably gullible,[71] or, to put the point more into the context of negligence, that D had not taken sufficient precautions against making the mistake he sought to rely on.

The law appears even more clearly in a passage in the judgment of Dixon C.J. in *Dowling* v. *Bowie*.[72] In that case, it will be recalled, D was charged with having unlawfully sold liquor to a half-caste. P had failed to prove that the person, S, to whom the liquor was sold was a half-caste and the appeal from conviction was allowed on the ground that this was an essential part of the offence charged which P had to prove. The defence of reasonable mistake of fact was also canvassed, however. Dixon C.J. dealt with this part of the appeal as follows:[73]

"The appellant supported his appeal not only upon the ground with which I have dealt but also upon the ground that he honestly believed on reasonable grounds that [S] was exempt by declaration. I am prepared to concede that under s. 141 this would be a defence if made out in fact. But I am not satisfied that it has been made out. Kriewaldt J.[73a] accepted the view that the appellant believed that [S] was exempt but considered that the grounds of that belief were inadequate to sustain the defence. I am not prepared to differ from this view or to say that the magistrate ought to have found that the grounds of his belief were reasonable."

It would be difficult to find a clearer statement of the requirement that reasonable grounds for the mistake relied on must be proved as a matter of law.

(iv) *Burden and quantum of proof*

"The burden of establishing honest and reasonable mistake is in the first place upon the defendant. . . . The burden possibly may not finally rest upon him of satisfying the tribunal in case of doubt."[74]

---

[71] *Cf. Thompson* v. *Ewens* [1958] S.A.S.R. 193, 205, *per* Reed J.
[72] (1952) 86 C.L.R. 136, above, p. 97.
[73] *Ibid.*, 141.
[73a] The judge in the court below.
[74] *Proudman* v. *Dayman* (1941) 67 C.L.R. 536, 541, *per* Dixon J. Followed in *McCrae* v. *Downey* [1947] V.L.R. 194, 204, *per* O'Bryan J. *Cf. Heaslop* v. *Burton* [1902] St. R. Qd. 259, 265–266, *per* Griffith C.J., 267, *per* Real J.

Another important characteristic of the defence of reasonable mistake of fact is that it is a true defence, the burden of establishing which rests upon D. It is not merely a means of denying part of the case to be proved by P. Therefore D cannot establish this defence merely by casting doubts on P's case; he must do something more positive, for by hypothesis the defence does not come into play until P has established a prima facie case against him.

These things follow inevitably from what has already been seen of the other characteristics of the reasonable mistake rule. It is difficult to think of any circumstances under which it would be possible for D to establish that he made a positive mistake of fact on reasonable grounds merely by casting doubt on something proved by P. If it were the case that P in this part of the law had positively to prove negligence in D, then if D merely satisfied the evidentiary burden of proof by introducing or pointing to evidence that he made a relevant mistake, he would have cast doubt upon the establishment of negligence by P and it would not be necessary to argue that he need do more. Whether he would be successful in his own defence would depend on the quantum of proof resting on P, so that if P had to prove negligence beyond reasonable doubt the raising of a reasonable doubt whether D had made a relevant mistake would be sufficient to dispose of the charge against him; but if P had to prove negligence only on the balance of probabilities, D would have to make it more probable than not that he had taken due care in order to avoid conviction.

But it is not the case that P has to prove negligence in D. The rule has emerged perfectly clearly that it is for D to exculpate himself, if he can, by proving that on reasonable grounds he made a positive mistake of fact such that if the facts had been as he reasonably supposed them to be he would have committed no offence. The mere proof by P of the external facts required by the definition of the offence in question raises a prima facie liability in D to conviction. To say that P thereby raises a prima facie presumption of negligence in D is true as a description of the underlying basis of the law and as an indication that negligence rather than *mens rea* is the relevant concept from a jurisprudential point of view; but it is misleading if applied literally to the actual course which a trial would take.

It has been seen in every case so far cited in this chapter that where D has failed he has failed because he has not succeeded in positively persuading the tribunal of either the facts or the interpretation of the facts necessary to make out the defence under discussion. There is in none of the cases any discussion of the question whether P has sufficiently established his case in view of the allegations made by D. In every case P's proof has been taken for granted and relied on as a factual basis to which D has tried, not to take something incriminating away, but to add something exculpatory as a gloss. The only exception has been the *Dowling* v. *Bowie*[75] type of case where P has omitted to prove one essential fact at all and argument has turned on whether the burden of proving that fact rested on P or the burden of disproving it on D; but in this type of case nothing turns on whether P has *adequately* proved the point in issue.

Therefore if this defence to regulatory offences is to work at all, and it has worked successfully now for many years, it must be on the basis that D undertakes more than a merely evidentiary burden of proof. Clearly he has to undertake a persuasive burden of proof so far as reasonable mistake is concerned. This does not mean, of course, that he is debarred from defending himself in any other way. If he wishes to cast doubt upon P's case, as by attacking the adequacy of the evidence that some event happened at all, or that at the relevant time he, D, possessed some relevant status, then it is open to him to do so in the same way as in any other criminal trial, namely, by satisfying the merely evidentiary burden of introducing or pointing to some evidence which casts sufficient doubt on that part of P's case.

The extract from the judgment of Dixon C.J. with which this discussion of burden of proof was prefaced above is hesitant and at first glance difficult to understand. His Honour first lays down the rule that it is for D to establish mistake but immediately qualifies it by saying "in the first place". It can be in the interest of no one but D to establish the defence at any stage, so that "in the first place" seems to be superfluous unless one assumes that reference was intended to the evidentiary and not to the persuasive burden of proof. This understanding is consistent with the doubt expressed in the next sentence as to whether any additional burden rests on D to satisfy the tribunal in case of doubt. The first sentence therefore apparently means that in all cases D must undertake the evidentiary burden of introducing or pointing to some evidence to support an assertion of reasonable mistake of fact. This is in accord with principle.

The second sentence seems in effect to express doubt whether in advancing this defence D undertakes any persuasive burden. It is

[75] (1952) 86 C.L.R. 136, above, pp. 97, 105.

submitted that such a doubt would be unjustified for the reasons advanced above, which come down to the fact that unless D does undertake a persuasive burden there is no way in which his defence can succeed. It is worth emphasising by repetition that unless D undertakes a persuasive burden there is no way in which he can come to grips with P's case through the medium of mistake, for initially P does not have to disprove mistake by D; and he does not have to disprove mistake because he does not initially have to concern himself with any state of mind in D at all.

There is, however, another possibility. Dixon C.J. may have been referring, not to any burden of proof, but to the quantum of proof upon D. In approaching this question it is best to start with the task confronting P. There is no reason to doubt that in Australia[76] the rule that P must prove his case beyond reasonable doubt applies as much to regulatory as to any other criminal offences. There is only one case contrary to this statement of the law and that is *Jackson* v. *Butterworth*[77] where an income tax prosecution was held to be a civil proceeding for the purpose of determining the quantum of proof upon P, which was then held[78] to be persuading the court to its "reasonable satisfaction"[79] that the facts asserted were true. It is not thought that this solitary decision affects the general principle for regulatory offences as a class.

The quantum resting on D under any circumstances was laid down by Dixon C.J. in *Sodeman* v. *The King*[80] as follows. "Where by statute or otherwise the burden of disproving facts or of proving a particular issue is thrown upon a party charged with a criminal offence, he is not required to satisfy the tribunal beyond reasonable doubt. It is sufficient if he satisfies them in the same manner and to the same extent as is required in the proof of a civil issue."

The quantum of proof of a civil issue is often said to be on the balance of probability only. This is a useful term to contrast with "beyond reasonable doubt" but as applied to the actual trial of a case Dixon C.J. has uttered a warning against taking it too literally.[81] "The truth is that, when the law requires the proof of any fact, the tribunal must feel an actual persuasion of its occurrence or existence

---

[76] *Cf.* p. 23 nn. 73, 74, above.
[77] [1946] V.L.R. 330.
[78] Following *Briginshaw* v. *Briginshaw* (1938) 60 C.L.R. 336, 362, *per* Dixon J.
[79] [1946] V.L.R. 330, 333.
[80] (1936) 55 C.L.R. 192, 216. See also *Barker* v. *Callaghan* [1941] V.L.R. 15, 19 and 24.
[81] *Briginshaw* v. *Briginshaw* (1938) 60 C.L.R. 336, 361.

before it can be found. It cannot be found as a result of a mere mechanical comparison of probabilities independently of any belief in its reality."

Keeping this warning in mind, it is nevertheless useful to continue to contrast "beyond reasonable doubt" with "on the balance of probability". Dixon C.J.'s own phrase was that the court must have a civil issue proved to its own "reasonable satisfaction",[82] but if a court is reasonably satisfied that something was so, it must be, *inter alia*, because the existence of that fact appears to the court to be more probable than not.

It has already been observed[83] that there cannot be both a quantum beyond reasonable doubt upon P and a quantum on the balance of probability upon D in relation to the same issue, for D can cast a reasonable doubt on P's proof without affirmatively establishing anything. The quantum resting upon D in a regulatory offence prosecution to which the defence of reasonable mistake of fact applies therefore varies according to the course taken by his argument. If he seeks merely to deny part of P's case all he has to do is cast a reasonable doubt upon the truth of the facts, or any of them, asserted by P. He does not have to establish any contrary fact. But if he seeks to set up reasonable mistake he must persuade the court of the truth of what he asserts on the balance of probability, to its "reasonable satisfaction".

It would be theoretically possible for some fact relevant both to P's case and to D's reasonable mistake defence to be asserted by the former and denied by the latter, and for D to fail to establish reasonable mistake but incidentally to cast a reasonable doubt on this fact. If this situation should occur, D would be entitled to be acquitted.

Other jurisdictions

There are three cases in overseas jurisdictions of particular interest in the present context, the English case of *Reynolds* v. *G. H. Austin & Sons Ltd.*,[84] the Canadian case of *Sawicki* v. *The Queen*,[85] and *Ewart*[86] in New Zealand.

Reynolds v. *G. H. Austin & Sons Ltd.* has already been commented

[82] *Ibid.*, 362.
[83] Above, Ch. 2, pp. 39–40.
[84] [1951] 2 K.B. 135.
[85] (1960) 128 C.C.C. 386.
[86] (1905) 25 N.Z.L.R. 709.

upon.[86a] Its interest lies in the use by Devlin J. of a number of expressions in the course of his judgment indicating a cautious movement towards deciding on the guilt of a person charged with a regulatory offence by reference to the reasonableness of his behaviour in the circumstances of the infringement charged. His hints, however, have not so far been taken up by his brethren in England.[86b]

The recent Canadian case of *Sawicki* v. *The Queen* has an interesting affinity with *Proudman* v. *Dayman*.[87] D was charged with allowing to be operated a motor vehicle which was not equipped with a muffler.[88] The defence was, in effect, ignorance. The vehicle in question was in need of a new muffler, and one had been bought for installation, but owing to some misunderstanding between D and the man he employed as a driver, the necessary repair had not been carried out. Thomson J. of the Saskatchewan Queen's Bench dismissed D's appeal from summary conviction, but the ground of his decision is not altogether clear. After an inquiry into the authorities, his Honour observed:[89]

"The appellant may have assumed that someone would install the muffler but that is not enough. The duty to see that the truck was properly equipped before it was put on the road was his and that duty was an absolute one. . . . The appellant, however, took no effective steps to see that the muffler was installed on the truck and made no inquiry or check to ascertain if it had in fact been installed. In my opinion the appellant did not take those precautions which a reasonable or prudent owner should have taken to see that the requirements of the statute had been complied with. Counsel for the appellant contends that *mens rea* is an essential ingredient of the offence with which his client was charged. . . . In my opinion his indifference and the negligence he displayed in disregarding his statutory duty was sufficient to constitute *mens rea* and I so hold."

This finding starts with strict responsibility[89a] and ends with negligence but it seems reasonable to interpret it as proceeding much more upon D's unjustifiable neglect to take proper precautions than upon any other ground. If this is correct, then *Sawicki* v. *The Queen*

[86a] Above, p. 79 n. 24.
[86b] Recently, in *Lim Chin Aik* v. *The Queen* [1963] A.C. 160, the Privy Council, including Lord Devlin, as he now is, passed over an excellent opportunity to give these dicta the weight they deserve.
[87] (1941) 67 C.L.R. 536.
[88] Vehicles Act, 1957 (Sask.), 113 (1) (*b*).
[89] (1960) 128 C.C.C. 386, 389–390.
[89a] Unless Thomson J. meant only that the duty could not be delegated.

is in line with the Australian law as laid down in *Proudman* v.
Dayman and *Ferrier* v. *Wilson*.[90]

Neither of the preceding two cases is more than an isolated
instance of a line of argument being adopted which is unusual in its
actual context although familiar enough to Australian lawyers. The
New Zealand case of *Ewart* is a different proposition altogether, for
it laid down a principle not dissimilar from the one adopted in
Australia and did so as long ago as 1905.[91] D was charged on indictment for selling an obscene newspaper having been previously
convicted of a similar offence. He was convicted and appealed to the
Court of Appeal substantially on the question whether it should have
been proved that he knew the publication to be obscene, or, in other
words, whether *mens rea* was part of the offence. The court held, by
a majority of three to two, that a new trial should be ordered on the
ground that the jury had not been adequately directed as to the
mental element in the offence.

The majority[92] held that crimes should be divided into three
classes for the purpose before them. In the first class were crimes for
which *mens rea* had to be proved by P; in the second, crimes of strict
responsibility; and in the third, crimes in which,[93] "although from
the omission from the statute of the words 'knowingly' or 'wilfully'
it is not necessary to aver in the indictment that the offence charged
was 'knowingly' or 'wilfully' committed, or to prove a guilty mind,
yet the person charged may still discharge himself by proving to the
satisfaction of the tribunal which tries him that in fact he had not a
guilty mind."

This rule goes further than reasonable mistake, for it comprises

[90] (1906) 4 C.L.R. 785. Above, p. 56.
[91] *Ewart* is frequently cited in both New Zealand and Australia. For New Zealand see
Tustin (1908) 27 N.Z.L.R. 506; *Dunn* v. *Monson* (1911) 30 N.Z.L.R. 399; *Linssen* v.
Hitchcock (1915) 34 N.Z.L.R. 545; *Eccles* v. *Richardson* [1916] N.Z.L.R. 1090;
Miller v. *Hood* [1921] N.Z.L.R. 998; *Carswell* [1926] N.Z.L.R. 321; *Hirst* [1932]
N.Z.L.R. 300; *O. F. Nelson & Co. Ltd.* v. *Police* [1932] N.Z.L.R. 337; *Nelson* v.
Braisby (No. 2) [1934] N.Z.L.R. 559; *C. L. Innes & Co. Ltd.* v. *Carrol* [1943] N.Z.L.R.
80; *Hazelwood & Co. Ltd.* v. *Richardson* [1948] N.Z.L.R. 1204; *Commissioner of
Taxes* v. *King* [1950] N.Z.L.R. 202; *Gould & Co. Ltd.* v. *Cameron* [1951] N.Z.L.R.
314; *Innes* v. *McKinley* [1954] N.Z.L.R. 1054; *Gordon* v. *Schubert* [1956] N.Z.L.R.
431; *Russel* v. *Shand* [1956] N.Z.L.R. 654; *Technical Books Ltd.* v. *Collector of
Customs* [1957] N.Z.L.R. 490; *Burney* [1958] N.Z.L.R. 745; *Walker* [1958]
N.Z.L.R. 810; *Cottle* [1958] N.Z.L.R. 999; *Hill* v. *Douglas* [1959] N.Z.L.R. 121;
Holland v. *Peterkin* [1961] N.Z.L.R. 769; *D'Audney* v. *Marketing Services (N.Z.)
Ltd.* [1962] N.Z.L.R. 51; *Transport Department* v. *McCutcheon* [1962] N.Z.L.R. 675.
[92] Williams, Edwards and Chapman JJ., Stout C.J. and Cooper J. dissenting.
[93] (1905) 25 N.Z.L.R. 709, 731, *per* Edwards J.

"honest ignorance"[94] or any other absence of *mens rea*, but it has in common with the Australian law that it supplies a compromise between the conflicting claims of P and D instead of making the choice between *mens rea* to be proved by P or strict responsibility. It amounts, in fact, to the adoption by a court of high authority of the suggestion referred to elsewhere[95] that *mens rea* should not be implied into an offence in the absence of such words as "knowingly" and "wilfully" but that their absence should have the effect merely of shifting the burden of proof of exculpation to D.

[94] *Ibid.*, 729, *per* Williams J.
[95] Above, pp. 63–64

CHAPTER 6

REASONABLE MISTAKE AND PARTICULAR WORDS

Introduction

It remains to see in detail how the reasonable mistake rule has been applied in practice in different statutory contexts. Since it is ultimately upon the language of the statute that criminal responsibility must depend, the most instructive method of approach seems to be the one used hitherto, namely, the classification of cases by reference to the actual forms of words used in the statutes upon which they were decided. In this way the working of the reasonable mistake rule will now be examined in relation to neutral words, status offences, "knowingly" and "wilfully", "permit" and its synonyms, "cause", "fraudulent", and "evade". There will then follow a discussion of the effect of the express inclusion of a defence in a statute with particular reference to the question whether such a statutory defence, on the *expressio unius est exclusio alterius* principle, necessarily excludes this common law defence by implication.

Although in the discussions which follow the scene is necessarily dominated by cases reported since *Proudman* v. *Dayman*[1] was decided in 1941, it would be misleading to confine comment only to that period. *Proudman* v. *Dayman* did not burst upon an astonished legal world without previous warning. Seven years previously, in *Maher* v. *Musson*,[2] the High Court in general and Dixon J. in particular had given a clear indication of the approach which would in future be made to regulatory offences in the matter of *mens rea* and mistake; and, as will be seen, ever since its inception the High Court has taken much the same line with almost unbroken consistency. All that *Proudman* v. *Dayman* did, or, to be more precise, all that Dixon C.J. did in that case, was to make a more exact and general statement of a doctrine to which for the most part there had up to that time been only scattered and intermittent references in the case-law.

Although it has since appeared that, by one of those mysterious

[1] (1941) 67 C.L.R. 536.
[2] (1934) 52 C.L.R. 100.

conjunctions of events which periodically give unexpected importance to cases not seen in advance as at all remarkable, *Proudman* v. *Dayman* was decided at a singularly appropriate time, this is not to say that the preceding case-law, especially in the High Court, is superseded. Undoubtedly, there are many old decisions of the State Supreme Courts which are no longer reliable, but even here this is not universally true.

Neutral words

Under this head come the cases of so-called plain words exemplified by the phrase "no person shall" do something, the meaning of which surpasses every other statutory formula in ambiguity. There is some grammatical ground for regarding the impersonal wording of status offences as imposing strict responsibility, just as there is ground for regarding such words as "knowingly" and "permit" as requiring *mens rea*; but such a term as "no person shall", or "any person who", cannot be very obviously placed on either side of the line as a matter of semantics. "Plain" words are therefore more properly regarded as neutral words in the sense that they tend in themselves neither for nor against a mental element in crime. For this reason this group of cases is the most important for the establishment of a general principle of criminal responsibility for regulatory offences. It is possible with greater ease here than elsewhere to keep clear of the enticements of minute distinctions between the meanings of words and to concentrate upon the desirability of a general rule.

The picture which emerges from the Australian cases shows, as one would expect, a gradual change of emphasis from strict responsibility in the nineteenth century and early twentieth century towards the reasonable mistake of fact defence at the present day. Uniformity is far from being achieved even now, but the current flowing through the cases towards a general adoption of the doctrine of *Proudman* v. *Dayman*[3] is a strong one.

(i) *Before* 1918

It would be a mistake to spend time over the older cases establishing strict responsibility.[4] In the light of developments since they are

[3] (1941) 67 C.L.R. 536.
[4] *Murphy* v. *Innes* (1877) 11 S.A.L.R. 56; *Persse* v. *Smith* (1878) 4 V.L.R. (L) 201; *Stephens* v. *Robert Reid & Co. Ltd.* (1902) 28 V.L.R. 82; *Dawson* v. *Jack* (1902) 28 V.L.R. 634; *Irving* v. *Gallagher* [1903] St. R. Qd. 121; *Martin* (1904) 4 S.R. (N.S.W.) 720; *Dugdale* v. *Dight* [1906] V.L.R. 783. Contrast *Hesford* v. *Gilliam* (1898) 4 A.L.R. (C.N.) 90.

of little or no persuasive value. Progress can be dated from the first definite stand against the spread of strict responsibility for neutral words, which in Australia was taken in a group of cases between 1907 and 1915.

The first of these was *Gleeson* v. *Hobson*,[5] in which D was charged with having sold liquor without a licence authorising the sale.[6] The main point in the case was as to the constituents of liquor within the meaning of the section, but Cussen J. also canvassed the question of *mens rea* because D had sold the spirit in question as a patent medicine without any idea that it might contain alcohol. Having found that the evidence offered by P was insufficient to establish that the spirit sold was intoxicating, his Honour discussed *mens rea* in statutory offences generally and concluded:[7] "I am not at present satisfied that the defendant cannot rely on her belief in good faith that the compound contained no intoxicating liquor."

The opportunity to expand this careful reservation against strict responsibility came seven years later in *Erson*.[8] D was charged, *inter alia*, with two offences against the Commonwealth Maternity Allowance Act, 1912, s. 10 (a), which said that any person who obtained a maternity allowance which was not payable should be guilty of an offence. At the trial before Cussen J. and a jury the jury found specially that D had been unaware that he was obtaining maternity allowances on the occasions charged (the claims for which were based on fictitious births); that the false claims were made out without his knowledge by a lady to whom he had delegated the filling-in of such forms and certificates; but that he had omitted "to take care" to see that they were properly filled in. Cussen J. stated a case for the Full Court to decide whether these findings required a verdict of guilty to be entered.

It was unanimously decided that they did not, Cussen J. himself taking the opportunity to expand his observation in *Gleeson* v. *Hobson* into the following ground for judgment.[9] "I am of opinion that the accused is entitled to be acquitted, because – (1) According to the findings of the jury, he must be taken to have honestly and reasonably believed in the existence of circumstances which if they had really existed would have made his acts entirely innocent; and (2) I cannot find sufficient in the Statute creating these offences to exclude the application of the facts first stated as an exculpation."

[5] [1907] V.L.R. 148.   [6] Licensing Act, 1890 (Vic.), s. 182.
[7] [1907] V.L.R. 148, 158.   [8] [1914] V.L.R. 144.   [9] *Ibid.*, 156.

It is evident that at that date his Honour was prepared to go further than the High Court has since thought desirable, for he found that D's mistake was reasonable even though the jury found that he had not taken due care. Of the other two members of the court, A'Beckett J.[10] distinguished between proof of *mens rea* by P and proof of absence of *mens rea* by D, held that the latter rule was applicable in the instant case, that D had discharged this burden, and that therefore he should be acquitted. Hood J.[11] held that *mens rea* formed part of the offence and had not been proved, and that therefore D should be acquitted. All three judges were strongly influenced by the consideration that this was a prosecution on indictment. The decision is given added weight by the refusal by the High Court of leave for P to appeal.[12]

Two years earlier, in *Spooner* v. *Alexander*,[13] the High Court itself had made a similar approach to a summary offence under the Masters and Servants Act, 1902 (N.S.W.), s. 4. D, who was one of thirty-two workmen concerned in the incident, was charged with absenting himself from his employment "without reasonable cause" before the expiration of the contract. The workmen had demanded the reinstatement of a man who had been dismissed by the common employer for having absented himself from work to attend a union meeting as delegate for the lodge to which they all belonged. D argued that he had reasonably believed that the delegate had been wrongfully dismissed (which was not the case) and that in such a situation he had an implied right under the contract of employment to strike if the demand for reinstatement were not at once complied with (which was also not the case). This argument in effect raised the two questions, first, whether the defence of reasonable mistake of fact was available, the fact being the existence of reasonable cause to strike; and secondly, if so, whether the beliefs alleged were reasonable in the circumstances.

All three members of the court[14] accepted the proposition that reasonable mistake of fact would be a defence to a charge of this kind. The clearest statement is to be found in the judgment of Griffith C.J.[15] "The existence of reasonable cause affords a defence to the charge, but whether it exists or not is a question of fact to be

---

[10] *Ibid.*, 149–153.   [11] *Ibid.*, 153–155.   [12] *Ibid.*, 157.
[13] (1912) 13 C.L.R. 704. See also *Mollison* (1876) 2 V.L.R. (L) 144, and *Marshall* v *Foster* (1898) 24 V.L.R. 155.
[14] Griffith C.J., Barton and Isaacs JJ.
[15] (1912) 13 C.L.R. 704, 708.

determined upon evidence. It is, however, sufficient for the defendant to show that he honestly and reasonably believed in the existence of a state of things which if it had existed would have established reasonable cause." The conviction was affirmed, however, on the ground that the evidence did not disclose a reasonable mistake.

The remaining case in this early group is *Laughton* v. *Master Butchers Ltd.*,[16] a decision of the Full Court of South Australia to which added weight is given, as in *Erson*, by the refusal of the High Court to grant special leave to the unsuccessful party to appeal.[17] The case was a civil action. The plaintiffs had sold two pigs to the defendants at an auction. It was a term of the contract that the buyer took the pigs with all faults and that the seller did not warrant them to be free of disease. The day after purchase the defendants had the pigs slaughtered, whereupon they were found to have been suffering from tuberculosis and the carcasses were condemned. The defendants refused to pay the price and the plaintiffs sued. The defendants' difficulty was the term in the contract that the seller did not warrant the pigs to be free of disease. They attempted to surmount it by arguing that the whole sale was illegal, the plaintiffs having committed an offence against the Health Act, 1898 (S.A.), s. 109, which said that "no person shall sell . . . for food any diseased animal". It was common ground that the plaintiffs neither knew nor reasonably could have known of the condition of the pigs when they sold them. The magistrate entered judgment for the defendants on the ground that an offence had been committed by the plaintiffs, but reserved for the Supreme Court the question whether he was right in this opinion, which involved treating the offence as one of strict responsibility.

The judgment of the Full Court took the course of building up as strong a case for strict responsibility as possible and then deciding against it. The argument in favour took three points. First, the conflict of principle between the English cases of *Cundy* v. *Le Cocq*[18] and *Sherras* v. *De Rutzen*[19] had been resolved, in the view of the court, in favour of *Cundy* v. *Le Cocq* and strict responsibility by the decision of the Court of Appeal in *Hobbs* v. *Winchester Corporation*.[20]

---

[16] [1915] S.A.L.R. 3.

[17] *Sub nom. Master Butchers Ltd.* v. *Laughton* (1915) 19 C.L.R. 349.

[18] (1884) 13 Q.B.D. 207.

[19] [1895] 1 Q.B. 918. It will be recalled that in *Cundy* v. *Le Cocq*, selling liquor to a drunken person was held to be an offence of strict responsibility, whereas in *Sherras* v. *De Rutzen*, selling liquor to a policeman was held to require *mens rea*. See above, p. 8 n. 27.

[20] [1910] 2 K.B. 471. See above, p. 80

Secondly, there was no "*a priori* improbability"[21] that strict responsibility was intended by the legislature in a regulatory offence of this kind, and there was nothing in the wording of section 109 to exclude it. Thirdly, several sections of the Health Act creating offences included the word "knowingly", which section 109 did not. Had the court been disposed in favour of strict responsibility, therefore, there would have been plenty of material to hand with which to support the decision.

Instead, their Honours turned to two other sections in the same part of the Act as section 109,[22] which expressly provided that lack of knowledge should not be a defence to charges under those sections unless D proved also that he could not reasonably have had knowledge of the disease or other fault charged. Now, at least two inconsistent inferences could have been drawn from this fact. It could have been argued that the express inclusion of such a defence elsewhere implied that lack of knowledge was not relevant to section 109 where it was not mentioned. Alternatively, it could have been said that lack of knowledge was normally a defence to any charge and that the express provisions in these two sections were intended only to cut down the scope of this defence by creating liability for negligence in those particular cases. The court followed the second alternative and found for the plaintiffs, holding that the sale was not illegal.

By 1915, therefore, it was clear that a strong stand had been taken by the High Court against strict responsibility for regulatory offences expressed in neutral language.[23] This was owing as much to the influence of the Chief Justice, Sir Samuel Griffith, a firm upholder of the general principles of the criminal law, as to any other single factor. It is not without significance that the only two cases which reverted to strict responsibility during this period were both decided by the High Court in the absence of the Chief Justice. Neither of these cases is of the same order of importance as those previously mentioned because the approach to the law which they represent has since been departed from, but each must be briefly referred to in order to avoid giving the development of the law a misleading appearance of uninterrupted continuity.

---

[21] [1915] S.A.L.R. 3, 11.
[22] Ss. 106 and 111.
[23] See also *Ross* v. *Sickerdick* (1916) 22 C.L.R. 197; *Pankhurst* v. *Porter* (1917) 23 C.L.R. 504.

The first was *Duncan* v. *Ellis*.[24] This case is unique in the annals of the High Court for its injustice to both P and D. D was charged with an offence against the Factories and Shops Act, 1915 (Vic.), s. 226, of paying an employee at less than the award rate. It was common ground that not only did D not know the employee's correct age (which was material to the wage rate he was entitled to be paid), but also that the reason why D did not know was that the employee had deliberately misstated his own age in response to inquiry. Nevertheless, the court held the offence to be one of strict responsibility and convicted D. It is impossible to see any point in the decision. The court itself recognised the injustice of the result and imposed a nominal fine of one shilling. Indeed, it went further and made the informant pay the costs of the appeal; yet the object of this manoeuvre is far from clear, for if the informant had the law on his side he was perfectly justified in appealing from the adverse (to him) decision of the Supreme Court of Victoria.

The second case is *Myerson* v. *Collard*,[25] decided on emergency legislation arising out of the First World War. D was charged with an offence against the War Precautions (Active Service Moratorium) Regulations, 1916, reg. 12,[26] which said in effect that goods held by a dependant of a member of the Australian Imperial Forces under a hire-purchase agreement could not be repossessed by the vendor. The court held unanimously that the statute imposed strict responsibility, although for a variety of reasons. There is little agreement in the judgments on the proper route to be followed to arrive at the result. The general dissatisfaction of the court with the regulation it was required to construe is expressed in the judgment of Higgins J. who, after remarking caustically that "it is not for us to improve on legislation by inserting words which would make it as we think just,"[27] went on to criticise the regulation as having been "drawn with a reckless disregard of the problems" it created and thrown "like a bomb" into the civil law of title to goods.

(ii) 1918–1945

From the end of the First World War until after the Second World War the balance between the two views was on the face of it held

[24] (1916) 21 C.L.R. 379. *Cf. Hall* v. *Bartlett* (1898) 24 V.L.R. 1.
[25] (1918) 25 C.L.R. 154.
[26] Made under the War Precautions Act, 1914–1916 (Cth).
[27] (1918) 25 C.L.R. 154, 168. An abdication of the judicial function fortunately rare in the High Court.

evenly. During this period there were six relevant State Supreme Court decisions on regulatory offences expressed in neutral language. Three of them were in favour of strict responsibility[28] and three of them against the doctrine.[29] There was only one High Court decision, *Francis* v. *Rowan*,[30] which is discussed below.

The picture thus presented is misleading, however, for the same reason that all analyses of the development of the law are to some extent misleading. In order to reduce an amorphous body of law to some kind of order for the purpose of exposition, the commentator must draw his lines of demarcation somewhere; and yet as soon as he does so he excludes from one class of cases certain factors which it is for his purpose more convenient to assign to a different context and yet which in actuality had an importance outside the category to which he assigns them. The present narrative affords an example.

Although it is true that during the period from 1918 to 1945 there was only one High Court decision on a regulatory offence expressed in neutral language, there were several High Court decisions on the criminal law generally of the highest importance, for it was during this period that the lines of the modern law on regulatory offences were drawn in *Maher* v. *Musson*[31] and *Proudman* v. *Dayman*[32] and emphatic reassertions of the doctrine of *mens rea* handed down both in these cases and in *Bond* v. *Foran*[33] and *Thomas* v. *The King*.[34] Therefore, although it is convenient in exposition to classify regulatory offences in the same manner as the courts themselves, namely, by loose groupings of forms of words, it is essential to keep in mind parallel developments in other categories.

If the previous decision in *Maher* v. *Musson* and the contemporaneous decision in *Proudman* v. *Dayman* are kept in mind in this way, the apparent importance of *Francis* v. *Rowan*[35] is much diminished. The subject-matter was once again emergency wartime legislation, a context in which enlightenment is rarely manifest. D was

---

[28] *Thompson* v. *Sampson* [1930] V.L.R. 191; *Heading* v. *McCubbin* [1936] V.L.R. 159; *Bond* v. *Clarke* [1938] S.A.S.R. 55.
[29] *Bollmeyer* v. *Daly* [1933] S.A.S.R. 295; *Hickinbotham* v. *Dawson* [1935] V.L.R. 47; *Hubbard* v. *Beck* (1947) 64 W.N. (N.S.W.) 20.
[30] (1941) 64 C.L.R. 196.
[31] (1934) 52 C.L.R. 100, above, p. 51
[32] (1941) 67 C.L.R. 536.
[33] (1934) 52 C.L.R. 364, above, p. 51
[34] (1937) 59 C.L.R. 279.
[35] (1941) 64 C.L.R. 196.

charged with an offence against the National Security (General) Regulations (1939–1940), reg. 42 (1) (a),[35a] which provided that a "person shall not endeavour whether orally or otherwise to influence public opinion . . . in a manner likely to be prejudicial to . . . the efficient prosecution of the war".

D had made a speech. The magistrate before whom he was charged as a result of this speech found as a fact that what he had said was likely to be prejudicial to the efficient prosecution of the war, but that he had not intended to influence public opinion in a manner likely to be prejudicial to the efficient prosecution of the war. He construed regulation 42 as requiring such an intention and dismissed the complaint. On appeal by P the High Court reversed this decision, holding that the magistrate had misconstrued the regulation in the matter of intention. It was beyond doubt that D had endeavoured to influence public opinion. The further question, whether the effect of the influence, if any, would be to prejudice the efficient prosecution of the war, required an objective answer which had nothing to do with D's intention.

With all respect, this reasoning strikes one as a little specious. A straightforward reading of the regulation gives the impression that the word "endeavour" was intended to qualify all the remainder of the offence and not just the influencing of public opinion, but the effect of the decision was to impose strict responsibility for the "likely" consequence of the endeavour.[36] The type of reasoning employed here is the same as was used in *Proudman* v. *Dayman*[37] shortly afterwards to separate the licence question from the elements of (1) driving (2) a motor vehicle (3) on a road, but with much less justification. The real ground of the decision seems to have been that people who choose to speak critically of the government in a time of national emergency must take the risk of uncomfortable consequences.[38] This may not be a particularly commendable basis for conviction but it helps to explain why in retrospect *Francis* v. *Rowan* is not seen as a significant departure by the High Court from its

---

[35a] Made under the National Security Act, 1939–1940 (Cth), s. 10.

[36] No member of the court went so far as to hold that there could be strict responsibility even for the endeavour, which, it is submitted, would be untenable. The word "endeavour" is a synonym for "attempt" and an attempt requires intention even where the completed offence is strict: *Gardner* v. *Akeroyd* [1952] 2 Q.B. 743.

[37] (1914) 67 C.L.R. 536, above, p. 60. McTiernan J. perceived the similarity of reasoning in the two cases (543).

[38] Nevertheless compare the more liberal attitude taken in *Pankhurst* v. *Porter* (1917) 23 C.L.R. 504.

usual opposition to strict responsibility. Its influence has not been comparable with that of *Maher* v. *Musson* and *Proudman* v. *Dayman*.

(iii) *Since* 1945

The period since 1945 has seen much development of the law. During this time the High Court has taken further opportunities to restate the applicability of the reasonable mistake of fact defence to regulatory offences expressed in neutral language, and the State Supreme Courts have shown an increasing tendency to take the same view.

There are four relevant High Court decisions, two of which need not be further mentioned here because they have previously come under discussion.[39] In each of them the reasonable mistake of fact rule was reaffirmed. Of the other two, the first is *Brown* v. *Green*,[40] where the court expressly refrained from deciding whether the reasonable mistake defence applied to an offence of receiving from a tenant a rent in excess of the permitted maximum[41] on the ground that on the facts the question did not arise. Such significance as the case possesses in the present context is from the pointed omission to rule that defence out in favour of strict responsibility.

The latest decision is the interesting case of *Ryall* v. *Carroll*.[42] D had been summarily convicted in the Northern Territory of an offence against the Observance of Law Ordinance, 1921, (N.T.), s. 11, which said: "Any person who, by threats, intimidation, violence, force or any physical act, interferes with the right of any person – (*a*) to carry on his lawful occupation ... shall be guilty of an offence."

On the instructions of his union D helped to picket a wharf to prevent the unloading or carrying away of goods from a ship. In so doing he prevented the driver of a truck belonging to a firm of carriers from loading goods from the ship. This interference was intentional, but it was held unanimously that it did not amount to an interference with the right of the driver or his employer to carry on their lawful occupations because they were left entirely free to carry them on elsewhere. It was only this particular job which was being frustrated. Two members of the court, Dixon C.J. and Taylor J.,

---

[39] *Dowling* v. *Bowie* (1952) 86 C.L.R. 136; *Bergin* v. *Stack* (1953) 88 C.L.R. 248; above, pp. 96–97.
[40] (1951) 84 C.L.R. 285.
[41] Landlord and Tenant (Amendment) Act, 1948–1949 (N.S.W.), s. 35.
[42] (1959) 102 C.L.R. 162.

made no further comment, but Fullagar J. went a little deeper into the question of intent.[43]

"It is obvious, I think, that *some* intent must be proved in order to establish the commission of an offence under s. 11 (*a*). The carrying on of a lawful occupation could no doubt be interfered with by a 'physical act' which was merely negligent or even accidental, but in such a case it would be impossible to say that there had been an interference with a 'right' to carry on a lawful occupation. The question is whether it is sufficient for the prosecution to prove an intention to do an act which in fact interfered with the right . . . or whether it is necessary to prove an actual intention to interfere with the right – a mind directed to interference with the right. . . . If the former view is correct, the fact that the object of the act done in the present case was not to injure [the driver] but to prevent the ship from being loaded will be irrelevant. If the latter view is correct, it will follow from that fact that no offence has been committed."

His Honour went on to decide in favour of the second view, that there must be an intention not merely to interfere with the exercise of the lawful occupation but also to interfere with the right to exercise it, reaching this conclusion chiefly by interpreting the words "physical act" *ejusdem generis* with the preceding nouns denoting states of mind. The distinction drawn by Fullagar J. is another manifestation of the method adopted in *Francis* v. *Rowan* and *Proudman* v. *Dayman* of analysing an offence into two parts for the purpose of either applying or excluding some mental element in relation to the second part. In this case the undoubted requirement of intention, which was also present in *Francis* v. *Rowan* through the word "endeavour" and in *Proudman* v. *Dayman* through the word "permit", could have been either stopped before the question of right arose or applied to that element also. In the event it was applied to that element also, a marked contrast with *Francis* v. *Rowan* but in line with *Proudman* v. *Dayman* except that here Fullager J. did not contemplate responsibility for negligence but only for full *mens rea*.

At the State Supreme Court level the reasonable mistake rule has received strong support in two recent Victorian decisions on neutral words and has been accepted without question in three other cases, including a decision of the Full Court of South

---

[43] *Ibid.*, 168.

Australia.[44] The two Victorian cases specially mentioned are *McCrae
v. Downey*[45] and *Bergin v. Stack*.[46] In the first of these O'Bryan J.
applied the reasonable mistake defence in its most precise modern
form to an offence of removing goods from a wharf without a permit.[47] The judgment, if one may respectfully say so, is a model
discussion of the correct basis of responsibility. It is deservedly
frequently cited. In *Bergin v. Stack* Barry J., after a similarly illumin-
ating discussion of the question at issue, applied the defence to an
offence of selling liquor without a licence.[48]

As against these cases there are five which take the opposite view
and even at the present day accept strict responsibility for neutral
words. In four of them,[49] however, the weight of authority to the
contrary was acknowledged by the express quotation of Dixon C.J.'s
judgment in *Proudman v. Dayman* for the purpose of attempting to
demonstrate that the instant case did not come within its purview.
In the fifth, *Smith v. Manno*,[50] the Full Court of South Australia was
asked to apply the reasonable mistake defence to an offence of driving
a motor vehicle whilst disqualified from holding a licence.[51] The facts
were unusual. D had been disqualified for six months. Towards the
end of this time he found himself uncertain of the exact date upon
which the disqualification ended. He telephoned the police to find
out and was misinformed. On this basis he set up reasonable mistake
of fact. The court found it "difficult to regard the supposed mistake
as one of fact" but in any event regarded the offence as "absolute".

No reasons were given for these odd conclusions. No ground
suggests itself for regarding the mistake as other than a mistake of
fact, and it is unsatisfactory, to say the least, at the present day to
classify any offence as "absolute" without giving reasons. It is
submitted that *Smith v. Manno* is more accurately seen as a lingering

[44] *Thompson v. Ewens* [1958] S.A.S.R. 193. See also *Belling v. O'Sullivan* [1950]
S.A.S.R. 43; *Gherashe v. Boase* [1959] V.R. 1. In *Murphy* [1957] V.R. 545, it was
held that a charge of using a car without the consent of the owner required knowledge in D that he did not have the consent of the owner.
[45] [1947] V.L.R. 194.
[46] [1952] A.L.R. 810.
[47] Reg. 123A (c) of regulations made under the Melbourne Harbour Trust Act, 1928
(Vic.). Unfortunately, the result of the decision in *McCrae v. Downey* was the
amendment of the regulations in such a manner that strict responsibility was
unavoidable: *Smith v. O'Grady* [1953] V.L.R. 303. See p. 67 n. 58, above.
[48] Licensing Act, 1928 (Vic.), s. 161.
[49] *Gepp v. Anderson* [1949] S.A.S.R. 135, (Full Court); *Lipshut v. McKay* [1950] V.L.R.
57 (a rare example of *Francis v. Rowan*, above, p. 120, being influential); *Hawthorn v.
Bartholomew* [1954] V.L.R. 28; *Georgeff v. Ryan* [1954] S.A.S.R. 234.
[50] [1961] S.A.S.R. 17.
[51] Motor Vehicles Act, 1959 (S.A.), s. 91.

survival of an outmoded approach to regulatory offences than as a significant departure from the doctrine of *Proudman* v. *Dayman*. Moreover, that case was mentioned in argument but not in the judgment. It is submitted that no decision at the present day in this part of the law which fails to take account of *Proudman* v. *Dayman* can be regarded as carrying much weight.

Status offences

There is still some divergence of view in Australia between the High Court and the State Supreme Courts on the correct method of dealing with the impersonal wording characterised herein as creating status offences.[52] These offences have been defined for present purposes[53] as those which attach criminal responsibility to someone merely by reason of his status, capacity or physical situation, apparently dispensing with the need for either act or omission as a prerequisite for conviction.

The High Court first manifested the unease about status offences which has always characterised its judgments on the subject in *Bear* v. *Lynch*,[54] the first case in which the question came before it. D was charged with an offence under the Liquor (Amendment) Act, 1905 (N.S.W.), s. 19 (4), in that he was the licensee of licensed premises upon which a person was found, outside permitted hours for the sale of liquor, otherwise than for a lawful purpose. He was convicted at summary trial, it being the fact that gambling had been taking place on his premises. The Supreme Court of New South Wales quashed the conviction on a point of evidence. This decision was sustained by the High Court but on the different ground that the gambling proved, playing cards for money, was not an unlawful purpose within the meaning of the section. The court regarded it as clear that some limitation had to be placed on the liability of the licensee for the

---

[52] Legislatures have for some time past been aware of the draconic potentialities of offences expressed in impersonal words. For this reason status offences are more often associated with express statutory defences than is the case with any other form of words. Status offence cases which turned on the effect of a statutory defence rather than on the wording of the offence itself have been omitted from the present discussion but referred to in the section on "Statutory Defences", below, p. 143. Such cases are, *Trenchard* v. *Ryan* (1910) 10 S.R. (N.S.W.) 618; *Dineen* v. *Nicholson* [1922] S.A.S.R. 1; *Fraser* v. *Dryden's Carrying Co.* [1941] V.L.R. 103; *Eclipse Motors* v. *Milner* [1950] S.A.S.R. 1; *Bergin* v. *Khyat* [1953] V.L.R. 695; *Young* v. *Paddle Bros. Pty. Ltd.* [1956] V.L.R. 38; *Myers* v. *Crabtree* [1956] V.L.R. 431; *O'Sullivan* v. *Friebe* [1956] S.A.S.R. 89; *Tully* v. *O'Sullivan* [1956] S.A.S.R. 106.
[53] Above, p. 46.
[54] (1909) 8 C.L.R. 592.

presence of others for an unlawful purpose, for otherwise he would be liable for the presence of a burglar.[55] The limitation suggested by the wording of the statute was that the purpose had to be unlawful in the contemplation of the Liquor Acts themselves. Since playing cards for money was not contrary to these Acts, the conviction could not be upheld.

The court was fortunate in being able to find this loophole in the legislation, but no one can seriously suppose that the only reason why D in that case would not have been liable for the presence of a burglar was that the Licensing Acts did not make burglary an offence. That Griffith C.J. at least was well aware of the real problem, which he regarded "as one of considerable difficulty",[56] appears from the following observation.[57] "I express no opinion on ... whether if it were found as a fact that a licensee had taken all reasonable care to prevent any person coming on his premises for a purpose which is not lawful, or had taken all reasonable care to ascertain that the purpose for which a person had come on his premises was lawful, that would be a good defence to a charge under this section."

Not until many years later, in *Maher* v. *Musson*[58] in 1934, was the High Court required to grasp the nettle, but when this case came before it the court did so in the firmest manner. D was charged with an offence against the Commonwealth Distillation Act, 1901–1931, s. 74 (4), which said that "no person shall ... have ... in his custody ... any illicit spirit."

Reasons have already been given for classifying this as a status offence.[59] It was not disputed that, literally speaking, D had had an illicit spirit in his custody. He was a chemist of good repute and had bought the spirit through a friend of his, another chemist of similarly unblemished character. Both were deceived by the plausible explanation of the vendor as to why the spirit was being sold at an unusually cheap price. In fact the spirit had been stolen. The magistrate apparently held that the offence was one of strict responsibility, but nevertheless dismissed the complaint on grounds which were not clear.[60] On appeal to the High Court the substantial question was whether the magistrate had been correct in excluding *mens rea* from

---

[55] *Ibid.*, 600, 603.
[56] (1909) 8 C.L.R. 592, 601.
[57] *Ibid. Cf. Gill* v. *Williams* (1916) 12 Tas. L.R. 67, 69.
[58] (1934) 52 C.L.R. 100.
[59] Above, p. 51.
[60] (1934) 52 C.L.R. 100, 104, *per* Dixon J.

the offence charged and, if so, what was the effect. With one dis-sentient[61] it was decided that to exclude *mens rea* did not conclude the issue against D because room was left for the operation of the reasonable mistake of fact rule. In reaching this decision the court was not in the least deterred by the form of words used in the definition of the offence.

Dixon J. made his first statement of the guiding principle which has become familiar in this and earlier chapters, distinguishing a positive requirement of knowledge amounting to full *mens rea* from reasonable mistake of fact in the following words.[62] "[T]he terms in which clause 4 of section 74 is expressed do not make knowledge of the illicit character of the spirits an essential element of the offence. To imply such a requirement would no doubt be possible, but in the case of a revenue statute of the tenor now in question, no presumption appears to arise in favour of that implication. Nevertheless, in the case alike of an offence at common law and, unless expressly or impliedly excluded by the enactment, of a statutory offence, it is a good defence that the accused held an honest and reasonable belief in the existence of circumstances, which, if true, would make innocent the act for which he is charged."

His Honour went on to decide that section 74 (4) did not go to the length of excluding even a defence of reasonable mistake of fact because the offence created was not of an "intrinsically nefarious"[63] character but depended on antecedent breaches of the law by persons other than D of which D might very well be unable to know. This is an interesting observation and an altogether welcome one. The more graphic expression of opinion by Evatt and McTiernan JJ. has already been referred to[64] but is worth repeating *in extenso*.[65] "In our opinion it would be a palpable and evident absurdity to suppose that the Legislature intended to expose the innocent messenger or carrier of spirits which are in fact illicit, but of whose character it is impossible that he should be aware to the drastic penalty imposed by section 74."[66]

This firm rejection of the idea that a status offence carried any magic in the words of its definition peculiarly apt to create strict

[61] Rich, Dixon, Evatt and McTiernan JJ., Starke J. dissenting.
[62] (1934) 52 C.L.R. 100, 104. Rich J. agreed with Dixon J. *in toto*.
[63] *Ibid.*, 105.
[64] Above, p. 51.
[65] (1934) 52 C.L.R. 100, 109. *Cf. Ewart* (1905) 25 N.Z.L.R. 709, 736, *per* Edwards J.
[66] The maximum penalty was a fine of £500.

responsibility was demonstrated again later in the same year in
Bond v. *Foran*,[67] described in an earlier chapter,[68] which went even
further by requiring *mens rea* to be proved by P and not merely
reasonable mistake by D.

The result of these cases if taken in isolation would be to reject
strict responsibility for status offences but to leave uncertain whether
a general rule of *mens rea* was to be adopted or merely the defence
of reasonable mistake of fact. In the light of developments since
1934, especially the decision in *Proudman* v. *Dayman*,[69] it seems clear
that it is the reasonable mistake rule that the High Court has adopted,
and that if the facts of *Bond* v. *Foran* recurred the case would
probably be decided on that basis rather than *mens rea*.

It would give a misleading impression, however, to state the High
Court decisions on this type of regulatory offence without recording
also their effect on the case-law of the State Supreme Courts. State
court decisions, as one might expect, fall into two groups: those
decided before *Maher* v. *Musson* and those decided after that case.
There are four relevant decisions in the earlier group. Each of them
is of doubtful authority on the question under discussion at the
present day, not only because of the subsequent development of the
reasonable mistake of fact principle, but also for more particular
reasons which will be mentioned in connection with each case.

The first is *Griffin* v. *Larum*[70] in 1915, which raised precisely the
question left open in *Bear* v. *Lynch*. D was charged with being the
licensee of licensed premises upon which a person was found after
permitted hours for the sale of liquor for an unlawful purpose.[71] The
unlawful purpose was the consumption of liquor outside permitted
hours, which was clearly a purpose the unlawfulness of which was
contemplated by the Liquor Acts themselves. The line taken by the
High Court in *Bear* v. *Lynch* was therefore inapplicable and Ferguson
J. drew attention to the dictum of Griffith C.J., leaving the question
of reasonable mistake of fact open. The drink had been served by an
employee to a person whom she reasonably believed to be a bona fide
traveller and therefore entitled to be served after hours. The character
of the licensee was exemplary and the legislation included a mandatory penalty of forfeiture of licence after three convictions within

[67] (1934) 52 C.L.R. 364.
[68] Above, p. 51.
[69] (1941) 67 C.L.R. 536.
[70] (1915) 32 W.N. (N.S.W.) 10.
[71] Licensing Act, 1912 (N.S.W.), s. 63 (4).

three years. Nevertheless, Ferguson J. expressly rejected the idea that reasonable mistake of fact or reasonable precautions could be a defence. Fortunately the decision would at any time be of limited authority as it was reached by a single judge in chambers only. It is submitted that in view of later developments it can now be disregarded.

The next case prima facie carries more weight as it was a decision of the Full Court of Victoria. In *Martin* v. *Whittle*[72] in 1922 D was convicted for being a licensee upon whose licensed premises liquor was disposed of outside permitted hours. The facts were that three bottles of beer had been given away by a lodger on the premises who handed them through a door to a woman outside. This happened without the knowledge or authority of D. *Bear* v. *Lynch* was referred to in argument but not in the judgments. Once again the case is not a formidable authority at the present day, this time not only because it was decided before the modern law of reasonable mistake had been formulated, but also because it has been restrictively distinguished by a later Full Court in *Charlesworth* v. *Federal Hotels Ltd.*[73]

The third antecedent case is *Lewis* v. *Brown*,[74] decided by the New South Wales Court of Criminal Appeal in 1931. It was held that the owner of cattle trespassing on unauthorised land was liable to conviction regardless of whether he had knowledge of, or had authorised, the trespass. No reference was made to the relevance, if any, of his having taken reasonable precautions against the occurrence. The court was much influenced by considerations of vicarious responsibility.

The fourth case is *Wells* v. *Noblet*[75] in 1933, where strict responsibility was imposed for the offence of being the occupier of a common gaming house.[76] It is quite clear from the report, however,[77] that the learned judge was satisfied of D's guilt and anxious that he should not escape conviction on a technicality.

With *De La Rue* v. *McNamara*[78] in 1939 a change in attitude is apparent. This is the first of the later group of decisions on status offences. D appealed from summary conviction for being the occupier

[72] [1922] V.L.R. 207.
[73] [1943] V.L.R. 88.
[74] (1931) 48 W.N. (N.S.W.) 196.
[75] [1933] S.A.S.R. 134, 135.
[76] Lottery and Gaming Act, 1917–1930 (S.A.), s. 48a.
[77] [1933] S.A.S.R. 134, 135.
[78] [1940] V.L.R. 128.

of a house whereon a contrivance was kept for gaming.[79] D had no knowledge of the offending contrivance because it had been installed by her son at a time when he had been left in charge of the premises whilst D took a holiday. In these circumstances the conviction was affirmed on the basis of vicarious responsibility, but on the question whether in the absence of vicarious responsibility there could have been a conviction, Martin J. of the Victorian Supreme Court made the following observation[80] after citing *Maher* v. *Musson.* "In view of the drastic nature of the penalty[81] which might be imposed on one who neither by himself nor his agent had any knowledge of the presence of the forbidden article in her house, I would hesitate before deciding that *mens rea* was not an element of the offence . . . in the sense that once the defendant showed want of knowledge in herself or her agent of the article in her house, no offence was proved."

Against this expression of caution by a single judge, however, there must be set the decision of the Victorian Full Court four years later in *Charlesworth* v. *Kissling*.[82] D appealed against summary conviction for being the secretary of a members' club on the premises of which liquor was drunk on a Sunday.[83] The conviction was affirmed on the basis of strict responsibility. The following passage contains the reasoning.[84] "It was further contended that the secretary should not be held liable in a case where he showed that the act complained of had taken place without his knowledge, sanction or connivance or that of any person for whose conduct he was responsible and that he was not responsible for the acts or conduct of members. But the terms of the section creating the offence are absolute. It is one of the class of enactments which is expressed impersonally and makes the mere fact that liquor is drunk on club premises on Sundays . . . an offence."

It is submitted that this decision cannot be supported. Neither counsel nor the court cited any of the relevant High Court authority on offences "expressed impersonally", nor was the general doctrine of reasonable mistake which was confirmed in *Proudman* v. *Dayman* referred to. By 1943 the Australian common law had moved far beyond the point where the mere fact that an offence is "expressed

---

[79] Police Offences Act, 1928 (Vic.), s. 155.
[80] [1940] V.L.R. 128, 134.
[81] The maximum penalty was a fine of £100 or imprisonment for three months.
[82] [1943] V.L.R. 129.
[83] Licensing Act, 1928 (Vic.), s. 178.
[84] [1943] V.L.R. 129, 131–132.

impersonally" creates strict responsibility. If the case was supposed
to come within some exception to the general doctrine, the exception
should have been stated. The very fact that the statute made the
secretary, as the court observed,[85] "a sort of artificial defendant"
should have made their Honours astute to avoid the obvious
injustice of their decision.

A similar but more careful approach to the construction of a
status offence was made by Reed J. of the South Australian Supreme
Court in the celebrated case of *O'Sullivan* v. *Fisher*[86] in 1954. D had
been charged with being drunk in a public place.[87] Reed J. concluded
that the "absolute" (by which he seems to have meant "impersonal")
form of words used in the statute and the fact that the object of the
offence was the preservation of public order meant that strict
responsibility was imposed. To reach this conclusion, however, he
traced a course through relevant authorities[88] and took the trouble
accurately to distinguish between proof of *mens rea* by P and proof
of reasonable mistake by D. Nevertheless, it is submitted that the
decision was wrong. There are the several cases already cited to show
that there is no necessary connection between impersonal wording
and strict responsibility; and the antithesis implied between cases
concerned with public order and others is untenable, for all crimes
are aimed either directly, as with murder, or indirectly, as with
forgery, at the preservation of public order. A view directly contrary
to that of Reed J. on the effect of impersonal wording had previously
been strongly expressed by Napier C.J. of the South Australian
Supreme Court in *Snell* v. *Ryan*.[89] The facts of this case and Napier
C.J.'s observations have already been given.[90] *Snell* v. *Ryan* is an
important reinforcement at the State Supreme Court level of the
attitude manifested by the High Court to status offences.

The conclusion to be drawn is that while the High Court has set
its face firmly against putting status offences into a special class and
making them subject to strict responsibility merely on the basis of
the form of words used, there is a certain amount of hesitation to
follow this lead in the Supreme Courts. It is reasonable to anticipate,

[85] *Ibid.*, 131.
[86] [1954] S.A.S.R. 33.
[87] Police Act, 1936–1951 (S.A.), s. 74 (1).
[88] *Laughton* v. *Master Butchers* [1915] S.A.L.R. 3; *Dayman* v. *Proudman* [1941]
S.A.S.R. 87; *Proudman* v. *Dayman* (1941) 67 C.L.R. 536; *Bergin* v. *Stack* (1953)
88 C.L.R. 248.
[89] [1951] S.A.S.R. 59.
[90] Above, p. 52.

however, that this hesitation is a temporary phenomenon only and will disappear as the general rule becomes more firmly established.

Knowingly: wilfully

The word "knowingly" has acquired in Australia the same odd characteristics as elsewhere[91] of being more usually important through its absence than its presence[92] and of being thought, if absent, to shift a burden of proof from P to D.[93] The effect at the present day is that if this word qualifies the definitions of some offences in a regulatory statute but not others, the way is left open for the application of the reasonable mistake of fact rule to the offences in which "knowingly" does not appear. Since this would be the case whether the word appeared in other adjoining offences or not, observations upon that circumstance, where it occurs, are superfluous.

In the Australian cases "knowingly" is usually found in conjunction with "permits" and "suffers".[94] Here it has been consistently held that[95] "the word is used for the evident purpose of ensuring that . . . *mens rea* shall be retained not only as an essential ingredient of the crime but with the full onus of proving it thrown upon the prosecutor." This means that where these forms of words are found there is no room for the application of the reasonable mistake rule because D is placed in a position sufficiently favourable for that defence to be unnecessary. It has been urged above[96] that in the interests of a uniform rule of responsibility for regulatory offences "knowingly" ought to add nothing to "permits" and "suffers", and it may be that in time the Australian law will reach this position; but the cases do not at present support this view.

A distinction was drawn in *O'Sullivan* v. *Harford*[97] between

[91] Above, pp. 62–64.
[92] *Stephens* v. *Robert Reid & Co. Ltd.* (1902) 28 V.L.R. 82, 88; *Cochrane* v. *Tuthill* (1908) V.L.R. 549, 558–560; *Erson* [1914] V.L.R. 144, 150; *Laughton* v. *Master Butchers* [1915] S.A.L.R. 3, 12; *Lewis* v. *Brown* (1931) 48 W.N. (N.S.W.) 196, 198; *Bond* v. *Foran* (1934) 52 C.L.R. 364, 369; *Lipshut* v. *McKay* [1950] V.L.R. 57, 59; *Green* v. *Sergeant* [1951] V.L.R. 500, 504; *Hawthorn* v. *Bartholomew* [1954] V.L.R. 28, 31. For a rare instance of presence see *Colyer* (1897) 8 Q.L.J. 27.
[93] *Maher* v. *Musson* (1934) 52 C.L.R. 100, 105.
[94] The effect of these terms used in isolation is the subject of the next section.
[95] *Turnbull* (1943) 44 S.R. (N.S.W.) 108, 112. See also *Cullen* v. *Ware* (1897) 3 A.L.R. (CN) 65; *Ex p. Rowan* (1891) 8 W.N. (N.S.W.) 35; *Ex p. McDermott* (1901) 18 W.N. (N.S.W.) 231; *Ex p. Dunn* (1902) 19 W.N. (N.S.W.) 38; *Canty* v. *Buttrose* [1912] V.L.R. 363.
[96] Above, pp. 65–66.
[97] [1956] S.A.S.R. 109, 115.

"knowingly" and "wilfully" on the ground that "the natural meaning of 'wilfully' can be satisfied either by knowledge, or by a state of mind which adverts to the possibility of the existence of the attendant circumstances, but forbears to make inquiry, and wills to do the act whether or no". The implication was that "knowingly" would not be apt to cover an instance of wilful blindness. It is submitted that this is untenable. There is no difficulty at all in attributing knowledge to D if he behaves in such a way as to avoid discovering what he does not want to know. There is and ought to be no distinction of substance between "knowingly" and "wilfully" where criminal responsibility is concerned.

It is clear law that where the word "wilfully" appears in the definition of an offence P must prove full *mens rea* for D to be convicted.[98] This rule has not been affected by the emergence of the reasonable mistake of fact defence.

Permit: suffer: allow

Very little weight can now be attached to Australian cases on permitting, suffering or allowing[99] which were decided before *Ferrier* v. *Wilson* in the High Court in 1906.[1] That case, it will be recalled,[2] was a prosecution for "allowing" rubbish to fall into Sydney Harbour from a lighter, the actual cause of the falling of the rubbish from the lighter into the harbour being unknown. It was held that the word "allow" was apt to create criminal responsibility for[3] "the case where somebody by negligence allows the event which ought to be prevented to happen". With this decision responsibility for permitting a for-

---

[98] *Henty* v. *Hardwick* (1866) Argus Newspaper, July 4; *Garside* (1884) 6 A.L.T. 152;, *Buttons* v. *Melbourne Justices* (1890) 16 V.L.R. 604; *Thomas* v. *Ivey* (1892) 13 A.L.T. 190; *Melling* v. *Melbourne Justices* (1895) 17 A.L.T. 205; *Duncan* v. *Keppert* (1900) 26 V.L.R. 182; *Moffat* v. *Hassett* [1907] V.L.R. 515; *Lowe* [1917] V.L.R. 155; *Marsh* v. *Newton* (1927) 44 W.N. (N.S.W.) 28; *Doulin* v. *Coulton* (1938) 55 W.N. (N.S.W.) 131; *Ex. p. Wolff* (1939) 56 W.N. (N.S.W.) 33; *Jackson* v. *Butterworth* [1946] V.L.R. 330; *Davies* v. *O'Sullivan No. 2* [1949] S.A.S.R. 208; *Fenwick* v. *Boucaut* [1951] S.A.S.R. 290.

[99] *Ex p. M'Kinnon* (1853) 1 Legge 792; *Cornish* v. *Elliott* (1873) 4 A.J.R. 152; *M'Queen* (1875) 1 V.L.R. (L) 18; *Doyle* v. *Sparling* (1881) 3 A.L.T. 63; *Shuter* (1883) 9 V.L.R. (L) 204; *Francis* v. *Smith* (1886) 2 W.N. (N.S.W.) 82; *Maloney* v. *Clifford* (1890) 6 W.N. (N.S.W.) 125; *Mowling* v. *Hawthorne Justices* (1891) 17 V.L.R. 150; *Martin* v. *McGinnis* (1894) 20 V.L.R. 556; *Hillard* v. *Fitzpatrick* (1901) 27 V.L.R. 380; *Tippett* v. *Heyman* (1902) 19 W.N. (N.S.W.) 6; *Ex p. Little* (1902) 2 S.R. (N.S.W.) (L) 444; *Ex p. Neilsen* (1903) 20 W.N. (N.S.W.) 4; *Ex p. Lambert* (1905) 22 W.N. (N.S.W.) 130.

[1] (1906) 4 C.L.R. 785.

[2] Above, p. 56.

[3] (1906) 4 C.L.R. 785, 790.

bidden state of affairs to occur or continue was placed squarely upon the basis of negligence, of unreasonable failure to prevent. With one recent exception, this rule has been applied in similar cases ever since.

The High Court rule was followed almost immediately in *Potts* v. *Knox*,[4] a prosecution for allowing a false statement to be on the board required to be kept by D as a poundkeeper.[5] On appeal the case was remitted to the magistrate[6] "to determine whether the statement was allowed to be on the board within the meaning of the decision in *Ferrier* v. *Wilson*." In *Hudson* v. *Hanlon*[7] in 1913 it was next held, without express reference to the principal case, that to be convicted of permitting cattle to stray on to a railway line it must be proved at least that D ought reasonably to have foreseen the likelihood of their straying and neglected to take reasonable precautions against it.

These were New South Wales cases. The first mention of *Ferrier* v. *Wilson* in this context in Victoria comes in *Gilbert* v. *Gulliver*,[8] where Cussen J. had to construe the offence of allowing cattle to graze on unfenced municipal land, contrary to a local by-law. He distinguished the principal case on the ground that the wording differed in form from the regulation before him, but appears nevertheless to have been prepared to accept the proposition that evidence of negligence on D's part would have been relevant.[9] It is submitted that fine distinctions of the kind made by Cussen J. in this case are undesirable. In both cases the material word was "allow" and on the meaning of that word there had been a clear pronouncement by the superior court.

The next relevant case is *Sangster* v. *Henry*[10] in 1920, where the master of a ship was charged with allowing his ship to be so loaded as to submerge in salt water the centre of the disc indicating the load line duly marked on the ship. A passage from the argument in *Ferrier* v. *Wilson*[11] was adopted which said, "allowing means not preventing that which ordinary care would prevent". The decision in favour of the master of the ship then proceeded in the clearest possible way on the ground that although he had made an error in the loading of the ship, in the circumstances the error was a reason-

[4] (1907) 24 W.N. (N.S.W.) 91.
[5] Impounding Act, 1898 (N.S.W.), s. 9.
[6] (1907) 24 W.N. (N.S.W.), 91, 92.
[7] (1913) 30 W.N. (N.S.W.) 85.
[8] [1918] V.L.R. 185.
[9] *Ibid.*, 189–191.
[10] (1920) 37 W.N. (N.S.W.) 135.
[11] (1906) 4 C.L.R. 785, 788.

able one to make; and the warning was given that he could not expect to be able to rely on a similar error again.

In South Australia the same rule was adopted in *Jolly* v. *Virgo*[12] in 1927 and *Horseman* v. *Cavanagh*[13] in 1930. In *Jolly* v. *Virgo* D appealed from summary conviction for unlawfully permitting liquor to be consumed on his licensed premises.[14] Napier J. made an unambiguous choice between the alternative possible meanings for the word "permit", citing *Ferrier* v. *Wilson* in support of the following observations.[15] "The first matter to be considered is the meaning of the word "permits" in this context. It might be used in the sense of "give leave", but an alternative, if not the more common meaning, is "not to prevent", and I think that the licensee may be said to permit the consumption of liquor if it takes place with his knowledge or connivance or by his failure to use due diligence to prevent it."

In *Horseman* v. *Cavanagh*[16] D appealed from summary conviction under a section whereby every member of the committee of management of a club who permitted the keeping of liquor on unregistered premises committed an offence.[17] Beer was found in lockers on unregistered club premises and D was a member of the committee which, in the absence of contrary evidence, was assumed to be the committee of management. In dealing with the question whether D had permitted, Richards J. made the same approach as Napier J., relying on both *Ferrier* v. *Wilson* and *Jolly* v. *Virgo*. "[I]t is not essential to show that he actually knew. It is sufficient if the liquor was in the lockers by his failure to use due diligence to prevent it."[18]

In view of these cases it is surprising to find in Victoria a recent decision, *Bond* v. *Reynolds*,[19] in which it was held on a charge against a licensee that he permitted liquor to be drunk on his licensed premises outside lawful hours that there could not be a conviction unless it were proved by P that either D or, on the basis of vicarious responsibility, someone to whom he had delegated his authority, actually knew that the unlawful drinking was taking place. In arriving at this decision Gavan Duffy J. declined to follow the earlier

[12] [1927] S.A.S.R. 188.
[13] [1930] S.A.S.R. 1.
[14] Licensing Act, 1917 (S.A.), s. 185.
[15] [1927] S.A.S.R. 188, 190.
[16] [1930] S.A.S.R. 1.
[17] Licensing Act, 1917 (S.A.), s. 94 (2).
[18] [1930] S.A.S.R. 1, 5.
[19] [1960] V.R. 601.

Victorian case of *Broadhurst* v. *Larkin*,[20] decided in 1954 by Herring C.J., on the ground that it was on a different statute. In *Broadhurst* v. *Larkin* D had been charged with permitting an employee to drive a motor vehicle over a period of time without taking sufficient rest.[21] The magistrate dismissed the information on the ground that there was no evidence that D actually knew that the driver was driving with insufficient rest. Herring C.J. allowed P's appeal for the express reason that the magistrate was wrong on this point, the word "permit" in the context meaning[22] "abstain from taking reasonable or proper steps to prevent those under [D's] control from driving without adequate rest".

The decision in *Bond* v. *Reynolds* occasioned such general surprise that in 1961 an attempt was made to test it by having an order to review the dismissal of an information in *Earl* v. *Jakus*[23] referred to the Full Court.[24] In *Earl* v. *Jakus* the charge was laid under a section prohibiting the suffering of gaming on premises where refreshments were being dispensed.[25] The Full Court decided the case on the evidence, no point material to the present discussion arising, and declined to make the comments requested on *Bond* v. *Reynolds* on the ground that the two cases were on different statutes and raised different issues on the facts. It is significant, however, that the Full Court did not approve the earlier decision in any way, which it would not have been difficult or unusual to do.

Two other cases should be mentioned. In *Ex parte Bruce*[26] D, a truck driver, appealed from summary conviction under traffic regulations that he permitted or allowed people to ride on a part of the vehicle not meant for the carriage of persons under such circumstances that there was a reasonable danger of their falling off, being thrown off, or being injured thereby.[27] Apart from saying that the words "permit" and "allow" excluded strict responsibility, McClemens J. of the Supreme Court of New South Wales, allowing the appeal, found it unnecessary to be explicit as to their precise meaning because it was clear on the evidence that D had not been

---

[20] [1954] V.L.R. 541.

[21] Transport Regulation Act, 1933 (Vic.), s. 39 (1) (c).

[22] [1954] V.L.R. 541, 545.

[23] [1961] V.R. 143.

[24] Herring C.J., Dean and Adam JJ.

[25] Police Offences Act, 1958 (Vic.), s. 32.

[26] (1957) 74 W.N. (N.S.W.) 452.

[27] Motor Traffic Regulations, reg. 110A, made under the Motor Traffic Act, 1909–1956 N.S.W.), s. 3.

proved by P even to have omitted to take reasonable precautions to prevent people riding in the forbidden manner. If not even that much had been proved, there could be no question of permitting or allowing.

In the older case of *Tennant* v. *Harris*[28] Cussen J. held that a dog owner had not permitted the animal to worry a turkey unless he knew the incident was taking place, even though the dog was known to have worried other animals before and the owner nevertheless allowed it to roam. This decision, however, seems to have been based on an application of the *ejusdem generis* rule of statutory interpretation, for the whole phrase which contained the word "permit" was "setting on, urging or permitting",[29] which conveys a sense of immediacy.

It can therefore be seen that, with one recent exception of doubtful authority, the doctrine of *Ferrier* v. *Wilson*, that the word "allow" and synonyms therefor are apt to create responsibility for failing to take reasonable steps to prevent some prohibited state of affairs, has become part of Australian law in reference to regulatory offences, as against the view that these words require actual knowledge by D or by someone for whom he is responsible.[30] In reaching this conclusion three classes of cases have been excluded from discussion: first, civil cases on the same words,[31] because quite different considerations from the problems of criminal responsibility arise when questions only of civil liability to damages are in issue; secondly, cases which turned on the doctrine of vicarious responsibility,[32] because it is of the utmost importance not to confuse liability for permitting with liability for someone else's permitting; and thirdly, cases where the statutory words were qualified by either "knowingly" or "wilfully" or both, because these have already been more conveniently dealt with as a separate class in the preceding section of this chapter.

Before leaving the subject, however, it is well to recall that *Proudman* v. *Dayman*[33] itself was on the word "permit" and laid down the reasonable mistake rule in its modern form in this very

[28] [1916] V.L.R. 557.
[29] Police Offences Act, 1915 (Vic.), s. 17 (9).
[30] *Cf. Gill* v. *Williams* (1916) Tas. L.R. 67, where on a charge of "failing to prevent" prostitutes remaining on licensed premises P had to prove knowledge in D that the women were prostitutes.
[31] *Adelaide Corporation* v. *Australasian Performing Right Association Ltd.* (1928) 40 C.L.R. 481, (H.C.); *Broad* v. *Parish* (1941) 64 C.L.R. 588, (H.C.).
[32] *e.g., Mahoney* v. *Le Page* (1900) 6 A.L.R. 23; *Charlesworth* v. *Penfolds Wines Pty. Ltd.* [1943] V.L.R. 76.
[33] (1941) 67 C.L.R. 536.

context. It follows that the nature of the relationship between the negligence rule of *Ferrier* v. *Wilson* and the reasonable mistake rule of *Proudman* v. *Dayman* needs to be stated.

It has already been observed[34] that in *Proudman* v. *Dayman* Dixon C.J. analysed the offence of permitting a person not being the holder of a licence to drive a motor vehicle on a road into two parts.[35] He first isolated (1) the driving (2) of a motor vehicle (3) on a road as being subject to the word "permit" in the sense that D must have "meant to consent"[36] to them. To arrive at the possibility of consent his Honour conceded that[37] "the very idea of permission connotes knowledge of or advertence to the act or thing permitted. In other words, you cannot permit without consenting and consent involves a consciousness or understanding of the act or conduct to which it is directed."

There are two modern cases which illustrate well this part of the reasoning in *Proudman* v. *Dayman*. The first is *Winton* v. *Wright*[38] in which D had been summarily convicted of permitting an unregistered vehicle to be driven on a public road.[39] He was the owner of a car sales business in the course of which he commonly sent out M, an employee, with a car for which M was to endeavour to find a buyer by driving round the district and offering it to people for sale. The business was situated in Victoria and the car was registered for driving in this manner in that state. On the occasion in question M had driven the car over the border into New South Wales, where the car was not registered. D's appeal against conviction was allowed on the ground that he could not be said to have permitted the driving in New South Wales unless it were shown that he had either expressly or impliedly authorised M to drive there; and there was no evidence of this.

Proudman v. *Dayman* and *Winton* v. *Wright* were expressly followed in the Tasmanian case of *Peterson* v. *Curran*[40] in 1950. D was charged with virtually the same offence[41] as in *Winton* v. *Wright*, which Morris C.J. regarded as being on all fours with the case before

---

[34] Above, pp. 60–61.
[35] *Cf.* the reasoning adopted in *Francis* v. *Rowan*, above, pp. 120–121; and for another example see *O'Sullivan* v. *Harford* [1956] S.A.S.R. 109.
[36] (1941) 67 C.L.R. 536, 541.
[37] *Ibid.*
[38] (1941) 58 W.N. (N.S.W.) 181.
[39] Motor Traffic Act, 1909 (N.S.W.), s. 6 (1) (c) (v).
[40] [1950] Tas. S.R. 9.
[41] Traffic Act, 1925–1947 (Tas.), s. 14.

him. D was the owner of two trucks, one registered to be driven on a public road and one not. He instructed a driver to take a load without specifying which truck to use. His reason for failing to specify the truck was that in his belief only the registered one could be used because the other was out of action owing to a mechanical fault. Unfortunately, unknown to D, the fault had been repaired and the driver by chance chose to take that vehicle, not realising that it was unregistered. The magistrates expressed the opinion that D would not intentionally have put an unregistered truck on the road but for some reason felt constrained to convict. Morris C.J. allowed the appeal on the ground that unless D knew the material facts, as to which there was no finding, he could not be convicted. A new trial was ordered.

Each of these cases was concerned with the element of permitting driving, and they show that the rule laid down for this part of such offences is narrower than the rule in *Ferrier* v. *Wilson*. It is not enough to be ignorant or mistaken about the fact of driving through negligence; actual knowledge must be proved. A distinction between *Proudman* v. *Dayman* and *Ferrier* v. *Wilson* seems to be thereby created, but it is reasonably clear that the difference is more theoretical than practical; for there is scarcely room for negligent error in relation to either "driving" or a "motor vehicle", and not much more for "road". In short, there is no real conflict between the two cases because on this part of the offence charged in *Proudman* v. *Dayman* there was no significant room for the application of the rule in *Ferrier* v. *Wilson*.

The situation is different, however, with regard to the second part of the offence as analysed by Dixon C.J., the status of the driver as a person not holding a licence. Here it is clear that absence of knowledge in D is admissible as a defence under *Proudman* v. *Dayman* only if it can be put in the form of a reasonable mistake of fact and is proved affirmatively by D. Under the doctrine of *Ferrier* v. *Wilson* it would have been for P to prove that if D was ignorant of the driver's lack of a licence, his ignorance was owing to a negligent failure to ascertain the true facts. Here there is a conflict between the two cases which must be reconciled.

Once again the basic difference between the two fact situations suggests the correct answer. It is true that the negligence doctrine of *Ferrier* v. *Wilson* could have been applied to this element of the offence in *Proudman* v. *Dayman*, but it is not true that the reasonable mistake doctrine of *Proudman* v. *Dayman* could have been applied to the facts in *Ferrier* v. *Wilson*. There was no mistake of fact involved in the unexplained falling of rubbish into Sydney Harbour. The same applies to the facts in the line of cases mentioned above in which the *Ferrier* v. *Wilson* rule has been adopted either expressly or in effect. The reason which reveals itself upon inspection of those cases is that they are differentiated from *Proudman* v. *Dayman* by the absence from the definitions of the offences concerned of any significant status element. If liability does not turn on the possession by some person or place or object of a status which is unlawful in the circumstances, it is difficult to find anything relevant about which to be mistaken.

The rule may therefore be formulated for regulatory offences of permitting, suffering or allowing activities or states of affairs, that if D's criminal responsibility turns on his ignorance of a question of status, he must prove that he made a reasonable mistake of fact as to that status if he is to escape conviction; but that if it turns on any other element of the offence P must prove that D's behaviour was either negligent or, if negligence is in the nature of the case inappropriate, intentional with respect to that element.

Cause

The High Court decision in *O'Sullivan* v. *Truth & Sportsman Ltd.*[42] has already been mentioned.[43] It decides that where the word "cause" appears in the definition of a statutory offence, D's criminal responsibility depends upon proof by P of[44] "the actual authority, express or implied, of the party said to have caused".

In that case D was a company charged under the Police Offences Act, 1953 (S.A.), s. 35 (1), which made it an offence to "cause to be offered for sale or sold to any person" a newspaper containing certain prohibited matter. The evidence established that D had supplied its offending newspapers to independent newsagents on sale or return. The question was whether D had thereby "caused" the newspapers to be sold or offered for sale. Applying the test quoted above, the court held that the offence had not been proved. Indeed, as the majority observed, if no limit were placed on the relevance of ante-

[42] (1957) 96 C.L.R. 220. *Cf. Miller* v. *Hilton* (1937) 57 C.L.R. 400; *Shakespeare* v. *Taylor* (1890) 24 S.A.L.R. 51.
[43] Above, p. 54 n. 32.
[44] (1957) 96 C.L.R. 220, 228.

cedent events, it might equally well be argued that it was the news-vendors who caused the paper to be printed by indicating their willingness to sell it. The result is that the word "cause" in Australia requires full *mens rea*. There is therefore no need for the reasonable mistake rule in this type of offence. Reasons for doubting whether this is the best rule for regulatory offences including the word "cause" have already been given.

It follows from *O'Sullivan* v. *Truth & Sportsman Ltd.* that the addition of the word "wilfully" or some synonym to "causes" adds nothing to the sense of the definition of an offence of causing.[45]

Fraudulent

One would scarcely expect strict responsibility to be an issue where D is charged with doing something fraudulently. Nevertheless, this occurred in the first case in which the problem of strict responsibility came before the High Court, *Hardgrave* v. *The King*,[46] which set the ball rolling in style by presenting the remarkable, and possibly unique, spectacle of D arguing in favour of strict responsibility and P arguing against it.

D was charged with an offence against the Commonwealth Audit Act, 1901, s. 64 (1) (a), of fraudulently converting money belonging to the Commonwealth Post Office. P tendered evidence of a similar misappropriation of money belonging to a State Savings Bank which he contended was admissible to rebut a possible defence of accident or negligence. To this D objected that the purpose of the evidence was to help prove the mental element in the offence, but that this was irrelevant since P would have made out his case if he proved merely the fact of the deficiency; and that therefore the evidence was not admissible.[47] Griffith C.J. dealt with the objection as follows:[48]

"Respecting the contention that it is not necessary to show anything more than the mere fact that there is a deficiency, I do not think that that is supported by the language of the section. The general rule is that a person is not criminally responsible for an act

---

[45] *Ex p. Ritchie* (1896) 12 W.N. (N.S.W.) 109; *Howell* v. *Bullen* [1915] V.L.R. 445. *Cf. Ex p. Hop Sing* (1887) 4 W.N. (N.S.W.) 59.

[46] (1906) 4 C.L.R. 232. *Cf. Foster* v. *Damyon* (1932) 38 A.L.R. 477.

[47] A last ditch defence if ever there was one. It is not easy to see how this evidence could have mattered if D was relying on being able to deny the fact of the deficiency *in limine*.

[48] (1906) 4 C.L.R. 232, 237. The other member of the court, O'Connor J., uttered a similar opinion at 239.

which is done independently of the exercise of his will or by accident.[49]
It is also a general rule that a person who does an act under a
reasonable misapprehension of fact is not criminally responsible for
it even if the facts which he believed did not exist. I do not think the
first rule has ever been excluded by any statute. I can see no foundation for the suggestion that a man who by accident places a sum of
money in a wrong drawer, honestly believing that it belongs to
himself or to the state, is criminally liable. I think it would be a good
defence to show that, although there was a deficiency in the
Commonwealth accounts, the money lacking was placed in to the
credit of another account by accident, or with a bona fide intention,
and I think that evidence bearing upon that point would have been
admissible."

It may be conceded that D had set himself an uphill task, for it is
unlikely that the court would have gone out of its way to find strict
responsibility merely in order to exclude cogent evidence. Nevertheless, it is noteworthy that in this first case the High Court declined
to make the choice proposed by D between full *mens rea* and strict
responsibility, pointing instead to the possibility of "reasonable
misapprehension of fact".

Evade

Another unusual case is *Wilson* v. *Chambers*,[50] which may show
that under very exceptional circumstances the defence of reasonable
mistake can extend even to a mistake of law.

D was charged with having "evaded" payment of import duty
contrary to the Commonwealth Customs Act, 1901–1920, s. 234. It
was common ground that D had made an arrangement whereby duty
was not paid at the time when it should have been, but that this
arrangement had been made with the concurrence of the local

[49] His Honour here used the wording he employed in s. 23 of the Queensland Criminal
Code, of which he was the draftsman, and which was copied thence into the Western
Australian Criminal Code (s. 23). On this see below, Ch. 7, *passim*. Griffith C.J. was
no friend of the term *mens rea*, which he often disparaged: "Few expressions in the
law have given rise to more confusion than *mens rea*." (*Ross* v. *Sickerdick* (1916)
22 C.L.R. 197, 200.) "An argument was addressed to us founded upon what is
known as the doctrine of *mens rea*. With the profoundest respect to the learned
persons by whom that doctrine has been discussed, I cannot help saying that I think
that, now at least, it has become a misleading expression." (*Bear* v. *Lynch* (1909)
8 C.L.R. 592, 600–601.) "I confess I do not know exactly what is meant" by an
argument based on the absence of *mens rea*. (*Ferrier* v. *Wilson* (1906) 4 C.L.R. 785,
792.) "The old doctrine of *mens rea*, the exact meaning of which has been the subject
of much discussion." (*Widgee Shire Council* v. *Bonney* (1907) 4 C.L.R. 977, 981.)
[50] (1926) 38 C.L.R. 131.

customs officer as a matter of convenience, and with no intention of failing to pay any duty leviable in due course. The truth of the matter was that the persons concerned had not realised that their arrangement of convenience might involve a technical breach of the law. The High Court held that D had not "evaded" payment of duty. The test of evasion enunciated by Isaacs J.[51] was "whether the Crown debtor has acted honestly and reasonably in relation to his public obligations". He drew a parallel with the defence of reasonable mistake of fact and held that where dishonesty on D's part was a prerequisite for criminal responsibility,[52] an action might still be honest even though founded on a mistake of law.

Perhaps it is wrong to regard *Wilson* v. *Chambers* as a case on mistake at all. What the court seems to have done in substance was to define an offence of evasion as requiring proof by P of an intent on D's part permanently to deprive the Crown of duty, and to hold that on the facts of the case P had failed to prove this intent. Nevertheless, the reference by Isaacs J. quoted above to an inquiry whether D's behaviour as a whole had been reasonable is interesting.

Statutory defences

Two problems arise with statutory defences to regulatory prosecutions. The first is as to the proper construction of the defences themselves. This problem is not relevant to the present discussion.[53] The second problem is as to the effect upon the common law of the enactment of a statutory defence; or, to put it differently, whether the enactment of a statutory defence carries with it the implication that common law defences are necessarily excluded from the offence in question.

The argument that an express defence necessarily excludes the common law depends upon the maxim *inclusio unius est exclusio alterius*. But this is only a statement of a point of view, not a proposition of logic. The mere enactment of a statutory defence has no necessary impact on the common law by way of superseding it unless

---

[51] *Ibid.*, 144.

[52] As opposed to the pleonastic use of the word "honest" in "honest and reasonable mistake of fact." See below, p. 150 n. 10.

[53] *Barrett* v. *Sullivan* [1900] S.A.L.R. 48; *Anstee* v. *Jennings* [1935] V.L.R. 144; *Broadhurst* v. *Cockcroft* [1937] V.L.R. 159; *Barker* v. *Callaghan* [1941] V.L.R. 15; *Freeman* v. *C. T. Warne Pty. Ltd.* [1947] V.L.R. 279; *Eclipse Motors* v. *Milner* [1950] S.A.S.R. 1; *Bergin* v. *Khyat* [1953] V.L.R. 695; *Young* v. *Paddle Bros. Pty. Ltd.* [1956] V.L.R. 38; *Myers* v. *Crabtree* [1956] V.L.R. 431; *Tully* v. *O'Sullivan* [1956] S.A.S.R. 106.

there is an inconsistency between the two, in which case the statute must prevail. As a matter of precedent this was established for the criminal law in *Tolson*[54] and has been confirmed for Australia in *Thomas* v. *The King*.[55]

The Australian decisions on statutory defences to regulatory offences show little or no awareness of this. There is a line of cases[56] going back to 1910 in which regulatory offences to which statutory defences applied have been held subject to the doctrine of strict responsibility, but in none of them is there any clear recognition of the point at issue and in only one or two are there more than the most perfunctory discussions of the question whether the offence under consideration is one to which strict responsibility ought to be applied. Because of this omission to consider expressly what effect a statutory defence has on the common law, the point passing *sub silentio* if at all, it is submitted that these cases constitute very doubtful authority on the question and are certainly not strong enough to prevail against the general rule to be derived from *Tolson* and *Thomas* v. *The King*.

Moreover, to these two cases there may be added the further authority in the regulatory offence area of *Spooner* v. *Alexander*,[57] a High Court decision in 1912 which has already been discussed.[58] It will be recalled that in that case the charge was that D absented himself from his employment "without reasonable cause", the existence of reasonable cause being a defence given by the wording of the statute. This did not prevent the common law defence of reasonable belief in the existence of reasonable cause being available to D. It will also be recalled that in a dictum quoted in the previous chapter[59] Lord Atkin expressed the same view in *Thorne* v. *Motor Trade Association*.[60]

It is therefore submitted that both reason and authority are in favour of the view that the mere presence in a statute of an express defence to a regulatory offence does nothing to exclude common law defences including the defence of reasonable mistake of fact.

[54] (1889) 23 Q.B.D. 168.
[55] (1937) 59 C.L.R. 279.
[56] *Trenchard* v. *Ryan* (1910) 10 S.R. (N.S.W.) 618; *Griffin* v. *Larum* (1915) 32 W.N. (N.S.W.) 10; *Dineen* v. *Nicholson* [1922] S.A.S.R. 1; *Fraser* v. *Dryden's Carrying Co.* [1941] V.L.R. 103; *O'Sullivan* v. *Friebe* [1956] S.A.S.R. 89.
[57] (1912) 13 C.L.R. 704.
[58] Above, p. 116.
[59] Above, p. 101.
[60] [1937] A.C. 797, 809.

CHAPTER 7

THE AUSTRALIAN CRIMINAL CODES

Introduction

A certain amount has already been said on this subject.[1] It will be recalled that in this book by a criminal code is meant a statute covering the whole of the criminal law to the exclusion of all other sources except for cases decided subsequently to the enactment of the code on the interpretation of the code. This definition does not mean that every regulatory offence must appear in the code, but that every regulatory offence which does not do so is subject to the same general principles of responsibility as if it were in the code, and that these general principles are set out in the code. Nevertheless, since a criminal code, although imposing in appearance, carries no greater weight *per se* than any other statute, an offence created after the enactment of the code may be defined in such a way as to exclude these general principles either expressly or by necessary implication, and thereby repeal the code *pro tanto*.

In this sense there are for the present purpose only two criminal codes in Australia, those of Queensland and Western Australia.[2] The general parts of these codes, which is all that we shall be concerned with in this chapter, are identical. The case-law has pursued a somewhat different course in the two states, however.

Interpretation

(i) *Introduction*

For the present purpose the key sections, which are the heart of criminal responsibility under the codes, are sections 23 and 24, the texts of which, so far as material, are as follows.

> *Section 23.* Subject to the express provisions of this Code relating to negligent acts and omissions, a person is not criminally responsible for an act or omission which occurs independently of the exercise of his will, or for an event which occurs by accident.

> *Section 24.* A person who does or omits to do an act under an honest

[1] Above, Ch. 4, pp. 74–75.
[2] On the Tasmanian Code see above, p. 78, n. 19.

and reasonable, but mistaken, belief in the existence of any state of things is not criminally responsible for the act or omission to any greater extent than if the real state of things had been such as he believed to exist.

The operation of this rule may be excluded by the express or implied provisions of the law relating to the subject.

The correct interpretation of these sections is of paramount importance but no little difficulty. First they must be put into context. They form part of Chapter V of the Code, which, by section 36, applies to anyone charged with a criminal offence against the statute law of the state. Since the effect of the enactment of the criminal codes of Queensland and Western Australia has been to make all offences statutory,[3] the effect of section 36 is to apply the general principles of responsibility set out in Chapter V to the whole of the criminal law. The exclusive nature of the codes is derived from section 2 of the Criminal Code Acts, whereby they "shall be the law ... with respect to the several matters therein dealt with".[4]

The effect of these rules is twofold. First, the general principles of criminal responsibility are to be found in Chapter V of the Code and nowhere else. This has the legal consequence that the common law doctrines of *mens rea* and strict responsibility are irrelevant in the code jurisdictions. There has been judicial disagreement whether section 23 is identical with the common law or enacts a different rule;[5] but since it is clear that in construing section 23 no reliance is to be placed on common law authorities on the doctrine of *mens rea*,[6] it is

---

[3] The only exception is contempt of court, which is expressly excluded from the operation of the codes: Criminal Code Act, 1899 (Q'ld.), s. 8; Criminal Code Act, 1913 (W.A.), s. 7.
[4] The Queensland Code was brought into force by the Act of 1899. The W.A. Code was first enacted in 1902, but repealed and re-enacted in 1913.
[5] For the common law, Chubb J. in *Walker* v. *Chapman* [1904] St. R. Qd. 330, 334, and Webb C.J. in *Callaghan* [1942] St. R. Qd. 40, 43–44. Compare the remarks of the draftsman of the Code, Sir Samuel Griffith, in his letter of October 29, 1897, which accompanied the first draft; and his later comments in *Hardgrave* v. *The King* (1906) 4 C.L.R. 232, 237. *Cf.* Dixon J. in *Thomas* v. *The King* (1937) 59 C.L.R. 279, 305–306, on claim of right and mistake (ss. 22 and 24 of the Code). Against the common law, Cooper C.J. and Lukin J. in *Thomas* v. *McEather* [1920] St. R. Qd. 166, 174–175; and Philp J. in *Anderson* v. *Nystrom* [1941] St. R. Qd. 56, 69, and *Callaghan*, above, at p. 50. In *Scarth* [1945] St. R. Qd. 38, 52, Philp J. is reported as saying the exact contrary to what he says elsewhere, but it is clear from the context that he was referring there only to the judge's duty in summing up in the particular case, which was not affected by any difference between s. 23 and the common law.
[6] Criminal Code Acts, s. 2. For judicial pronouncements to the same effect see *Widgee Shire Council* v. *Bonney* (1907) 4 C.L.R. 977, 981–982, *per* Griffith C.J.; *Thomas* v. *McEather* [1920] St. R. Qd. 166, 174–175, *per* Lukin J.; *Anderson* v. *Nystrom* [1941] St. R. Qd. 56, 69, *per* Philp J.

immaterial which view one takes. Secondly, the general principles of responsibility set out in the Code protect not only a defendant charged with an offence against a section of the Code itself, but also a defendant charged with an offence, however minor, against any of the statute laws of the state in question.

These matters are preliminaries to the real problem, which is the nature of the relationship between sections 23 and 24; or, put differently, what these sections mean. There are two words upon which all discussion turns. The first is "act" in section 23 and the second is "reasonable" in section 24. The meaning which is given to sections 23 and 24 in this book is the following.

(ii) *Section 23*

Section 23 lays down the basic rule that no one is to be criminally responsible for an act or omission which occurs independently of the exercise of his will or for an event which occurs by accident. The reference to accident should not be forgotten, but it will be convenient to concentrate attention on the volition requirement. This rule is subject to the express provisions of the code relating to negligent acts and omissions. It is therefore clear at the outset that whatever meaning is to be attributed to "act" and "omission", this meaning must be such that it makes sense to talk of a "negligent act" or a "negligent omission". The conclusion immediately follows that a negligent act or omission is one which occurs independently of the exercise of the actor's will; for if this were not the case there would be no point in making the main rule subject to express provisions relating to negligent acts and omissions.

Now, if a negligent act or omission is one which occurs independently of the exercise of the will, it follows that the words "act" and "omission" must include a reference to some degree of mental advertence in addition to so much volition as is required merely to perform an act or make an omission in a purely physical sense. An act can be defined, and, indeed, usually is quite adequately defined, in a purely physical sense as a "muscular contraction or bodily movement";[7] and such a meaning is consistent with a distinction

[7] This is the meaning apparently adopted by the American Law Institute's Model Penal Code, Tentative Draft No. 4, s. 2.01 (2). See also Comment, 119. But *cf.* s. 2.01 (4), where possession as an act is defined to include knowledge. The meaning of "act" in s. 13 of the Tasmanian Criminal Code, a section corresponding to s. 23 of the Queensland Criminal Code, was considered by the High Court in *Vallance* v. *The Queen* (1961) 35 A.L.J.R. 182, but the drafting of s. 13 is materially different from the drafting of s. 23.

drawn between volitional acts and acts which occur independently of the exercise of one's will. It is also consistent with a reference to negligent acts if by a negligent act is understood an act performed negligently. But it is not consistent with a scheme which classifies negligence with lack of volition, for negligence refers to the state of mind with which an admittedly volitional act was done.

If D is charged with committing an offence and his liability to conviction depends on whether P proves that he has performed the forbidden act negligently, he can defend himself at one or both of two levels. He can say, and this is the usual case, that he was not negligent. Here he does not deny the facts proved by P but argues that they do not amount in law to negligence. Alternatively (leaving out of account a defence that the facts alleged by P never occurred at all) he can deny that his act was voluntary, as where he claims that he acted in a state of automatism after sustaining concussion.[8] In the first of these two defences, in the normal use of language, D is saying that his act was voluntary, although his conduct was not negligent. In the second he is saying that his act was involuntary, so that the question of negligence does not arise. In the normal use of language it would be said that in the first case D's act occurred in accordance with the exercise of his will but in the second case it did not.

The point of these hypothetical examples is to show that the question of negligence is different from the question of volition so far as "act" in a purely physical sense is concerned. There can be a volitional act with or without negligence, although there cannot for legal purposes be negligence without a volitional act or omission. But the same cannot apply where, as in the codes, a negligent act is classified as an act which occurs independently of the exercise of one's will. In this situation it follows inevitably that the word "act" must include some degree of knowledge or advertence over and above that which would be required for an act as an exclusively physical phenomenon.

If this much be granted, the question remains, what degree of knowledge or advertence is included in the words "act" and "omission" in section 23? The obvious answer is, knowledge of such facts as render the act criminal in the circumstances. This would mean knowledge of the fact that pulling the trigger of a gun would

---

[8] *Kay* v. *Butterworth* (1945) 61 T.L.R. 452; *Minor* (1955) 112 C.C.C. 29; *Coates* v. *R.* (1957) 31 A.L.J.R. 34; *Re a Barrister* (1957) 31 A.L.J.R. 424; *Hill* v. *Baxter* [1958] 1 Q.B. 277; *Wakefield* (1958) 75 W.N. (N.S.W.) 66; *Cooper* v. *McKenna* [1960] Qd. R. 406; *Bratty* v. *Att.-Gen. for Northern Ireland* [1963] A.C. 386.

kill a human being, or knowledge of the fact that the milk one was about to sell was adulterated. If an act in the narrow sense is done with this degree of knowledge, then the fact that it is done voluntarily, as required by section 23, supplies what at common law would be called *mens rea*, the intention to do the forbidden act.

The result is that the paragraph of section 23 quoted above enacts a rule very like *actus reus* and *mens rea* at common law, for it says in effect that normally D cannot be convicted unless there is proof of a volitional act, and that D can deny the volitional element by demonstrating that the occurrence in question took place either by accident, or through his negligence and not his intention, or without volition in the more usual sense. Section 23, in short, requires intention for all crimes except those which contain in their definitions an express requirement of negligence only.

This interpretation of section 23 derives support from several incidental factors. First, there is the absence in the rest of the general part of the Code of any other words which could be understood as creating a requirement equivalent to *mens rea* at common law. Since this requirement must be somewhere, and since section 23 is the obvious place to look for it, there is a persuasive implication that section 23 should be interpreted in such a way as to import an adequate mental element into the general principles of the Code.

Secondly, there is the second paragraph of section 23, immediately following the paragraph quoted above: "Unless an intention to cause a particular result is expressly declared to be an element of the offence constituted in whole or part, by an act or omission, the result intended to be caused by an act or omission is immaterial." This rule envisages intentional acts and puts a restriction upon a presupposed requirement that an act, to be criminal, must be intentional as to the criminal result. The presupposition would be incomprehensible unless there were in the previous paragraph of section 23 a requirement of intention, which must include knowledge. Such a requirement can be arrived at only by interpreting "act" and "omission" in the manner adopted above.

Thirdly, it is a little difficult to fit the word "omission" into a pattern which regards the word "act" in the Code as referring to a purely physical phenomenon. In no sense which suggests itself can an omission be sensibly referred to in the same way, for an omission is in physical terms nothing. There is no "muscular contraction or bodily movement" about an omission. There the very equation of

omissions with acts tends to suggest that the latter are to be understood in a wide sense.

Finally, it is interesting that in his letter of October 29, 1897, to the
Attorney-General which accompanied the draft Code, the draftsman,
Sir Samuel Griffith, explained his omission to use the words "malice"
or "maliciously" in the definitions of offences relating to the person
or property as follows.[9] "[These words mean] no more than that the
offender did the act in question voluntarily (that is, not accidentally)
and knowing what he was doing. The general rules of criminal responsibility set out in section [23] render it unnecessary to express these
elements in the definition of an offence."

Although what the draftsman thought he was doing is not strictly
admissible as evidence of what he did, the significance of this passage,
with particular reference to the words italicised, should not be overlooked. It is clear that in Sir Samuel Griffith's view section 23
contained a clear requirement of intention as to the criminal result
of a voluntary action. Such a requirement can be arrived at only in
the way shown above, namely, by giving a wide meaning to the words
"act" and "omission" so as to include in them not only the necessary
element of volition to produce a purely physical result but also so
much knowledge and intention with respect to surrounding circumstances that the physical act or omission becomes a criminal act or
omission.

(iii) *Section 24*

Turning now to section 24, a different kind of difficulty presents
itself. The problems posed by section 24 arise entirely out of the
inclusion of the word "reasonable", with the effect that a mistake of
fact[10] cannot amount to an exculpation within the meaning of
section 24 unless it is a reasonable one to have made in the circumstances. A mistake which was reasonable in the circumstances is one
which, in the customary euphemism of the courts, would have been
made by a reasonable man. The reasonable man is in law the man
who is not negligent. A reasonable mistake is therefore in substance
a non-negligent mistake, and it is to this type of mistake that section

[9] Italics added. In the draft referred to in this letter what is now s. 23 was s. 25.
[10] Section 24 also refers, as is customary, to an "honest" mistake. Logically the word
"honest" adds nothing to what the sense would be without it, for to speak of a
dishonest belief implies (if it means anything at all) that the "belief" is not held at all.
Nevertheless, it may be wise in directing a jury to refer to an honest belief as an
indirect means of emphasising that wilful ignorance does not amount to mistake for
the purposes of the criminal law.

24 is by its own words expressly confined. This being so, the question arises, what is the relationship between section 24 and section 23, which is not restricted in its application to reasonable behaviour?

An example will elucidate the point at issue. The following hypothetical case has been chosen because it shows the difficulties clearly although it has nothing to do with regulatory offences. D is driving some sheep along a country road at dusk. He sees a small shape move towards the flock some way ahead. Thinking it is a dingo about to attack the sheep, he shoots and kills the intruder. When he reaches the body he discovers that he has killed, not a dingo, but a child. He is charged under section 301 of the Queensland Code[11] with wilful murder. The jury find that D honestly believed that he was shooting at a dingo but that the mistake was not a reasonable one to make in the circumstances. By section 301 wilful murder is committed by a person who unlawfully kills another, intending to cause his death or that of some other person. By section 291[12] an unlawful killing is one which is not authorised, justified or excused by law. Should D be convicted of wilful murder?

The opposing arguments may be shortly stated. D relies on the fact that an essential element in the crime of wilful murder is proof by P of an intention on D's part to kill a human being. Since, owing to D's mistake, P cannot prove this element, D cannot be convicted of wilful murder. P's reply, however, is formidable, although the absurdity of the result leaves one in no doubt that it cannot be the law.

According to P, D cannot be heard to say that the element of intention to kill has not been proved, for the only way in which D can demonstrate this is by pointing to his own mistake. Mistake of fact is governed by section 24. This section clearly restricts the defence to reasonable mistakes and the jury have found that D's mistake was not reasonable. Therefore D cannot rely on his mistake as an answer to any element in the offence charged. Therefore D must be convicted of wilful murder.

Obviously P's argument cannot be correct, for it is unthinkable that had the jury's findings been made as a preliminary to a request for a direction on the law to assist them in arriving at their general verdict, the trial judge would have been obliged to tell them that it was their duty to convict of wilful murder. Equally obviously, the

[11] W.A. Code, s. 278.
[12] W.A. Code, s. 268.

difficulty arises from the inclusion in section 24 of the word "reason-able". Since it cannot be assumed that the requirement of reasonable-ness is merely to be overlooked or explained away, the problem is to retain it but fit section 24 into an interpretation of the Code which does not lend itself to anomalies of this kind.

The clue is to be found in the second sentence of section 24: "The operation of this rule may be excluded by the express or implied provisions of the law relating to the subject." At first sight the sentence seems to be superfluous, for any part of any statute[13] may be expressly or impliedly excluded by any later statute.[14] But this sentence is far from superfluous. Indeed, it would be remarkable to find a passage of such length in such a place to be serving no useful purpose. Its function is to indicate that the first paragraph of section 24 does not necessarily stand or fall as a whole, but applies only so far as its terms accord with the elements of the particular offence under consideration. By virtue of this sentence, the first paragraph of section 24 does not apply to offences with the definitions of which it is inconsistent, to the extent of the inconsistency. Irreconcilable conflicts between the general and the particular in the Code are thereby avoided.

The answer to P's argument in the example above is therefore that the requirement of reasonableness in section 24 may be disregarded in relation to wilful murder because it is inconsistent with the express requirement in the definition of that offence that D be proved to have an intention at the material time to kill a human being. Therefore D's mistake operates to prevent his conviction for wilful murder. Whether he should be acquitted altogether or convicted of man-slaughter instead[15] is not clear on the facts of the problem. The jury have established in effect that D was negligent, but to support a conviction for manslaughter there would have to be a finding, not merely of negligence, but of criminal negligence, for under the codes,

---

[13] Saving problems of constitutional law which do not arise in the present connection.
[14] In *Anderson* v. *Nystrom* [1941] St. R. Qd. 56, 70–71, Philp J. suggested that in view of the conflicting common law decisions on strict responsibility in statutory offences, the draftsman of the Code was trying to emphasise that only a clear exclusion on normal principles of statutory interpretation would suffice. In *Hunt* v. *Maloney* [1959] Qd. R. 164, 184, Mack J. suggested that since no such sentence appears in s. 23, the intention was to make it clear that s. 23 could be excluded only by express words, whereas mere implication, if strong enough, would do for s. 24. In *Brimble-combe* v. *Duncan* [1958] Qd. R. 8, 18, Stanley J. held that the words "provisions of the law relating to the subject" mean "provisions of the relevant statute law of Queensland relating to the subject of the offence charged".
[15] Under the power in s. 576 (W.A. Code, s. 595).

as at common law, a higher degree of negligence is required for criminal than for civil liability.[16]

It may be observed in passing that in *Anderson* v. *Nystrom*[17] Philp J. rejected an argument by counsel to the effect that section 24 had no application to offences under the Code which contained the word "knowingly" as "unthinkable", on the ground that it would then have no application to homicide and stealing and that to exclude the defence of mistake from these offences would be absurd. His Honour's comment suggests that there may have been some mis-understanding between himself and counsel. It is quite clear that the first paragraph of section 24 cannot apply in its entirety to offences which can be committed only "knowingly", any more than it can apply in its entirety to offences requiring a specific intent. But equally, the first paragraph of section 24 applies to any offence so far as it is not inconsistent with the definition of that offence, and there-fore applies, except for the word "reasonable", to offences which can be committed only "knowingly".

(iv) *Relationship between sections 23 and 24*

The meaning and effect of section 24 having been established in relation to the definitions of particular offences, it remains to carry the argument the further step necessary to establish its relationship with section 23. Here it is well to bear in mind that the second sentence of section 24 is quite general in its terms. It does not refer merely to the "provisions of the offence charged", but to the "pro-visions of the law relating to the subject".[18] This means that it would be possible for the requirement of reasonableness in the section, which is inconsistent with the main rule in section 23, to be excluded from operation by virtue of that inconsistency. This, however, cannot be the law because it would prevent the requirement of reasonable-ness from ever taking effect, which can hardly be the purpose of the careful wording of section 24.

The true relationship between sections 23 and 24 is indicated, not by the closing words of the latter, but by the opening words of the former. Section 23 takes effect, "Subject to the express provisions of

[16] *Callaghan* v. *R.* (1952) 87 C.L.R. 115. But see the criticism of this case by Brett, "Manslaughter and the Motorist" (1953) 27 *Australian Law Journal*, 6 and 89.
[17] [1941] St. R. Qd. 56, 72. *Cf. Waterside Workers' Federation* v. *Birt* [1918] St. R. Qd. 10. In *Foreman* v. *Bowser* (1918) 12 Q.J.P.R. 108, where s. 24 was applied to an offence of "intentional or deliberate" infliction of unnecessary pain on an animal, no difficulty was encountered because the mistake was regarded as reasonable.
[18] *Cf.* Stanley J. in *Brimblecombe* v. *Duncan*, above, p. 152, n. 14.

this Code relating to negligent acts and omissions". By virtue of the word "reasonable" the first paragraph of section 24 is an express provision of the Code relating to negligent acts or omissions.[19] Therefore section 23 takes effect subject to the first paragraph of section 24, which in turn can be displaced either expressly or by necessary implication from the definition of the offence charged.

Where regulatory offences are concerned the result is that section 24 applies to neutral words and status offences in its full form, so that a mistake of fact has to be reasonable to constitute a defence to the charge; but that where some such word as "knowingly" or "permit" is used, which according to the usual view imports *mens rea* at common law, the section applies as if the word "reasonable" did not appear. Section 23 applies in the former case subject to the negligence rule in section 24, but in the latter case it applies in its full form, so that the ground covered by section 24 where words requiring *mens rea* are used is incidentally also covered by section 23. This duplication, which follows logically from the process of interpretation adopted, is immaterial.

(v) *Comparison with common law*

The rule thus laid down is similar to the reasonable mistake rule developed in the Australian common law. It is not identical because there is under the codes no burden of proof on D except where he sets up insanity.[20] The codes are therefore even further from strict responsibility than is the common law rule, for the mere proof of external facts by P will not lead to conviction in the absence of proof by D of a reasonable mistake of fact, which is what happens under the common law.

(vi) *Simple ignorance*

The effect of reasonable simple ignorance is just as obscure under the codes as at common law.[21] Suppose that D is charged with selling

---

[19] It is true that a mistake is not apt to be called either an act or an omission; but this is a hair-splitting objection because the point of s. 24 is not to regulate mistakes, but the acts or omissions flowing from mistakes.

[20] Since the decision in *Woolmington* v. *D.P.P.* [1935] A.C. 462, there has been no doubt in the Code states that the same rule as to burden of proof applied under the codes, although as a matter of dispassionate statutory construction there is little to support this view and much to support the view of the law commonly held before *Woolmington*. See on this *Mullen* v. *The King* [1938] St. R. Qd. 97. *Cf. Heaslop* v. *Burton* [1902] St. R. Qd. 259, 265–266, *per* Griffith C.J., 267, *per* Real J.

[21] Above, pp. 91–95.

sub-standard milk contrary to a statute regulating the production and sale of milk. His defence is that he did not know that the milk was sub-standard in fact. This defence can be put in two ways. If it is put as a mistake of fact, the offence being couched in such neutral words as, "No person shall sell sub-standard milk", it follows from what has been previously said that this mistake must have been a reasonable one to make if D is to be acquitted. But if the defence is put as simple ignorance, a doubt may arise. The argument put forward by D would be that the act prohibited by the statute was selling sub-standard milk, and that since he did not know that the milk was sub-standard this act occurred independently of the exercise of his will in a material particular.

Reasons have already been given for regarding this as a correct understanding of the effect of section 23. The difficulty now is not the meaning of the word "act" but the apparent inconsistency that if D makes the error of framing his argument under section 24 he can be convicted for negligence, whereas if he puts it under section 23 he can be convicted only on proof of actual knowledge. The argument which produces the inconsistency rests on a very literal interpretation of the opening words of section 23, "Subject to the express provisions of this Code relating to negligent acts and omissions". It is argued that even though the operation of section 23 is limited in this way, it is limited only to the extent of the express wording of the provision in question. Thus in the case of section 24, the operation of section 23 is limited in its application to positive mistakes but not in its application to simple ignorance, for section 24 does not expressly refer to mere ignorance.

There are two ways out of the difficulty. The first is to try to distinguish simple ignorance situations from mistake of fact situations, the court classifying the nature of the defence in order to decide under which section it should fall to be decided. This expedient should be rejected for two reasons. First, it is unwieldy. No court would willingly saddle itself with such a task if it could be avoided. Secondly, there is no sound distinction between simple ignorance and mistake,[22] which are matters of degrees of consciousness only.

A more attractive way out of the difficulty is to point to the absurdity of the result reached in the example above and to argue that since it is just as easy to interpret the opening words of section 23 as referring to necessary implications from express provisions relating

[22] Above, pp. 91–95.

to negligent acts and omissions as not, a rule requiring reasonable mistake by implication requires also reasonable simple ignorance.

Case-law

It remains to give a brief account of the relevant case-law of Queensland and Western Australia. This account will not be found to have much relation to the foregoing analysis, not because the courts have rejected any such analysis, but because the questions which it raises have received very little judicial attention hitherto. Nevertheless, it is thought that the present state of the scanty case-law is not inconsistent with the rules arrived at above by statutory interpretation.

(i) *Queensland*

It has never been doubted in Queensland that section 23 has the effect of requiring knowledge by D of all the elements of the offence charged. Thus it was early decided that on a charge of being found in possession of the skin of an animal reasonably suspected of being stolen, contrary to section 446 of the Code, P had to prove knowledge by D that the skin was among his possessions. Mere proof that the skin was found among his possessions was not enough.[23] The same principle was extended to offences of possession under statutes other than the Code in a series of opium cases. The clearest example is *Lawrence* v. *Lake*[24] where D was charged with "unlawfully" having opium in his possession contrary to the Aboriginals Protection and Restriction of the Sale of Opium Act, 1897 (Q'ld.), s. 22. Shand J. held that the offence charged required "a knowledge of all the facts constituting the offence, and that a man who was ignorant that a parcel in his possession contained opium would be protected by the provisions of s. 23 of the Criminal Code".

In that case his Honour held that this conclusion followed from the use of the word "unlawfully" in the statute, but this was not necessary for the decision. The offence was charged under a statute

---

[23] This was held in *Crudginton* v. *Cooney* [1902] St. R. Qd. 176, without reference to the Code, but in the following year in *Molloy* v. *Hallam* [1903] St. R. Qd. 282, the requirement of proof of knowledge was based squarely on s. 23.

[24] [1921] Q.W.N. 30. See also *Aitkin* [1942] St. R. Qd. 57, where the requirement of knowledge was assumed *sub silentio*. Opium offences also arose under Commonwealth legislation, as in *Macarthur* v. *Hing* [1909] St. R. Qd. 179, and the confusing case of *Walker* v. *Chapman* [1904] St. R. Qd. 330. On Commonwealth legislation see p. 163, n. 63, below.

enacted in 1897. It has already been observed that by section 36 of
the Code, which came into force on the first day of the twentieth
century, January 1, 1901, section 23 was applied "to all persons
charged with any offence against the statute law of Queensland".
Therefore, although there was nothing to prevent the legislature
restricting the operation of section 36 in its application to statutes
enacted after the Code,[25] there could be no doubt that section 23
applied in *Lawrence* v. *Lake* regardless of the word "unlawfully".
Shand J.'s reasoning in this respect is perhaps the first example
among many of a general failure to appreciate the full effect of the
Code for about two decades after it came into force.[26]

A decision of the High Court of Australia illustrating the effect
of section 23 is *Widgee Shire Council* v. *Bonney*.[27] D had been
charged with an offence against a by-law designed to prevent
damage to the drainage gutters of roads by driving vehicles on them.
The enabling statute was the Divisional Boards Act, 1887. The only
question before the High Court was whether the by-law was valid.
One objection made was that the by-law purported to prohibit an
act absolutely, without reference to *mens rea*, and therefore could not
be lawful as dispensing with a fundamental prerequisite for criminal
liability. Griffith C.J. disposed of the objection[28] in a well-known
dictum: "So far as this last objection is concerned it may be dismissed
with the observation that under the criminal law of Queensland, as
defined in the Criminal Code, it is never necessary to have recourse
to the old doctrine of *mens rea*, the exact meaning of which has been
the subject of much discussion. The test now to be applied is whether
this prohibited act was, or was not, done accidentally or independently
of the exercise of the will of the accused person (section 23)."

His Honour did not enlarge on this reasoning, which as it stands
is manifestly incomplete, for D could have replied that the by-law
was invalid because it purported to dispense with section 23, instead
of because it purported to dispense with *mens rea*. The true answer

[25] *Cf. Anderson* v. *Nystrom* [1941] St. R. Qd. 56, 70–71, *per* Philp J., and *Hunt* v.
Maloney [1959] Qd. R. 164, 184, *per* Mack J., on the same point in relation to s. 24.
[26] The tide began to turn with *Thomas* v. *McEather* [1920] St. R. Qd. 166, below, p. 160.
A notable exception to the general unawareness was the draftsman of the Code, Sir
Samuel Griffith, but even he failed to perceive all the implications. See the discussion
of *Widgee Shire Council* v. *Bonney* (1907) 4 C.L.R. 977, which follows.
[27] (1907) 4 C.L.R. 977, on appeal from the Supreme Court of Queensland.
[28] *Ibid.*, 981–982. Isaacs J. agreed with him. The third member of the court, Higgins J.,
did not deal with this argument. For the avoidance of confusion it should perhaps
be mentioned that Sir Samuel Griffith was successively Chief Justice of the Supreme
Court of Queensland and of the High Court of Australia.

to the objection was that since, by section 36 of the Code, section 23 had to be read into the enabling statute, and therefore into the by-law, the statement that the by-law purported to dispense with guilty knowledge was wrong at the outset. But the importance of the case in this context is that it is clear that the High Court recognised that section 23 had to be taken into account, and that therefore, had the question been before them, they would not have considered the offence to have been one of strict responsibility.

A case where section 23, although not mentioned, must be taken to have been deprived of operation by the express words of a later statute, is *Loch* v. *Deakin*.[29] A regulation made under the Traffic Act, 1905 (Q'ld.),[30] required motor vehicles to carry lighted tail lamps at night. Another regulation, under the heading "Excuse", said: "No person shall be liable to a penalty for any breach of any regulation relating to general traffic if he proves to the satisfaction of the Court that such breach was the result of accident, and could not have been avoided by the exercise of reasonable care on his part." It was held that on proof of the material facts D must be convicted of failing to carry a lighted tail lamp on his vehicle unless he could discharge the burden placed on him by the regulations of proving reasonable care and accident.

There remains for consideration under section 23 only the curious case of *Hussie* v. *Williamson*.[31] D was charged with selling loaves "purporting" to be of a prescribed denomination, but deficient of the weight required for the denomination, contrary to the Weights and Measures Act, 1951 (Q'ld.), s. 28 (3) (ii). The magistrate dismissed the complaint on the ground that there was no evidence that D knew of the deficiency. The Full Court reversed this decision on the ground that the word "purporting" referred to the loaves alone, treating the word as synonymous with "appearing". The effect of the decision, however it was presented, was to impose responsibility for selling a loaf deficient in weight when that deficiency was not known of by the defendant. Since section 23, which was not mentioned in the case, would operate to prevent such a result, it must be supposed that

[29] [1925] St. R. Qd. 237. For a similar case on the National Security (Rationing) Regulations see *Wulf* v. *Moore* [1948] St. R. Qd. 95.
[30] Since repealed, but *cf.* the current statute, the Traffic Acts, 1949–1957 (Q'ld.), s. 49 (1) (*q*): "The burden of proof that any person, vehicle, tram, train, vessel, or animal was at any time exempt from any provision of this Act or that any such provision was not at any time applicable to any person, vehicle, tram, train, vessel, or animal shall be on the defendant."
[31] [1955] Q.W.N. 48. The report at 49 Q.J.P.R. 59 omits the arguments of counsel.

the use of the word "purporting" was taken to exclude it from the Weights and Measures Act.

It is submitted that this reasoning cannot be supported. Apart from being contrary to the principles already discussed, a glance at any dictionary will confirm the common impression that "purporting", as applied to inanimate objects, means in normal usage "being *intended* to seem". One cannot sell underweight loaves intended to seem to be of the correct weight when the fact of the deficiency is not known. It is submitted that *Hussie* v. *Williamson* should be confined strictly to its own facts until overruled.

The function served by section 23 is sometimes duplicated by including in the definition of an offence, both under the Code and under other statutes, such words as "knowingly", "knowingly permitting", or "suffering". In such cases it is clear that knowledge of all the elements of the offence must be proved by P.[32]

Section 23, however, is subject to section 24. Therefore if strict responsibility is to be imposed, the task before the court is the exclusion from the offence charged of the defence of reasonable mistake in section 24. This section may be excluded either expressly or by implication. No instance of express exclusion has yet been before the courts. The test of implied exclusion is as follows.

Section 24 is impliedly excluded by statute if the terms of the statute creating an offence are inconsistent with the existence of a defence of reasonable mistake of fact. This test was first enunciated by Real J. in *Thomas* v. *McEather*[33] and has since become firmly established.[34] It has been applied to statutes concerned with moving stock,[35] carrying goods by road,[36] using constructional timber,[37] and selling milk.[38] But the value of any such test lies less in the words in which it is expressed than in the spirit in which it is applied.

In Queensland inconsistency has been taken to mean "plain

[32] *Hill* v. *Richardson* (1904) 6 W.A.L.R. 85; *Dendle* v. *Williams* [1918] St. R. Qd. 50; *Burke* v. *Williams* [1918] St. R. Qd. 118; *Dixon* v. *Seiler* [1928] St. R. Qd. 93. *Kelly* v. *Wigzell* (1907) 5 C.L.R. 126 ("permitting") is not contrary to this principle; the whole question there was whether knowledge had been proved and it was held that it had been.
[33] [1920] St. R. Qd. 166, 177.
[34] *Anderson* v. *Nystrom* [1941] St. R. Qd. 5, 65 and 71; *Loveday* v. *Ayre* [1955] St. R. Qd. 264, 273; *Brimblecombe* v. *Duncan* [1958] Qd. R. 8, 12.
[35] *Thomas* v. *McEather* [1920] St. R. Qd. 166.
[36] *Anderson* v. *Nystrom* [1941] St. R. Qd. 56.
[37] *Loveday* v. *Ayre* [1955] St. R. Qd. 264.
[38] *Brimblecombe* v. *Duncan* [1958] Qd. R. 8.

repugnancy";[39] and plain repugnancy is what has been looked for
and, so far, not found. Thus it was argued in *Loveday* v. *Ayre*[40] that
the words "shall not use" indicated an intention on the part of the
legislature to impose strict responsibility. The contention was brushed
aside:[41] "So far as concerns the application of s. 24 of the code
to offences against the statute law of Queensland, I see no distinction
between the creation of an offence by words which say that a person
shall or shall not do an act, by words which say that if a person does
an act or omits to do an act he shall be guilty of an offence or be
liable to a penalty, and by words which require an act to be done
and then impose a penalty for a failure to do the act."

This firm refusal to dabble in distinctions between forms of words
which are synonymous in substance is altogether to be welcomed. A
similar fate met attempts in *Anderson* v. *Nystrom*[42] and *Brimblecombe*
v. *Duncan*[43] to persuade the court that in inquiring whether section 24
had been impliedly excluded, regard should be had to the subject-
matter of the statute.[44] The prevailing judicial attitude is well illustrated by a remark made by Philp J. in the first of these two cases:[45]
"It seems to me that legislation enacting offences should be made as
certain as possible, and if the Legislature intends to exclude the rule
in question it would best be done by an express provision to that
effect so that the subject will be in no doubt as to his liability."

This was not always so. For many years after the enactment of the
Code there was a tendency to regard it merely as a consolidating
statute. The argument that regard should be had to the subject-
matter of the statute in inquiring if section 24 had been impliedly
excluded, was really an aspect of another argument which was
advanced with a fair chance of success during the first two decades
of this century.

In *Thomas* v. *McEather*[46] a Full Court of six judges considered,
inter alia, the applicability of section 24 to a statutory offence[47] of

[39] *Anderson* v. *Nystrom* [1941] St. R. Qd. 56, 65; *Brimblecombe* v. *Duncan* [1958] Qd. R. 8, 19.
[40] [1955] St. R. Qd. 264.
[41] [1955] St. R. Qd. 264, 273–274, *per* Hanger J. Fifty-one years earlier Chubb J. had thought that no language could more plainly create strict responsibility than the words, "No person shall...": *Walker* v. *Chapman* [1904] St. R. Qd., 330, 345.
[42] [1941] St. R. Qd. 56.
[43] [1958] Qd. R. 8.
[44] See [1941] St. R. Qd. 56, 71, and [1958] Qd. R. 8, 12, *per* Philp J.
[45] [1941] St. R. Qd. 56, 72.
[46] [1920] St. R. Qd. 166.
[47] Under a local by-law.

moving stock without giving notice to the appropriate authority. The complaint had been dismissed by the magistrate on the ground that D had acted in good faith under a reasonable mistake of fact. On appeal P argued that section 24 was impliedly excluded if the offence would have been one of strict responsibility before the Code was enacted, for the Code was merely declaratory of the common law; that at common law the offence would have been one of strict responsibility; and that therefore section 24 was excluded. The novelty of the question is shown by the fact that the appeal was argued twice, each time, for some reason which does not appear, before an even number of judges, and on each occasion the court divided evenly over whether the appeal should succeed.[48] However, their Honours did not divide evenly in their grounds for judgment.

All six members of the court were apparently of opinion that section 24 applied to the case unless excluded.[49] Five of them held that section 24 had not been impliedly excluded by the statute.[50] Cooper C.J., Lukin and Real JJ. were explicitly of opinion that since the enactment of the Code such a question as the one before the court should not be decided by reference to common law authority.[51] McCawley J. was equally clearly of opinion that it should be.[52] The opinions of the other two judges, Chubb and Shand JJ., were less emphatic on this point, but they do not appear to have objected to the application of the common law tests.[53] Of the three who held that the common law did not apply, only Real J. framed an alternative test (the inconsistency one now accepted), Cooper C.J. and Lukin J. being content in a joint judgment to state their conclusion that section 24 was not excluded without giving any reasons.[54] This produced yet another division of opinion which cut across the others, for whereas Cooper C.J., Lukin and Chubb JJ. decided that the magistrate's finding of reasonable mistake was supportable on the evidence, Real and Shand JJ. decided that it was not. Once again

[48] [1920] St. R. Qd. 166, 180 *per* Chubb J.
[49] This point passed *sub silentio*, but there could hardly be any argument about it in view of s. 36 of the code.
[50] McCawley J. was the odd one out on this point.
[51] [1920] St. R. Qd. 166, 174–175 and 176–177.
[52] *Ibid.*, 189: "... I fail to perceive any reason why the question whether the rule is impliedly excluded, should not be approached just as it would have been approached in Queensland before the Criminal Code, or as it would have been approached in England...." This is a remarkable avowal of judicial ignorance. By s. 2 of the Criminal Code Act, 1899, the code "shall be the law of Queensland with respect to the several matters therein dealt with."
[53] *Ibid.*, 184, 188.
[54] *Ibid.*, 175.

McCawley J. was the odd one out, for he was the only judge to hold not only that the common law tests applied, but also that they excluded section 24, thus rendering a consideration of the evidence superfluous, since the offence was one of strict responsibility on this view. To complete the confusing picture it need only be added that Real J., having formulated the inconsistency test, proceeded on the "assumption"[55] that section 24 was not thereby excluded; and that Chubb and Shand JJ., apparently applying the common law, decided that it was not excluded.[56]

Thomas v. *McEather*[57] is important as being the first case in which the Full Court had occasion to discuss the scope of section 24, but the difference of opinion in the judgments would make it difficult to say for what propositions the case, taken in isolation, could stand as authority. Fortunately later cases have now made it clear in what sense *Thomas* v. *McEather* is to be understood. In *Anderson* v. *Nystrom*[58] the majority expressly accepted it as establishing that the law of reasonable mistake of fact in Queensland is to be found in section 24 without reference to the common law; and in *Brimblecombe* v. *Duncan*[59] all three members of the court treated this point as having been settled beyond argument by *Thomas* v. *McEather* and *Anderson* v. *Nystrom*.

(ii) *Western Australia*

In Western Australia the only case in which the relevance of either section 23 or section 24 to an offence charged under a statute other than the Code has been observed is *Sharp* v. *Caratti*.[60] D was charged with cutting forest produce in a state forest without lawful authority contrary to the Forests Act, 1918 (W.A.). His answer was that he made a reasonable mistake within the meaning of section 24 as to where the boundary was, and therefore failed to realise that he was on the wrong side of it. He succeeded before the magistrate but

[55] *Ibid.*, 177.
[56] *Ibid.*, 185, 188. Shand J. was "not prepared to hold" the section excluded.
[57] [1920] St. R. Qd. 166.
[58] [1941] St. R. Qd. 56, 65, 71, *per* Douglas and Philp JJ. respectively. Webb C.J. dissented, preferring an approach substantially the same as that of McCawley J. in the earlier case.
[59] [1958] Qd. R. 8.
[60] (1922) 25 W.A.L.R. 133. But see *Snow* v. *Cooper* (1944) 57 W.A.L.R. 92, and *Wilson* v. *Dobra* (1955) 57 W.A.L.R. 95, on s. 7 of the Code, relating to principals and accessories. This section does not form part of Chapter V of the Code and is therefore not extended generally by s. 36. These cases applied the section to statutory offences outside the Code, however.

failed on review before the Full Court. Such interest as the case possesses lies in the recognition by the Full Court of the possibility that section 24 might apply to the offence. Unfortunately even this degree of interest is slight.

In the first place, it was not found necessary to discuss, still less to decide, the question since it was held that D's mistake was not a reasonable one even if his own story were accepted in full. Secondly, it does not seem likely that their Honours were directing their minds to the true nature of the question involved because they refer[61] not to Chapter V of the Code as possibly applying, but to the doctrine of *mens rea*. Any attempt to decide by reference to the common law doctrine of *mens rea* what can be decided only by reference to the Code can result only in confusion. *Sharp* v. *Caratti* is therefore of no great weight. There can be no doubt that section 24 applied to the offence charged, and the most one can say is that the Supreme Court did not express a contrary opinion.

The other cases, in none of which was the Code mentioned, fall into two groups. First there are those of which it is possible to say that although the court failed to see the relevance of section 36, and therefore omitted to consider the question whether Chapter V of the Code or any part of it had been impliedly excluded by the particular statute, yet the actual decisions arrived at are not contrary to what one would expect. Into this group fall offences of unlawful possession, where, as elsewhere, P is required to prove knowledge on D's part of the presence of the article in question among his belongings.[62]

Another example is *Gee* v. *Wills*.[63] D was charged with accepting from a consumer a rationing coupon which under the current rationing regulations the consumer was prohibited from using. The facts were that an employee of D served a customer with some butter

[61] The brief judgment of the court was delivered by McMillan C.J., Burnside and Draper JJ. concurring.
[62] *Wightman* v. *Copperwaite* (1930) 32 W.A.L.R. 101, 103, *per* Dwyer J.; *Coleman* v. *Richards* (1941) 43 W.A.L.R. 21, 25, *per* Dwyer J. This may have been the ground of the decision in *Savage* v. *Hungerford* (1902) 4 W.A.L.R. 135.
[63] (1945) 47 W.A.L.R. 24. Both this case and *Coleman* v. *Richards*, cited in the previous footnote, arose on Commonwealth legislation. By the Commonwealth Judiciary Act, 1903, s. 80, the common law of England applied to a Commonwealth offence tried in a State, "as modified by the . . . statute law in force in the State". The point may be doubtful, but for the present purpose it is assumed that this section would make the Western Australian Criminal Code applicable to Commonwealth offences tried in that State. The doubt is cast by the argument that the Code did not modify the English common law, but replaced it. An even more technical and even less convincing doubt might be cast by arguing that it was not the English but the Australian common law that was modified or replaced.

in return for currently valid coupons, but when he cut these coupons from the customer's ration book he also cut out five expired coupons intending merely to destroy the latter as useless. The charge was dismissed on the ground that the employee's act was innocent.[64] P based his argument on the word "accept", contending that once it was proved that the coupons were accepted in a physical sense, it became immaterial with what intention, if any, they were accepted. It is clear that section 23 of the Code operated to prevent liability arising on this basis, whatever the evidence, but the actual ground of the decision was that the word "accept" conveyed "the idea of an intention to receive and keep the coupons—an intention which was absent here."[65]

Similarly, in *Mouritzen* v. *White*[66] the phrase "knowingly allow" led to the same requirement of guilty knowledge and intention as would have followed under section 23; and in *Stephens* v. *Taufik Raad*[67] a similar consequence followed on a charge that D, an unqualified person, "held himself out" as a qualified medical practitioner when he had merely misdescribed his qualifications in an advertisement designed to promote sales in his shop and had no intention of practising at all.

Into the second group fall those cases in which the court has imposed strict responsibility. The difficulty about these cases is that since no regard was paid in them to the question whether the particular statute by its terms impliedly excluded sections 23 and 24, it cannot be said with any confidence whether they are to be treated as correct or not. It would be unrealistic to try to deduce exclusionary rules from them. One can only record the decisions and wait to see if they will be followed in future, and, if so, for what reasons.

The first in point of time is *Durham* v. *Ramson*,[68] in which a licensee was charged with having on his premises adulterated liquor for the purposes of sale. D was convicted even though it was found as a fact that he knew nothing about the adulteration and had not been negligent. The ground of the decision was said to be that the

[64] For which reason vicarious responsibility could not arise.
[65] (1945) 47 W.A.L.R. 24, 26, *per* Wolff J.
[66] (1910) 12 W.A.L.R. 158. Cf. *Ashbury* v. *Reid* [1961] W.A.R. 49.
[67] (1908) 8 W.A.L.R. 183. Cf. *Sanderson* (1910) W.A.L.R. 92, where the trial judge attempted to impose strict responsibility by treating the requirement of wilfulness in an electoral offence as a question of law and withdrawing it from the jury. See also *Isherwood* v. *O'Brien* (1920) 23 W.A.L.R. 10.
[68] (1907) 9 W.A.L.R. 76.

section under which the offence was charged[69] was "one of those sections which make persons offenders although they have no guilty mind".[70] This decision is the less defensible in that the statute concerned ante-dated the code. In *Brown* v. *Shennick*,[71] an honest but mistaken belief by D that, although unlicensed herself, she was entitled to sell liquor as the agent of a licensed person was held to be no answer to a charge of selling liquor without a licence. The ground of the decision was that the statute[72] imposed strict responsibility, but the result can perhaps be supported on the basis either that the mistake was one of law, or was unreasonable,[73] or both.

In *Robinson* v. *Torrisi*,[74] D was held strictly responsible for having "operated" a public vehicle on a road without a licence contrary to the State Transport Co-ordination Act, 1933 (W.A.), s. 51. Here again the ground of the decision was that an intention to dispense with guilty knowledge should be inferred from the words of the statute. The learned judge came to this conclusion "for three reasons: (1) from the wording of section 51 itself; (2) because the proviso to that section affords to a driver[75] the defence of want of knowledge of the non-existence of a license (*sic*) and such defence is not given to an owner; (3) by comparison with a prior section of the Act, section 15, where knowledge is necessary. There the requirement of knowledge is plainly set forth by the use of the word "knowingly". . . . I do think that the omission of the word "knowingly" in section 51 is deliberate."[76]

None of these reasons necessarily amounts to a ground for inferring an implied exclusion of section 23 and 24 of the Code. The omission of the word "knowingly" might conceivably be taken to exclude full guilty knowledge under section 23, but it is hard to see how it could affect reasonable mistake of fact under section 24. The same applies to points (1) and (2) also.

Lastly, in *Sweeney* v. *Denness*,[77] D was charged with knowingly

[69] Sale of Liquors Amendment Act, 1897 (W.A.) s. 7.
[70] (1907) 9 W.A.L.R. 76, 77, *per* McMillan J.
[71] (1908) 10 W.A.L.R. 107.
[72] Wines, Beer and Spirit Sale Act, 1880 (W.A.).
[73] The parties had previously failed to obtain permission from the magistrates to transfer the licence to D.
[74] (1938) 40 W.A.L.R. 62.
[75] D was charged as the owner of a vehicle, not on the basis of vicarious responsibility, but as having contravened a duty placed on him personally by s. 51. This was therefore a status offence.
[76] (1938) 40 W.A.L.R. 62, 65, *per* Dwyer J.
[77] (1954) 56 W.A.L.R. 52.

supplying liquor to "a person under the age of twenty-one years" contrary to the Licensing Act, 1911–1951 (W.A.), s. 147 (1). Dwyer C.J. treated the case as turning[78] "on one point, and one point only, and that is whether it was established by the prosecution that Moriarty[79] was a person under the age of twenty-one years". With all respect, the inquiry should have been directed also to ascertaining whether the statute in question excluded sections 23 and 24, for, if they applied, P should have been required to establish, not merely that Moriarty was under twenty-one, but also that D knew or ought to have known this fact.

Conclusion

The conclusion is that whilst the Australian criminal codes lay down a rule differing from the Australian common law rule only, so far as can be ascertained at present, as to burden of proof, the courts of the code states have hitherto paid little attention to the implications of the statutory wording in its application to regulatory offences. The meaning and effect of the general sections 23 and 24 arrived at herein is not self-evident and may be wrong; but until corrected by judicial decision it has the virtue of producing a result consistent with what one would expect of the codes themselves and not too dissimilar from the law in other parts of Australia.

[78] *Ibid.*, 53.
[79] The person supplied.

CHAPTER 8

THE MODEL PENAL CODE

Introduction

The American Law Institute's Model Penal Code was cited in Chapter 4 as an example of the marking-off in a comprehensive criminal code of regulatory offences as a class of infringements of penal law separate from the criminal law. The method adopted is a highly interesting and important contribution to the theory and practice of the criminal law[1] and merits detailed critical study.

The Model Penal Code tries to confine strict responsibility to a new class of infractions of penal law called "violations". The basic scheme is as follows.[2]

> *Section 1.04. Classes of Crimes: Violations*
>
> (1) An offense defined by this Code or by any other statute of this State, for which a sentence of [death or of] imprisonment is authorized, constitutes a crime. Crimes are classified as felonies, misdemeanors or petty misdemeanors.
>
> [(2), (3), (4): definitions of felonies, misdemeanors and petty misdemeanors.][3]
>
> (5) An offense defined by this Code or by any other statute of this

---

[1] The drafts of the Model Penal Code so far published are already "having a substantial influence upon substantive law revision" in the U.S.A. The most conspicuous example to date is the Illinois Criminal Code of 1961. See Remington and Rosenblum, "The Criminal Law and the Legislative Process", [1960] *University of Illinois Law Forum*, 481, 483–484.

[2] Proposed Official Draft (1962).

[3]   (2) A crime is a felony if it is so designated in this Code or if persons convicted thereof may be sentenced [to death or] to imprisonment for a term which, apart from an extended term, is in excess of one year.

   (3) A crime is a misdemeanor if it is so designated in this Code or in a statute other than this Code enacted subsequent thereto.

   (4) A crime is a petty misdemeanor if it is so designated in this Code or in a statute other than this Code enacted subsequent thereto or if it is defined by a statute other than this Code which now provides that persons convicted thereof may be sentenced to imprisonment for a term of which the maximum is less than one year.

   (6) Any offense declared by law to constitute a crime, without specification of the grade thereof or of the sentence authorized upon conviction, is a misdemeanor.

   (7) An offense defined by any statute of this State other than this Code shall be classified as provided in this Section and the sentence that may be imposed upon conviction thereof shall hereafter be governed by this Code.

State constitutes a violation if it is so designated in this Code or in the law defining the offense or if no other sentence than a fine, or fine and forfeiture or other civil penalty is authorized upon conviction or if it is defined by a statute other than this Code which now provides that the offense shall not constitute a crime. A violation does not constitute a crime and conviction of a violation shall not give rise to any disability or legal disadvantage based on conviction of a criminal offense.

Sections 2.01 to 2.04 lay down the general principles of criminal responsibility and define the terms used.[4] The two basic rules are that there must be a voluntary act (or the culpable omission to perform an act of which the defendant was physically capable); and that this act must be performed purposely, knowingly, recklessly or negligently. A causal relationship must be established between the relevant state of mind and any particular result specified in the definition of an offence. "When causing a particular result is a material element of an offense for which absolute liability is imposed by law, the element is not established unless the actual result is a probable consequence of the actor's conduct."[5] There is a general defence of ignorance or mistake. There then follows:

Section 2.05. When Culpability Requirements are Inapplicable to Violations and to Offenses Defined by Other Statutes: Effect of Absolute Liability in Reducing Grade of Offense to Violation

(1) The requirements of culpability prescribed by Sections 2.01 and 2.02 do not apply to:

(a) offenses which constitute violations, unless the requirement involved is included in the definition of the offense or the Court determines that its application is consistent with effective enforcement of the law defining the offense; or

(b) offenses defined by statutes other than the Code, insofar as a legislative purpose to impose absolute liability for such offenses or with respect to any material element thereof plainly appears.

(2) Notwithstanding any other provision of existing law and unless a subsequent statute otherwise provides:

(a) when absolute liability is imposed with respect to any material element of an offense defined by a statute other than the Code and a conviction is based upon such liability, the offense constitutes a violation; and

[4] S. 2.01 deals with the requirement of a voluntary act, omission as a basis of liability, and possession as an act; 2.02 with states of mind, distinguished as purposely, knowingly, recklessly and negligently; 2.03 with causal relationships; and 2.04 with ignorance and mistake as defences.
[5] S. 2.03 (4).

(*b*) although absolute liability is imposed by law with respect to one or more of the material elements of an offense defined by a statute other than the Code, the culpable commission of the offense may be charged and proved, in which event negligence with respect to such elements constitutes sufficient culpability and the classification of the offence and the sentence that may be imposed therefor upon conviction are determined by Section 1.04 and Article 6 of the Code.

The effect of the reference in the last subsection to section 1.04 and article 6 of the Code is to emphasise that the conversion of a violation charged and proved to have been committed culpably into a crime has consequential results in the realm of punishment. So long as the offence remains a violation, punishment is regulated by section 1.04 (5) above, which says that by definition only "a fine, or fine and forfeiture or other civil penalty" may be imposed on conviction; by section 1.04 (7), which says that "[a]n offense defined by any statute of this State other than this Code shall be classified as provided in" section 1.04 and that "the sentence that may be imposed upon conviction shall . . . be governed by this Code"; and by the following sections.

Section 6.02. Sentence in Accordance with Code; Authorized Dispositions
   (4) The Court may suspend the imposition of sentence on a person who has been convicted of a violation or may sentence him to pay a fine authorized by Section 6.03.
Section 6.03. Fines
   A person who has been convicted of an offense may be sentenced to pay a fine not exceeding:
   (4) $500, when the conviction is of a petty misdemeanor or a violation;
   (5) any higher amount equal to double the pecuniary gain derived from the offense by the offender;
   (6) any higher amount specifically authorized by statute.

The Code distinguishes between elements of an offence and material elements of an offence. The latter are defined in section 1.13 (10) as elements that do not "relate exclusively to the statute of limitations, jurisdiction, venue or to any other matter similarly unconnected with (i) the harm or evil, incidental to conduct, sought to be prevented by the law defining the offense, or (ii) the existence of a justification or excuse for such conduct".

Before discussing this scheme in detail it is appropriate to quote the explanatory comments of the reporter appended to an earlier

draft of the foregoing sections which was in substance the same as
the proposed official draft from which they have been taken. Referring to section 2.05 he said:[6] "This section makes a frontal attack on
absolute or strict liability in penal law, whenever the offense carries a
possibility of sentence of imprisonment. The method used is not to
abrogate such liability but to provide that when conviction rests
upon that basis the grade of the offense is reduced to a violation,
which is not a 'crime' and under sections 1.04 (5) and 6.02 may result
in no other sentence than a fine or fine and forfeiture or other civil
penalty. If, on the other hand, the culpable commission of the offense
has been established, the reduction in grade does not occur. Negligence is, however, treated as sufficient culpability in cases of this
kind.

"This position is affirmed not only with respect to offenses defined
by the Penal Code; it is superimposed on the entire corpus of the
law, so far as penal sanctions are involved. Since most strict liability
offenses are involved in special regulatory legislation, this super-
imposition is essential if the problem is to be attacked. We have no
doubt that the attempt is one that should be made. The liabilities
involved are indefensible, unless reduced to terms that insulate
conviction from the type of moral condemnation that is and ought
to be implicit when a sentence of imprisonment may be imposed. In
the absence of minimal culpability, the law has neither a deterrent
nor corrective nor an incapacitative function to perform.

"It has been argued, and the argument undoubtedly will be
repeated, that absolute liability is necessary for enforcement in a
number of areas where it obtains. But if practical enforcement cannot
undertake to litigate the culpability of alleged deviation from legal
requirements, we do not see how the enforcers rightly can demand
the use of penal sanctions for the purpose. Crime does and should
mean condemnation and no court should have to pass that judgment
unless it can declare that the defendant's act was wrong. This is too
fundamental to be compromised. The law goes far enough if it
permits the imposition of a monetary penalty in cases where strict
liability has been imposed. . . .

"Paragraph (1) (*a*) of the section accepts strict liability for all
offenses which are graded as violations, *i.e.*, for which a sentence of
imprisonment may not be imposed, unless a culpability requirement
is included in the definition of the offense or the Court determines

[6] Tentative Draft No. 4, Comment, 140–146.

that the application of such a requirement is consistent with effective enforcement of the law defining the offense. The assumption is, in short, that when the offense is of this grade, culpability requirements ordinarily will be expressly stated when the legislative purpose is that they be included in the elements of the offense. If the law is silent, the Court must make an affirmative determination that they are consistent with effective enforcement or the liability will be construed as absolute. This device should greatly reduce the uncertainty upon the issue that is typically so pervasive until it is settled by the courts.

"... Paragraph (1) (*b*) accepts strict liability when [offenses][7] are defined by a statute other than the Code 'insofar as a legislative purpose to impose absolute liability for such [offenses] or with respect to any material element thereof plainly appears'. That such a purpose should not be discerned lightly by the courts seems very clear. [The elliptical manner in which criminal statutes are ordinarily expressed] makes it tempting to provide . . . that the 'intention to create strict responsibility ought always to be evidenced by the words of the statute', *i.e.*, by an explicit statement and not merely by the absence of a form of words denoting a requirement of culpability. This is, however, too severe a test for practical purposes since so much existing legislation that would not satisfy the test has been construed to impose strict liability. Legislative acquiescence in such constructions, without amendment of the statute, may reasonably be regarded as evincing legislative purpose that the liability obtain. Accordingly, the weaker requirement that such a purpose 'plainly appears' goes as far as we think it wise to go. In practice this might well mean either a settled interpretation or explicit statement in the statute. That is, however, left deliberately to judgment of the courts.

"It need not be added that the Code itself will not impose strict liability for any [offense][8] which it undertakes to define."

This is the case made out by the reporter for the scheme adopted in the Model Penal Code. Before embarking on detailed construction and criticism a *caveat* previously entered[9] should be renewed. In so far as the framers of the Code have been influenced by considerations of prudence, it is beyond the present purpose either to agree or to disagree with them. It may or it may not be wise in the United States

---

[7] As originally drafted this rule was confined to crimes. The word "offenses" has been substituted in the proposed official draft.

[8] In the original comment the word here was "crime", but in view of the amendment referred to in the previous footnote "offense" seems now more appropriate.

[9] Above, p. 71.

of America to attempt to circumscribe and confine strict responsibility in the criminal law rather than abolish the doctrine altogether; there is no need to come to a decision on the point in the present chapter.

The reporter of the Model Penal Code Project, Professor Wechsler, writing in 1952 *à propos* the object of drafting such a code, remarked that "when legislation is in prospect legislators do not seek a treatise but a legislative model".[10] In other words, it would be idle to criticise a practical undertaking on the ground that it had not attempted the utopian. This is true, but there should also be borne in mind another view expressed by the same writer in the same context that it would nevertheless "be unfortunate if the enterprise should operate to 'freeze' existing law or practice into rigid mold without exploration of the larger underlying questions".[11] Whatever the current practicability of the Model Penal Code scheme for regulatory offences, the underlying questions remain open for discussion.

In order to assess at their true value the contributions made by the Model Penal Code to the solution of the problem of regulatory offences it is necessary to discover precisely what are those contributions. It may be that what the draftsmen of the Code have actually done differs from what they think they have done. Even if this is not the case, it may still be that the Code as it stands is not entirely appropriate to the arguments put forward in its justification because it either goes beyond those arguments or else falls short of them. Points of interest may prove on inspection to turn merely on minor accidents of wording susceptible of simple cure by amendment; but they may also prove to conceal serious basic faults. Whatever the result, further discussion can proceed only in the context of a detailed analysis of the relevant code sections themselves.

The definition of violation

(i) *Introduction*

The obvious place to start is with the definition of "violation", for the basic premise of the whole scheme in relation to strict responsibility is that the evils of the doctrine may be mitigated by the creation of this new type of offence outside the criminal law. The definition is a little complex, both in itself and because it is distributed between

[10] "The Challenge of a Model Penal Code" (1952) 65 *Harvard Law Review*, 1097, 1131.
[11] *Ibid.*, 1133. Professor Goodrich expressed a similar view in the foreword to Tentative Draft No. 4 (1955).

two different sections. Both have already been quoted. The first, section 1.04 (5), runs in part as follows:

> An offense defined by this Code or by any other statute of this State constitutes a violation if it is so designated in this Code or in the law defining the offense or if no other sentence than a fine, or fine and forfeiture or other civil penalty is authorized upon conviction or if it is defined by a statute other than this Code which now provides that the offense shall not constitute a crime.

The second is section 2.05 (2) (*a*):

> [W]hen absolute liability is imposed with respect to any material element of an offense defined by a statute other than the Code and a conviction is based upon such liability, the offense constitutes a violation.

The two branches of this definition will be discussed separately, starting with section 1.04 (5).

(ii) *First branch*

It may be taken as certain that the definition in section 1.04 (5) is intended to specify four different ways in which an offence may be recognised as a violation, although as a matter of grammar this conclusion is not inevitable. The four different types of violation intended appear clearly: (1) definition of an offence and its designation as a violation by the Code itself; (2) definition of an offence and its designation as a violation by some other statute; (3) an offence defined either in the Code or elsewhere for which no other sentence than fine, or fine and forfeiture or other civil penalty, is authorised upon conviction; and (4) an offence defined by a statute other than the Code which is stated in the defining statute not to be a crime.

The first alternative needs no comment. Examples of violations designated as such in the Code itself are criminal mischief in section 220.3 (2) and criminal trespass in section 221.2 (2), each of which is capable of being an offence of different grades but constitutes only a violation in its least antisocial form. Alternative (4) is merely an instance of alternative (2), the instance being where the designation of an offence in a statute other than the Code as a violation occurs by implication instead of by express statement; for by section 1.04 (7) all statutory offences, whether in the Code or elsewhere, are to be graded in accordance with the Code scheme, and the result of applying this rule where the offence in question is stated not to be a crime is that it must be a violation. Alternative (3) leaves obscure the meaning of "civil penalty" upon which it depends. This matter will be discussed separately below.

There remains the question whether two other alternatives which are logically possible on the wording of section 1.04 (5) were intended by the draftsmen of the Code. Alternatives (1) and (2) above were arrived at by the natural method of applying the principle *reddendo singula singulis* to the section, reading "an offense defined by this Code" together with "constitutes a violation if it is so designated in this Code", and reading "an offense defined by any other statute of this State" together with "constitutes a violation if it is so designated in the law defining the offense". It is, however, logically possible to read the opening words of section 1.04 (5) to arrive also at alternatives (5) "an offense defined by this Code constitutes a violation if it is so designated in the law defining the offense", and (6) "an offense defined by any other statute of this State constitutes a violation if it is so designated in this Code".

As to these possibilities, it is obvious that (5) merely duplicates the first alternative specified above, namely, an offence both defined and designated in the Code itself. Since the framers of the Code would hardly go out of their way to repeat themselves, it is to be presumed alternative (5) was not intended and that the natural application of *reddendo singula singulis* is correct. This conclusion, however, at once disposes of alternative (6). Before accepting it, it is as well to see if alternative (6) has any practical content. What is in question is whether an offence defined in another statute becomes a violation by being so designated in the Code.

As soon as the question is formulated the answer becomes obvious. There is no instance in the Code of an offence defined elsewhere being specifically designated a violation. The Code grades other statutory offences only through the application of general rules. Since these general rules would apply, or not apply, as the case might be, to any particular offence elsewhere without reference to alternative (6), it follows that alternative (6), like alternative (5), is merely repetitive of other parts of the Code and therefore devoid of practical content. The conclusion follows that alternatives (1) to (4) above are exclusive so far as section 1.04 (5) is concerned.

It should be observed that these various definitions of "violation" are capable of overlapping. For example, a statute other than the Code may create an offence which it states is a violation, is not a crime, and may not be punished otherwise than by a fine. This appears to be quite immaterial. If an offence becomes a violation under any head, its status is not up-graded to a more serious offence merely because by every other test it would be a crime; and no amount of overlapping makes a violation any the less a violation.

(iii) *Civil Penalties*

Alternative (3) above says that an offence is a violation if no other sentence than a fine, or a fine and forfeiture or other civil penalty is authorised upon conviction. This rule may make the meaning of "civil penalty" of critical importance to a defendant, but the term is left undefined. The contrast in section 1.04 (5) itself is with "forfeiture", so that forfeiture becomes by implication a civil penalty. Another contrast is to be found in section 6.02 (5) which, in connection with punishment, saves powers of the court derived from sources other than the Code "to decree a forfeiture of property, suspend or cancel a license, remove a person from office, or impose any other civil penalty".

That formula adds suspensions and cancellations of licences and removals from office to the list of civil penalties and thereby further identifies the class of objects with which the term "civil penalty" is to be construed *ejusdem generis*.[12] Nevertheless that precision which ought to be the particular characteristic of a penal statute, especially where the area of strict responsibility is being demarcated, is still lacking.

It may be accepted that definition of "civil penalty" by enumeration is impracticable. The minor ways in which a person may be subjected to punishment short of a fine or imprisonment are for all practical purposes inexhaustible. Another alternative is definition by exclusion. This would make a civil penalty any sentence authorised upon conviction except for punishments expressly excluded from that class. Unfortunately the wording of the Code itself seems to prevent precision being arrived at by this route.

By section 6.02 (1) no person convicted of an offence shall be sentenced otherwise than in accordance with article 6 of the Code, which governs punishments. However, an exception to the rule thus

---

[12] See also Tentative Draft No. 2, Comment, 12, where the reference is to "forfeitures of property, suspension or cancellation of licenses, removal from office and the like".

laid down is created by section 6.02 (5) which says that article 6 does not deprive the court of any authority conferred by law (*i.e.*, a statute other than the Code) to decree a forfeiture of property, suspend or cancel a licence, remove a person from office, or impose any other civil penalty. The effect of these two sections read together is that no one may be sentenced otherwise than in accordance with article 6 except where the court has power derived from a statute other than the Code to impose a civil penalty, in which case that civil penalty may be imposed. Therefore, since the Code does not state what does *not* amount to a civil penalty within the meaning of article 6, it is impossible to define the term by exclusion.

It seems therefore that for the present the vagueness of the term "civil penalty" will have to be accepted as one of the incidental consequences of the attempt made in the Model Penal Code to place in a class separate from true crimes those minor infractions of penal law which the community at large does not regard as criminal in a moral sense. A civil penalty may be taken to be a punishment which does not carry a criminal stigma according to current public opinion.

There is only one exception to this rule according to the scheme of the Code, and that is where a person is fined. As to this, the suggestion may be made that if community attitudes were the sole test of the criminality of a penalty, a mere monetary fine would be classed as civil rather than criminal, for it is the commonest of all sanctions employed in penal law and is not to be compared in stigma with even the shortest term of imprisonment. Nevertheless a fine cannot be classed as a civil penalty for the reason that under the Code,[13] as at common law, the court can always punish crime by means of a fine unless there is some special law to the contrary.

The conclusion is therefore that in the scheme of the Model Penal Code a civil penalty is a punishment other than a fine which does not carry the stigma of criminality according to current public opinion. The view has already been expressed[14] that this classification of punishments is a serious underestimate of the gravity, to the persons who suffer them on the basis of strict responsibility, of these so-called "civil" penalties. A penalty is none the less a penalty for being called civil.[15]

The observation may be made on this conclusion that the problem

[13] S. 6.03.
[14] Above, p. 35 n. 11.
[15] See also above, p. 73 nn. 10, 11.

presented by the meaning of "civil penalty" seems to be quite unnecessary. The evident purpose of the Code with respect to violations is to define them, *inter alia*, as offences for which imprisonment[16] may not be imposed on conviction. There seems to be no reason why this should not be reflected more precisely in the definition of alternative (3) above in the following way: An offence defined by this Code or by any other statute of this State constitutes a violation if a sentence of imprisonment [etc.] may not be imposed upon conviction.

(iv) *Second branch*

We turn now to the second branch of the definition of "violation" in section 2.05 (2) (*a*): "when absolute liability is imposed with respect to any material element of an offense defined by a statute other than the Code and a conviction is based upon such liability, the offense constitutes a violation."

The addition of this definition to the preceding one means that in statutes other than the Code in which no express designation of the grade of the offence appears, violations may be identified by reference either to the punishment authorised upon conviction or to the basis of criminal responsibility. These two identifications of violations are by far the most important of the five specified in the Code. For most practical purposes violations will be found in statutes other than the Code and will be recognised by virtue of the fact, either that no other sentence is authorised upon conviction than a fine, or fine and forfeiture or other civil penalty; or that strict responsibility is imposed with respect to a material element; or that both conditions apply.

It has already been seen that the first of these methods of identification is rendered vague by the uncertainty of the term "civil penalty", although in practice this can be overcome by assuming that it means nothing else than "a punishment other than imprisonment or a fine". The second method suffers from a more serious uncertainty: the absence of any criterion of when strict responsibility has been imposed. Section 2.05 (2) (*a*) says that where strict responsibility is imposed for a material element of an offence, that offence shall be a violation, but does not say how it is to be discovered when that condition obtains. This presents no difficulty in the rare case where the legislature expressly states that responsibility is to be strict; and

[16] Or capital or corporal punishment.

it may be that the section envisages only express statements, although it does not say so;[17] but the problem of implication, which is the usual method of arriving at the basis of responsibility for a regulatory offence, must be dealt with.

There are two possibilities. Either the tests of strict responsibility at present employed by the courts are to be preserved under the Code, or some different test is to be derived from the Code. The first possibility requires no comment at this point. As to the second, attention focuses on section 2.05 (1) (b), which says that strict responsibility applies to "offenses defined by statutes other than the Code, insofar as a legislative purpose to impose absolute liability for such offenses or with respect to any material element thereof plainly appears". The question is whether the requirement that a legislative intention to impose strict responsibility "plainly appear" makes any change in the criteria applied by the courts at present.

The reporter's comments quoted above[18] make it clear that the term "plainly appears" was deliberately chosen to indicate to the courts that while the framers of the Code hoped that strict responsibility would not lightly be implied into any statute, in the last resort the courts must use such criteria of implication as they think fit; and indeed it seems that the enactment of section 2.05 (1) (b) into law would have this effect. Any change in the present law would therefore depend upon the weight the courts were willing to give the term "plainly appears". With the greatest respect to the draftsmen of the Code, it requires almost an act of faith to anticipate that any court would modify its previous practice on the strength of these words. Without this guidance the courts have hitherto drawn conclusions about the meanings of regulatory statutes by reference to those aspects of the legislation which seemed to them most significant. Where the meaning has appeared to be that strict responsibility was intended, this meaning has seemed to the courts to be reasonably clearly indicated. It is difficult to believe that in any such case the decision would have been different had the court been required to say that such a meaning not merely appeared, but appeared "plainly".

The conclusion on this branch of the definition of violation is therefore that where the courts, for whatever reason, actually impose strict responsibility for any offence defined by a statute other than

---

[17] The reporter's comments (above, p. 171) accept that a requirement of express statutory statement would be impractical.
[18] Above, p. 171.

the Code, that offence, by virtue of the imposition of strict responsibility as a basis for conviction, becomes a violation.

(v) *Summary of definition and conclusions*

The Model Penal Code distinguishes between crimes and violations. The former are identified by the possibility of a sentence of imprisonment being imposed on conviction. Imprisonment cannot be imposed on conviction of a violation. The Code further distinguishes between violations created by the Code itself and violations created by statutes other than the Code.

For practical purposes violations created by the Code are identified by express designation in the Code. Violations created by other statutes may also be identified by express designation as such, or, alternatively, by implied designation through being stated not to be crimes; but in practice violations in other statutes are more likely to be identified by reference to the fact either that imprisonment may not be imposed upon conviction, or that conviction is based upon strict responsibility.

Since in this last case it may frequently not be possible to identify an offence as a violation until the courts have passed upon it, and since in practice this class of violations is likely to contain overwhelmingly the largest group of such offences, it follows that the Model Penal Code scheme does not make it significantly easier than under the present law to foresee the incidence of strict responsibility in regulatory penal law absent a judicial decision covering the particular offence in question.

Culpability requirements

(i) *Introduction*

Violations having been identified, the next task is to state the legal consequences of being charged with and convicted of a violation. The first consequence is a modification of the general principles of responsibility prerequisite to conviction.

The basic principles of responsibility under the Model Penal Code are set out in sections 2.01 and 2.02, which has already been referred to.[19] They are called "culpability requirements" and it may be helpful to summarise them again here. The two basic rules in sections 2.01 and 2.02 are, first, that there must be a voluntary act

[19] Above, p. 168.

(or the culpable omission to perform an act of which the defendant was physically capable), and secondly, that this act must be performed purposely, knowingly, recklessly or negligently. These culpability requirements apply to all infringements of penal law with the following two exceptions, created by section 2.05 (1):

(*a*) offenses which constitute violations, unless the requirement involved is included in the definition of the offense or the Court determines that its application is consistent with effective enforcement of the law defining the offense; or

(*b*) offenses defined by statutes other than the Code, insofar as a legislative purpose to impose absolute liability for such offenses or with respect to any material element thereof plainly appears.

The second of these exceptions adds nothing for the present purpose to the first, for it has already been seen that the effect of imposing strict responsibility for any offence is to reduce that offence to a violation. Once an offence becomes a violation, by whichever of the several possible routes it arrives at that grade, the rule is that the culpability requirements of the Code do not apply unless either they are included in the definition of the violation itself or the court determines that their implication is inconsistent with effective law-enforcement.

(ii) *Criticism*

The comments of the reporter are as follows.[20] "The assumption is ... that when the offense is of this grade, culpability requirements ordinarily will be expressly stated when the legislative purpose is that they be included in the elements of the offense. If the law is silent, the Court must make an affirmative determination that they are consistent with effective enforcement or the liability will be construed as absolute. This device should greatly reduce the uncertainty upon the issue that is typically so pervasive until it is settled by the courts."

This argument fails to convince. The assumption that culpability requirements ordinarily will be expressly stated goes counter to all previous experience, if by this is meant that the legislature is believed in all cases to have stated exactly what it intended. This may be a misinterpretation. The comments may mean only that an arbitrary assumption is being made as a basis for statutory construction in future. If this is so, then the whole weight of the arrangement pro-

[20] Tentative Draft No. 4, Comment, 145.

posed falls on the second part of the rule, namely, that if culpability requirements are not expressly stated, they do not apply unless the court affirmatively decides that they do because they are consistent with effective law enforcement.

It is far from clear how this arrangement can reduce uncertainty. There are two weaknesses in the scheme. The first is that until the courts have passed upon any particular offence it cannot be known whether they will decide that some or all of the culpability requirements may be implied consistently with effective law enforcement. The practical disadvantage of the law as it now stands in most jurisdictions is the uncertainty which prevails until a decision is handed down on the particular offence in question. The Code scheme does not appear to affect this position, for the rule it lays down is open to just as much difference of judicial opinion as the present law.

The second weakness in the scheme is the ambiguity of the idea of express statement in this context. It is to be observed that although the commentary envisages express statement of the elements of the offence, section 2.05 (1) (*a*) does not actually say this. The statutory wording is, "included in the definition of the offence". This formula appears to leave inclusion by implication open just as much as inclusion by express statement. Nevertheless, even if the section is understood in the sense attributed to it in the commentary, ambiguity remains.

Take for example the simple prohibition, "No person shall sell . . .". There is no necessary unanimity of view on what these words expressly state or "include". An obvious uncertainty is whether a person can complete certain kinds of contracts of sale if he does not know what he is selling. Some may say that there can be a sale within the meaning of the statutory words regardless of whether D knows what is in the packet he is supplying; others can argue with equal logic that the word "sell" necessarily implies an intention to supply that which is demanded, so that if the demand relates to the contents of the packet, and not merely to the packet regardless of the contents, D cannot be said to sell unless he knows what is in the packet; others may agree with this second view but argue that the word "sell" by definition expressly says the same thing and does not merely imply it; and yet others may with no less cogency take the view that whether "sell" says these things expressly or by implication, it certainly "includes" them.

The significance of this obscurity in meaning is that unless the court decides that a culpability requirement is not "included" in the definition of the particular offence, it is not open to the court to make or not make an affirmative determination that implication of the requirement would be consistent with effective law enforcement. The Model Penal Code does not give the court power to modify the definition of an offence against the defendant, but only in his favour. Therefore the ambiguity inherent in nearly all regulatory offences has to be resolved against D before the discretion given to the court comes into play.

Although it is quite possible that such a rule would lead the courts to construe regulatory offences in a uniformly literal way, in effect always deciding against D on the first point to leave themselves with a discretion on the second, this consequence is not certain. Some judges might well prefer to base themselves on what they conceived to be the meaning in law of the definition of the offence rather than on a discretion about the exercise of which they might legitimately have reservations. In the present state of the evidence on the matter, one could well understand the predicament of a member of the judiciary who came to the opinion that he was quite unable to make a meaningful determination as to whether any particular culpability requirement was consistent with effective law enforcement.

(iii) *Status offences*

Some further difficulties arising out of the Code rule that prima facie culpability requirements do not apply to regulatory offences may be explored. The very first culpability requirement is the following, in section 2.01:

> (1) A person is not guilty of an offense unless his liability is based on conduct which includes a voluntary act or the omission to perform an act of which he is physically capable.

The reporter comments,[21] and one may agree without reservation, that this rule is one without which "penal sanctions can not be employed with justice". Nevertheless, the structure of the Code is such that it does not necessarily apply to violations.

Most regulatory offences are defined in such a way that the requirement of a voluntary act will be deemed to be part of the offence. It is for this reason that automatism has been judicially accepted as affording an answer to a charge based on strict respon-

---

[21] Tentative Draft No. 4, Comment, 119.

sibility as much as to any other type of offence.[22] The considerations which affect the rule that there should not be responsibility for the omission to perform an act of which the defendant was physically capable, however, are different. This rule does not relate to volition but to the general defence of necessity, of which it is an instance. The extent to which situations of necessity afford a defence to a strict responsibility charge is uncertain, and discussion of this issue is deferred until the next chapter.[23]

But all the difficulties are not disposed of by accepting that a voluntary act is normally required and that impossibility is linked with the general defence of necessity. There remains the problem of the status offence, the offence defined in impersonal wording which attaches liability by virtue, not of anything that D either did or omitted to do, but of his having at the material time a status to which the law attaches penal consequences for a state of affairs which has no necessary connection with anything done or omitted to be done by D.[24] The most celebrated instance of arbitrary injustice being occasioned by the imposition of strict responsibility for a status offence is *Larsonneur*,[25] which has already been discussed in detail.[26] It is the opinion of the reporter of the Model Penal Code that the voluntary act rule in section 2.01 (1) "would have precluded a conviction"[27] in this case. Much as one would like to accept this view, there are two reasons for not doing so.

Both objections arise out of the impersonal form of words used for the definition of the offence in *Larsonneur*, which was being "found" in the United Kingdom when possessing the status of a prohibited immigrant. The first is that such a form of words does not compel a literal-minded court to find either that the culpability requirement of section 2.01 (1) is included in the definition of the offence or that its implication would be consistent with effective law enforcement. It is abundantly clear that the English Court of Criminal Appeal would have decided against the defendant in *Larsonneur* on both points. Section 2.01 (1) refers to acts and omissions. On the literal view which courts not uncommonly take of status offences, neither act nor omission need be relevant.

[22] *Hill* v. *Baxter* [1958] 1 Q.B. 277, 283, *per* Lord Goddard C.J.; *Carter* [1959] V.R. 105; *Watmore* v. *Jenkins* [1962] 2 Q.B. 572.
[23] Below, p. 204.
[24] Above, p. 46.
[25] (1933) 24 Cr. App. R. 74.
[26] Above, p. 47.
[27] Tentative Draft No. 4, Comment, 120.

The second objection is that even if the court does decide that this culpability requirement is included in the definition of a status offence, or that its implication is consistent with effective law enforcement, there is no need for the court, on a literal view, to regard section 2.01 (1) as making any difference. Whether the section is included or implied or not, acts and omissions by D remain irrelevant to the offence charged.

No doubt the reporter founds his opinion on the inclusion in section 2.01 (1) of the words "based on". The section does not say that all offences must be deemed to include a requirement of either a voluntary act or an avoidable omission. It attempts to reach the same result by saying that the court must look beyond the precise definition of the offence before it and decide whether in substance the liability sought to be imposed is founded on a voluntary act or avoidable omission. If this is the effect of section 2.01 (1), then it is true that it would have prevented a conviction in *Larsonneur*; but it is hard to accept that the intention of the draftsmen of the Code has here been translated into effect with sufficient certainty to produce the result aimed at.

The weakness upon which the literal approach to criminal statutes thrives is ambiguity of expression, for the spirit of the literal approach is restrictive, and if more than one meaning can reasonably be derived from the statutory words it is always open to the court to choose the more restrictive. It has already been observed[28] that although a restrictive approach to penal statutes is supposed to be a safeguard for the defendant, and no doubt fulfils that function when attention is directed to the scope of the offence rather than to prerequisites for conviction, in this part of the criminal law such an approach works against the defendant and not in his favour.

In the present case the ambiguity which undermines the attempt of the Model Penal Code draftsmen to circumvent status offences lies in the words "based on". One meaning which can be attached to them is the meaning evidently intended: that the court should look to the substance of the matter and not merely to the form. But as against this view a literal-minded court could argue that liability is based on what the statute says it is based on, and the statute in *Larsonneur* said that it was based upon being found in the United Kingdom after being refused permission to land there.

It is therefore concluded that the Model Penal Code has not

[28] Above, p. 12 n. 38.

succeeded in coping satisfactorily with the problem of the status offence.

(iv) *Conclusion*

It would be tedious to repeat the foregoing arguments in relation to each of the culpability requirements specified in the Model Penal Code. It is clear that so far as the general part of the law is concerned, the overall effect of the Code in relation to regulatory offences is to leave the courts exactly where they are at present, namely, in possession of a discretion to read the definitions of these offences in as liberal or as literal a manner as they see fit. This result is no doubt in accordance with the main object of the Code in relation to this type of offence, which is to modify the consequences of conviction in terms of punishment and social stigma rather than to modify the doctrine of strict responsibility.

Admittedly the Code emphasises one avenue of escape for a court which does not like the doctrine of strict responsibility, and also invites it to exercise a judgment extending beyond the literal meanings of words, by the rule that culpability requirements may be read into a violation if the court thinks them consistent with effective law enforcement. A further persuasion in the same direction is the rule[29] that P may bring down a more serious punishment on D, and convert the violation into a crime, by proving that the violation in question was committed culpably. These tentative and gentle pressures, however, would not be enough to make a significant difference to the law in a jurisdiction where strict responsibility for regulatory offences had taken firm root.

Punishment

It is in the realm of punishment that the Model Penal Code takes a firm stand against strict responsibility. There are two basic rules, the significance of which become clear if it is remembered that the Code itself does not impose strict responsibility for a material element of a crime,[30] as opposed to a violation, and that if a statute other than the Code makes such an imposition the crime is *ipso facto* converted into a violation.[31] The first rule is that a violation may not be punished with imprisonment. The second is that,

[29] S. 2.05 (2) (*a*).
[30] Tentative Draft No. 4, Comment, 146. Above, p. 171
[31] S. 2.05 (2) (*a*).

A violation does not constitute a crime and conviction of a violation shall not give rise to any disability or legal disadvantage based on conviction of a criminal offense.[32]

The second of these rules needs no comment. Its purpose and effect is to keep a conviction based on strict responsibility off the defendant's record, and thereby to abolish one of the more outstanding injustices of the doctrine. The first rule, that a violation may not be punished with imprisonment, is founded in the first instance upon section 6.02 (1), which says,

No person convicted of an offense shall be sentenced otherwise than in accordance with [article six of the Code].

By contrast with the culpability requirements, which do not necessarily apply to violations, the rules governing sentencing are to be found without exception in article 6 of the Code. The following subsections of section 6.02 are also relevant to the present discussion:

(4) The Court may suspend the imposition of sentence on a person who has been convicted of a violation or may sentence him to pay a fine authorized by Section 6.03.

(5) This Article does not deprive the Court of any authority conferred by law to decree a forfeiture of property, suspend or cancel a license, remove a person from office, or impose any other civil penalty. Such a judgment or order may be included in the sentence.

The effect of subsection (4) taken in conjunction with subsection (1) is that, except for the saving as to civil penalties in subsection (5), a person convicted of a violation may not be sentenced to any punishment other than a fine, and in particular may not be sentenced to imprisonment. The discussion above under the heading "Civil penalties" has already led to the conclusion that this term seems to mean any punishment other than imprisonment.[33] It may therefore be that subsection (5) could be made more exact by appropriate redrafting.

The fines which may be imposed on conviction of a regulatory offence are set out in section 6.03 (4)–(6). They are either $500, or any higher amount equal to double the pecuniary gain derived from the offence by the offender, or any higher amount specifically

[32] S. 1.04 (5).
[33] Or capital or corporal punishment.

authorised by statute. The object of the second of these rules is said[34]
to be to ensure that the primary purpose of a fine, in theory at least,
that D should gain no pecuniary advantage from his offence is
preserved. Presumably the extension of liability to double any such
gain is to allow for deterrence to operate by imposing actual loss in
appropriate cases. The object of the third category, any amount
higher than $500 specifically authorised by statute, is to preserve
particular penalties enacted as being appropriate to special cases.

The actual scale of punishments envisaged by the Model Penal
Code does not call for comment. Any such scale is related to necessarily transient economic conditions and is therefore open to
periodical amendment. As to the principles on which the powers set
out above are based, they appear to be unexceptionable once the
object of the Code with reference to violations is conceded. It is
better to confine strict responsibility to penalties less drastic than
imprisonment than to extend it to imprisonment as well. Whether it
is either necessary or desirable to expose a defendant to any penalty
at all on the basis of strict responsibility has already been debated at
length in Chapter 1. If the conclusion is reached, as it has been
reached by the framers of the Model Penal Code, that strict responsibility must be accepted for fines and other penalties short of
imprisonment, then the scheme of punishments set out in the Code
seems to be a reasonable one.

Burden of proof

It is of interest that the Model Penal Code makes no distinction
between violations and other offences in the rules governing proof.
The fundamental rule is set out in section 1.12 (1):

> No person may be convicted of an offense unless each element of such
> offense is proved beyond a reasonable doubt. In the absence of such
> proof, the innocence of the defendant is assumed.

This rule is modified in various ways in the remainder of section
1.12. The modifications do not require comment here because they
also apply indifferently to both crimes and violations.

Conclusions

The aim of the draftsmen of the Model Penal Code in relation to
the doctrine of strict responsibility for regulatory offences was to

[34] Tentative Draft No. 2, Comment, 22.

diminish the injustice caused by this doctrine by excluding from its operation offences for which a sentence of imprisonment might be imposed on conviction. This aim is achieved in the Code, but some detailed modification of the drafting may be desirable.

It appears also to have been the hope, as opposed to the specific aim, of the draftsmen to discourage the continuance of the doctrine of strict responsibility by holding out to the courts various inducements to apply instead some or all of the culpability requirements set out in the Code. The scheme of the Code as drafted gives little ground for anticipating the realisation of this hope if the Code is translated into law.

Nothing in the detailed drafting of the Code reduces the disquiet previously expressed[35] at the probable long-term consequences of appearing to acquiesce in the preservation of strict responsibility in penal law by the device of declining to call the offences for which it may be imposed criminal offences.

[35] Above, pp. 72–73

CHAPTER 9

THE GENERAL DEFENCES

Introduction

Sayre is the only writer who has devoted any significant amount of space to the relationship between the regulatory offence and the general defences normally available to the defendant accused of crime.[1] In the course of a brief discussion he reviews infancy, coverture, insanity, and intoxication. Whilst regarding the question as largely or entirely academic except in the case of coverture, he comes to the following conclusions.

That class of infants, under seven years of age at common law but under eight years of age by statute now in most jurisdictions, which is elsewhere totally protected from criminal responsibility should also be incapable of incurring responsibility for regulatory offences; but children over the relevant age should be on the same footing as adults. Coverture should not apply, not merely because it is inappropriate in most circumstances to this class of offence, but also because "the defense based upon the husband's coercion is so antiquated and unsuited to the conditions of modern life that it ought to be abolished altogether".[2]

Insanity should not apply for the rather inconsistent reasons, first, that it is not likely to be raised in answer to a summary prosecution, and secondly, that lunatics at large can hardly be allowed to make themselves a social menace by breaking traffic laws without discouragement through the normal sanction of a fine.[3] No problem arises with intoxication because that defence operates only to negative a specific intent required by the definition of a crime, a contingency which does not arise with regulatory offences.

Unique though Sayre's discussion appears to be, it is none the less superficial and unsatisfactory because he did not regard the subject as having any practical importance. In relation to some of the general defences, such as insanity, he was no doubt right, but it is unfortunate

---

[1] Sayre, "Public Welfare Offenses" (1933) 33 *Columbia Law Review*, 55, 75–78.
[2] *Ibid.*, 77.
[3] *Ibid.*, 78.

that he confined himself to a somewhat narrow concept of general defence. It would have been interesting to know his views on the application to a regulatory offence of a plea of necessity in one of the many forms in which it can arise.

It must be remembered that Sayre was writing from the point of view of those who accept the inevitability of strict responsibility in this part of the law. His line of argument appears to have been that since no mental element was required, the very basis of most of the general defences to crime was removed and that therefore these defences became irrelevant. This approach must be met at two levels in a book written from the standpoint that strict responsibility is neither necessary nor desirable. In the first place, the argument based on lack of a mental element may fail because strict responsibility is replaced by another rule to which it cannot be applied. Secondly, the argument may fail even as applied to strict responsibility.

It is submitted that Sayre's approach to the general defences was wrong on both grounds. In so far as this view is based on general disagreement with Sayre and others about the merits and necessity of strict responsibility in the criminal law, the particular problem of the general defences raises no issue not already covered in Chapter 1. On this part of the argument the general defences can be examined afresh in relation to the reasonable behaviour rule advanced as the best rule of law for regulatory offences in Chapter 2. But on a strict responsibility basis Sayre's apparent assumptions in regard to the mental element in crime must be specifically rebutted.

Strict responsibility and the mental element in crime

The argument that no defence which is in substance a denial of all or part of the mental element in crime can apply to an offence of strict responsibility[3a] confuses *actus reus* with *mens rea*. The distinction between *actus reus* and *mens rea* is not the same as the distinction between the physical and the mental elements in crime. This is one of the reasons why the doctrine of strict responsibility, although superficially simple, is fundamentally confusing.

Although there is no doubt that different people use the customary terms *actus reus* and *mens rea* in different ways, it is thought that for an analysis of strict responsibility the following usage might command general acceptance. *Actus reus* includes not only the physical

[3a] *Ibid.*, 78.

or outward circumstances of an offence, but also so much of the mental element in that offence as pertains to the definition of the physical or outward circumstances.[4] In the normal case, *actus reus* is a physical act by D, and therefore includes so much of the mental element in the offence as is necessarily included in the definition of an act for the purposes of the criminal law. *Mens rea* is the residue of the mental element required by the definition of the offence in question.

On this analysis, if murder by shooting were charged, the voluntary act of pulling the trigger of the gun would pertain to *actus reus* and the knowledge of the surrounding circumstances and the intention to kill would form part of the *mens rea*. Thus, if the gun went off by accident, the defence of accident might be directed either at the *actus reus* requirement, or at both *actus reus* and *mens rea*, according to the circumstances. If D had *mens rea* but the gun went off by accident, he would be attempting to deny *actus reus*.[5] But if the whole affair were accidental, the possibility of killing somebody having been present to the mind of no one, the defence would be a denial of both *actus reus* and *mens rea*.

It is the common confusion between defences which deny both *actus reus* and *mens rea* and those which deny *mens rea* only; or alternatively, between defences which deny the whole of the mental element in crime and those which deny only part; which has occasioned much uncertainty about the true nature of the doctrine of strict responsibility. Strict responsibility does not deprive the defendant of any defence which denies *actus reus*, but only of defences which deny *mens rea*. Each defence raised to a strict responsibility charge should therefore be examined with precision to ascertain what it is that is being argued in relation to the definition of the offence.

There are two classes of cases which at first sight seem to form an exception to the proposition that strict responsibility eliminates *mens rea* only, and not *actus reus*. One is the status offences and the other cases of vicarious responsibility.[6] In both these types of cases defendants have been convicted without either *actus reus* or *mens rea* in any significant sense. Neither of them, however, affects the validity of the general proposition that strict responsibility as a general doctrine eliminates *mens rea* only. The remarkable results reached in

[4] Glanville Williams, *Criminal Law: The General Part* (2nd ed.), 22.
[5] He would not succeed, of course, because the *actus reus* of reckless killing includes creating a situation in which someone is likely to be killed.
[6] Above, pp. 46, 49.

the status offences have been thought to follow from the particular wording of the statutes concerned and not from any general rule. Under vicarious responsibility the theory is that D has acted through another under circumstances which estop him from denying that that other's act was his own.

It is not the case that outside these two classes of offences strict responsibility extends even to the mental element in *actus reus*. On this basis the general defences will now be considered individually in relation both to strict responsibility and to the proposed reasonable behaviour rule.

Infancy

There appears to be no reasonable ground for suggesting that the general rule that children under the ages of seven or eight years, or such other minimum age as may be prescribed in any particular jurisdiction, are incapable of incurring criminal responsibility should be modified for regulatory offences, whatever the doctrine which governs the responsibility of adults.

Equally there appears to be no ground for modifying the rule that persons under the age of fourteen years, or such other age as may be relevant in the particular jurisdiction, are incapable of incurring criminal responsibility unless they are affirmatively proved to have the capacity to understand that they ought not to do that which they are charged with having done. At first sight there might appear to be a problem here in cases of strict responsibility, but it is submitted that there is in reality no need for difficulty. Unless D is proved to have the capacity to have known that he ought not to do that which he is charged with doing, he is on the same basis as a child incapable of incurring any criminal responsibility. Once that capacity is proved, however, he is on the same basis as an adult and liable to be convicted or acquitted, as the case may be, on the same principle as an adult.[7]

Coverture

It can be only very rarely that infancy is of importance as a defence to a regulatory prosecution. The same cannot be said of the presumption of marital coercion. Particularly is this the case with the licensees of licensed premises, where it is a common arrangement for both husband and wife to hold licences, either jointly or severally.

---

[7] Sayre, *op. cit.*, 76–77.

The present scope of the presumption of marital coercion is some-what uncertain. "What is perhaps entitled to be spoken of as the majority view, is that except in cases of treason, murder, and offenses 'conducted by the intrigues of the female sex' such as keeping a house of ill fame, there is a prima facie presumption that a wife was coerced by her husband, and is therefore entitled to an acquittal, if she committed a prohibited act jointly with him, or while he was present."[8]

If this view is correct, the presumption applies to summary offences, and therefore to regulatory offences, as much as to any others. This view appears to have been accepted in some American cases,[9] but it has been consistently rejected in Australia.[10] It is sub-mitted that the Australian view is the better one for the reason given by Sayre[11] that the presumption of marital coercion is an anachronism at the present day. If this view is accepted it follows that where there is doubt as to its application, as with summary offences, the decision ought to be in favour of restricting rather than extending its scope. This consideration applies as much to the doctrine of strict respon-sibility as to any other.

Compulsion

For what it is worth, the decision in *Larsonneur*[12] is some authority, although the point passed *sub silentio*, for the view that compulsion is no defence to a charge to which the doctrine of strict responsibility applies. It will be recalled that in that case the charge was "being found" in the United Kingdom, D being a person to whom permis-sion to land had been refused; but the only reason why D was in the United Kingdom at the material time was that she had been brought there by the police acting under lawful authority. The more recent South Australian case of *O'Sullivan* v. *Fisher*[13] raises the question whether the decision would, or ought to have been, different had the compulsion under which D was brought to the United Kingdom been unlawful.

In *O'Sullivan* v. *Fisher* D was charged with being drunk in a public

[8] Perkins, *Criminal Law*, 800–801.
[9] Sayre, *op. cit.*, 77.
[10] *Reidy* v. *Herry* (1897) 23 V.L.R. 508; *Manuels* v. *Crafter* [1940] S.A.S.R. 7; *Ewart* v. *Fox* [1954] V.L.R. 699.
[11] Above, p. 189 *Cf.* Perkins, *op. cit.*, 804–805.
[12] (1933) 24 Cr. App. R. 74. Above, p. 47
[13] [1954] S.A.S.R. 33.

place.[14] The facts were unfortunately not as clear as they might have been. D was sitting in certain private premises when two policemen entered. There was no dispute that he was drunk. After some conversation the three of them went downstairs and out into the street. After walking about ten yards D was arrested and charged. It was not clear why he had gone from the private premises into the public street with the two policemen, but the story he advanced at his trial was that he believed himself to be under lawful compulsion to do so. On this basis the magistrate dismissed the complaint. P's appeal was allowed and the case remitted for rehearing.

Reed J. distinguished between lawful and unlawful compulsion, holding that neither the former nor a reasonably mistaken belief in the former was a defence to a charge of strict responsibility such as the one before him. To this proposition he made a tentative exception, however, and that was if D was in the street by reason only of the fact that he had been arrested on the private premises and was in the course of conveyance elsewhere whilst in custody. His Honour did not explain the distinction between this kind of lawful compulsion and any other kind of lawful compulsion beyond saying that "[s]uch a defence, if valid, would . . . rest upon a general ground not of the same nature" as the compulsion which had been suggested in the case before him. What this general ground would be was not specified.

It appears, therefore, that Reed J. would not have been inclined to decide *Larsonneur* in the same way as did the English Court of Criminal Appeal, for the lady in that case was brought to where she was "found" in custody after lawful arrest. It is submitted that so far as lawful arrest is concerned, the view tentatively expressed by Reed J. is much to be preferred. It is absurd, and indeed if the matter were not so serious it would be ludicrous, to suggest that the police have power forcibly to put a person who has no right to resist (because his arrest is lawful) into a position where he becomes guilty of some offence for which he was not originally arrested. The question is whether it follows that any other form of lawful compulsion ought to be a defence to crime.

Lawful compulsion other than arrest might quite easily arise in connection with being drunk in a public place through the expulsion from his home by the owner of a guest who had become objectionably drunk. According to *O'Sullivan* v. *Fisher*, in which the similar case of

[14] Police Act, 1936–1951 (S.A.), s. 74 (1).

customers being ejected from a bar at closing time was referred to,[15] if a passing policeman then charged the defendant, he would have no answer. And yet if it is the case that unlawful compulsion may be a defence, it may be argued that the success or failure of the prosecution depends on the question, possibly quite immaterial to the drunken man, whether the houseowner used more force than was necessary to eject him. This problem may be deferred until unlawful compulsion has been considered.

Owing to the uncertainty of the circumstances under which D left the private premises in *O'Sullivan* v. *Fisher*, Reed J. on appeal thought it advisable to express an opinion on the effect of unlawful compulsion. "Being called upon to express an opinion, I state my view as being that if the respondent in the present case proved that he was compelled by physical force, used by a person or persons having no lawful right or authority to remove him from the premises, to go out into the street, he has established an answer to the charge."[16]

It will be observed that this opinion is carefully limited to a certain set of circumstances by two conditions. The first is the need for physical compulsion and the second that the person applying that physical compulsion have no lawful right to remove the defendant from the premises. Many questions arise on these limitations. It is probable that under the head of physical compulsion there may be included the immediate threat of physical compulsion. What is not clear is whether a reasonable belief in the threat of physical compulsion would be a defence.

It is in such a case as this that the vagueness which is so marked a characteristic of strict responsibility becomes prominent. If the rule is that D may be convicted only if the court concludes that he has been negligent in the sense that he has not behaved reasonably, there is no difficulty; for if D proves that he reasonably believed he was under the immediate threat of physical compulsion, he is clearly entitled to be acquitted on the ground that his behaviour in all the circumstances was reasonable. But if strict responsibility is the rule, it is not clear whether this belief is relevant. On the one hand it can be argued that all beliefs at all points of time are irrelevant, and that therefore D should be convicted; or, on the other, that since the effect of compulsion is to remove from the *actus reus* the element of volition which is as requisite for strict as for any other basis of

---

[15] [1954] S.A.S.R. 33, 35–36.
[16] *Ibid.*, 39.

criminal responsibility, there is no rational ground for distinguishing between causes of lack of volition and that therefore D should be acquitted.

It is submitted that even under strict responsibility a reasonable belief that one was under unlawful physical compulsion to do the forbidden act ought to be a defence. If a tobacconist is compelled by threats to sell a packet of cigarettes after lawful trading hours by a young man who threatens to beat him if he does not, it is unreasonable to make the tobacconist's guilt or innocence turn on the question whether the young man was bluffing. Yet if the threat of physical compulsion is a defence, but a reasonable although mistaken belief in the genuineness of such a threat is not, that is the result which follows.

Another question arising out of Reed J.'s formulation of the defence of unlawful compulsion concerns the source of the unlawful character of the compulsion. It was suggested above that compulsion might be unlawful for this purpose if its unlawful character came from its being disproportionate to the occasion which called it forth, as where a householder uses excessive force in ejecting a drunk from his home. If Reed J.'s words are to be taken literally, this form of unlawful compulsion would not furnish the drunk with a defence to a charge of being drunk in a public place because the householder has a "lawful right" to remove him, even if that lawful right was resorted to in an unlawful manner. Possibly this result is less undesirable than the alternative of making the drunkenness charge depend on the degree of force with which D was removed from the private premises.

The position might also arise where the person removing D reasonably thought he had lawful authority to do so when in fact he had not. It should be borne in mind that in the commonest case, that of an arrest which is technically unlawful for some reason not apparent to the person arresting, such as a flaw in a warrant, the difference between lawfulness and unlawfulness would be immaterial on the rule laid down in *O'Sullivan* v. *Fisher*; for if lawful arrest furnishes a defence to a charge based on removal elsewhere in custody, then unlawful arrest furnishes such a defence *a fortiori*. If the result is the same whatever the facts, it is immaterial what the arrester thought. However, it is quite possible for a reasonable mistake to be made as to powers of ejection from premises without an arrest situation arising.

It might be argued that something ought to turn on the state of mind of the person ejected. Thus the very ground upon which the prosecutor's appeal was allowed in *O'Sullivan* v. *Fisher* was that the magistrate had erred in holding that a reasonable belief by D that he was under lawful compulsion to leave the private premises was a defence. The reasoning of the appeal court was that since lawful compulsion was no defence, a reasonable belief in lawful compulsion could not be a defence. At this point several different situations have to be distinguished.

If the compulsion is lawful and the defendant to the charge of drunkenness believes it to be lawful, then the compulsion, provided that it does not amount to an arrest, is no defence and D's belief cannot affect the matter. If the compulsion is lawful but D believes it to be unlawful, it is difficult to see how this can affect the situation either. The fact is that D had no right to resist being removed to a public place. However relevant his beliefs may be to a charge arising out of resistance to lawful arrest, they cannot be relevant in the present situation. Next, the compulsion may be unlawful but D complies because he reasonably believes it to be lawful. This may have been the case in *O'Sullivan* v. *Fisher*, but the facts were not clear. It is submitted that on the general principle that a defendant's reasonable mistakes ought not to prejudice him, even if they do not help him, attention should once more be directed to the legal status of the compulsion rather than to D's state of mind. Lastly, the compulsion may be unlawful and D reasonably believe it to be unlawful. In this situation he obviously has a defence, subject, as in the previous situation, to the artificially limited meaning of "unlawful" which may apply in this part of the law.

The conclusion which follows from the distinguishing of these four situations is that D's beliefs as to the lawfulness or otherwise of the compulsion under which he believes himself to be acting are irrelevant. The question still remains whether the state of mind of the person exercising the compulsion is relevant, as, for example, if in *O'Sullivan* v. *Fisher* the policemen had reasonably believed they were answering a request from the owner of the premises to assist in removing the drunk, and had used force in this belief, whereas their actions were in fact unlawful because the request they had received was a practical joke by some third party. It is submitted that if the distinction between lawful and unlawful compulsion is to be preserved for the purpose of testing a defence of compulsion to a later charge against the person compelled to move, the beliefs of the person using the compulsion must also be dismissed as irrelevant. No amount of belief, however reasonable, can make lawful that which is unlawful. The most which erroneous beliefs can do is furnish an excuse for doing that which is prima facie penalised by law.

It is time to draw the discussion together to see whether the position arrived at is satisfactory. The broad rule suggested by *O'Sullivan* v. *Fisher* is that unlawful physical compulsion should furnish a defence to a charge of strict responsibility but that lawful compulsion should not. This is subject to two qualifications. First, arrest is a defence whether lawful or unlawful. Secondly, compulsion which is prima facie lawful because it is exerted in pursuance of a lawful power does not become so unlawful as to furnish a defence if it becomes unlawful by reason only of excessive force. Where there is no compulsion in fact, a reasonable belief in the immediate threat of unlawful physical compulsion is a defence but an equivalent belief as to lawful compulsion is not. For all purposes the threat of immediate physical compulsion is to be equated with actual physical compulsion.

It is immediately clear that once it is taken out of the context of the offence of being drunk in a public place the rule that lawful compulsion is no defence is unworkable. Take the case of a motorist who is about to drive away from a metered parking space, immediately before the lawful parking period expires, when he is stopped by a policeman to allow free passage along the road for an ambulance. The meter flag drops and he is charged with illegal parking. The compulsion exercised by the policeman was perfectly lawful but it is incredible that the motorist should be convicted. If the rule were reasonable behaviour, of course he would not be; it is only strict responsibility which creates the problem.

Or suppose again that D gets drunk at a private party. He has no intention of leaving the premises until next day when he will have sobered up. He has lawfully parked his car in the street outside. There is an accident and to allow free access to the area the police come to the house and lawfully order the defendant to remove his car. As soon as he has done so he is charged with being drunk in a public place and driving the car whilst under the influence of drink. It may be said that there would be no defence here because the police have no authority to compel him physically to remove the car. They can either remove the car themselves or charge D with obstructing them in the course of their duty, or both, but they are not entitled to lay hands on him and take him outside. This is so, but none the less D may quite reasonably believe the contrary and go outside for that reason only; or, indeed, he may even quite wrongly but nevertheless reasonably fear the use of unlawful force. Here again it is hard to envisage conviction for obeying the lawful commands of the police, which is what the situation would in substance amount to.

It is submitted that the only satisfactory rule is that compulsion, or a reasonable belief in compulsion, should be a defence whether it is lawful or unlawful. Thus if a drunken man refuses to leave a bar at closing time and is forcibly ejected, he cannot complain about being put outside because he knew very well when he went into the bar that he could remain there only for a limited period. He is not being compelled at closing time to do something which he would not otherwise do, as is the case with a man who is unexpectedly ejected from private premises to which he has been invited, but merely being obliged to abide by an obligation which he undertook voluntarily.

There seems to be no good reason why a general defence of compulsion as outlined above should not be available in all strict responsibility prosecutions. If reasonableness of behaviour is the test, here, as elsewhere, there is no need to construct a separate general defence; for the facts relevant to the defence would be equally relevant to the question of reasonableness.

Insanity and automatism

Although it might be theoretically interesting, no discussion of insanity as a defence to regulatory offences, or to offences of strict responsibility, is called for here because the subject is of no practical importance. It is inconceivable that on such a charge D would wish to raise this defence and, subject to what follows about automatism, highly unlikely that the evidence will disclose any matter from which the court might think that it appeared[17] that D was of unsound mind. If an opinion is called for, it is submitted that insanity gives rise to a personal incapacity to commit crime of any order in the same way as the incapacity of infancy; and that therefore insanity should be a complete defence to any criminal charge.

Automatism may be a rather more practical question, although its importance is easily capable of exaggeration. The reason is that

[17] The wording usually used in statutes regulating verdicts of not guilty on the ground of insanity is that such a verdict is to be returned "if it appears" from the evidence, or to the jury, that D was insane when he committed the act. See, *e.g.*, Trial of Lunatics Act, 1883 (Eng.), s. 2, which has been generally copied in Australia.

200 The General Defences

whereas a verdict of not guilty on the ground of unsoundness of mind[18] leads to indefinite incarceration in an institution, automatism calls for acquittal.[19] This is why there are signs that automatism may be developing into a general defence in a manner that insanity never has.[20]

Automatism may be defined for the present purpose as involuntary action performed in a state of unconsciousness not amounting to insanity.[21] As such it is now clearly established that automatism may constitute an answer to a criminal charge distinct from, and with none of the incidents of, a defence of insanity.[22] The action must be unconscious to distinguish it from irresistible impulse and involuntary to constitute an answer to the charge.[23] The preponderance of

[18] Under which head is included the self-contradictory English verdict of guilty but insane.

[19] See the cases in the following footnotes.

[20] Of the fourteen cases, *Cogdon* (unreported, Victorian Supreme Court, 1950); *Harrison-Owen* [1951] 2 All E.R. 726; *Charlson* [1955] 1 W.L.R. 317; *Minor* (1955) 112 C.C.C. 29; *Hill* v. *Baxter* [1958] 1 Q.B. 277; *Wakefield* (1958) 75 W.N. (N.S.W.) 66; *Cottle* [1958] N.Z.L.R. 999; *Carter* [1959] V.R. 105; *Foy* [1960] Qd. R. 225; *Holmes* [1960] W.A.R. 122; *Bentley* [1960] 7 C.L. 355; *Cooper* v. *McKenna* [1960] Qd. R. 406; *Bratty* v. *Att.-Gen. for Northern Ireland* [1963] A.C. 386; *Watmore* v. *Jenkins* [1962] 2 Q.B. 572; only three were charges of murder. The others were made up of one motor manslaughter, three lesser offences against the person, three dangerous driving, and four offences against property. Two of the offences against the person, however, arose out of dangerous driving, so that property and traffic offences are in the majority. Since such offences form the bulk of the offences committed, this may be some evidence that the defence of automatism is on its way to becoming general in a manner that insanity never is likely to.

[21] Unconscious involuntary behaviour is what the courts seem to understand by automatism. The clearest statement is given by Gresson P. in *Cottle* [1958] N.Z.L.R. 999, 1007 and 1020. For England, see *Hill* v. *Baxter* [1958] 1 Q.B. 277; *Watmore* v. *Jenkins* [1962] 2 Q.B. 572; for Northern Ireland, *Bratty* v. *Att.-Gen. for Northern Ireland* [1963] A.C. 386; for Australia, *Carter* [1959] V.R. 105; and for Canada, *Minor* (1955) 112 C.C.C. 29 (disapproving *Kasperek* (1951) 101 C.C.C. 375).

[22] *Charlson* [1955] 1 W.L.R. 317; *Minor* (1955) 112 C.C.C. 29; *Hill* v. *Baxter* [1958] 1 Q.B. 277; *Cottle* [1958] N.Z.L.R. 999; *Carter* [1959] V.R. 105; *Holmes* [1960] W.A.R. 122; *Cooper* v. *McKenna* [1960] Qd. R. 406; *Bratty* v. *Att.-Gen. for Northern Ireland* [1963] A.C. 386.

[23] For modern statements of the ancient rule that the criminal act must have been voluntary see *Woolmington* v. *D.P.P.* [1935] A.C. 462, 482; *Vickers* [1957] 2 Q.B. 664, 672. See also the Model Penal Code of the American Law Institute, Tentative Draft No. 4, s. 2.01 (1) and (2). For recent academic discussions see Glanville Williams, *Criminal Law: The General Part* (2nd ed.), 11–13; Perkins, *Criminal Law*, 660–661. The old writers did not deal with involuntariness, apart from insanity, in any way relevant to automatism. Thus Hale's example in 1 *P.C.* 434 is of physical compulsion by another, and Hawkins' example in 1 *P.C.*, Ch. 29, s. 3, does not seem to involve an act by the rider of the horse at all. Prevezer, "Automatism and Involuntary Conduct" [1958] *Criminal Law Review*, 361, 365, classifies duress and coercion as forms of conscious involuntary action, but it is thought that this approach obscures the issue. The act performed under duress or coercion is normally voluntary, although the willingness to perform it may have been brought about by threats. See Stephen, *History of the Criminal Law of England*, Vol. 2, p. 102; Hall, *Principles of Criminal Law* (2nd ed.), 419, 421–425.

opinion in the common law jurisdictions is now in favour of the view that it is for the defence to carry the evidentiary burden of producing some evidence in support of a plea of automatism, but for the prosecution to carry the persuasive burden of disproving automatism beyond reasonable doubt.[24]

If the analysis made earlier in this chapter[25] of *actus reus* and *mens rea* in relation to the whole mental element in crime is accepted, it becomes apparent that there is no difficulty in applying the defence of automatism to strict responsibility; for if D was in a state of automatism at the relevant time, not only is he devoid of the irrelevant element of *mens rea*, he also lacks the volitional element in *actus reus*. As Lord Goddard C.J. put it in relation to dangerous driving, "I agree that there may be cases where the circumstances are such that the accused could not really be said to be driving at all. Suppose he had a stroke or an epileptic fit, both instances of what may properly be called acts of God; he might well be in the driver's seat even with his hands on the wheel, but in such a state of unconsciousness that he could not be said to be driving."[26]

In other words, if the driver were in any of these states, no question of *mens rea* would arise because there was no *actus reus*. It is therefore submitted that automatism is a complete defence to a criminal charge, including a criminal charge based on the doctrine of strict responsibility. If the rule were that D could not be convicted if he had behaved reasonably in all the circumstances, the same result would follow, for the strict analysis would be that he had not "behaved" at all.

Intoxication

Although no case has been traced in which intoxication has been raised as a defence to a regulatory or strict responsibility prosecution, the subject, in view of the universal addiction to alcoholic beverages, may well have some practical importance. Fortunately no problems seem to arise.

If the intoxication alleged has no further or other effect than to

---

[24] *Charlson* [1955] 1 W.L.R. 317; *Minor* (1955) 112 C.C.C. 29; *Hill* v. *Baxter* [1958] 1 Q.B. 277; *Cottle* [1958] N.Z.L.R. 999; *Wakefield* (1958) 75 W.N. (N.S.W.) 66; *Carter* [1959] V.R. 105; *Bentley* [1960] 7 C.L. 355; *Bratty* v. *Att.-Gen. for Northern Ireland* [1963] A.C. 386; *Watmore* v. *Jenkins* [1962] 2 Q.B. 572.

[25] Above, n. 31 *et seq.*

[26] *Hill* v. *Baxter* [1958] 1 Q.B. 277, 283. See also *Carter* [1959] V.R. 105; *Watmore* v. *Jenkins* [1962] 2 Q.B. 572.

negative some form of *mens rea*, then it is clearly irrelevant to strict responsibility. If the importance of the intoxication is that it occasions some other condition, such as a form of temporary insanity or automatism, then the defence falls for consideration according to the principles which have been advanced under those heads. In neither case does it seem to be relevant to inquire whether the intoxication was deliberately induced or unintentional except where deliberately induced intoxication is resorted to as a means of producing a condition which would otherwise form a defence. It is difficult to envisage a regulatory offence the commission of which would be sufficiently attractive to provoke this course of action on the part of the defendant, but should there be one it is submitted that D's self-induced incapacity should be treated as a wrongful act for the purpose of the general rule that he should not be allowed to benefit through his own wrongdoing.[27]

If the doctrine of strict responsibility is replaced by the reasonable behaviour rule, the questions arise whether what is reasonable be judged by the standard of the drunken man or the sober man, and whether the voluntariness or involuntariness of the drunkenness is relevant. These questions need occasion no great difficulty. It must be remembered that the situations which arise in the context of regulatory offences are not particularly serious ones. It may not be reasonable for the law to compel a convivial man to take the risk that through intoxication he will commit a murder that he would not have committed when sober; but it is quite reasonable to expect him to take the risk of committing minor infractions of the law from the same cause. Voluntary intoxication should not be taken into account either in D's favour or against him on a regulatory offence charge, assuming that the intoxication does not occasion some more serious incapacitation of another legal kind. On the other hand, involuntary intoxication should prima facie operate in favour of D if his condition may have had something to do with the act he is charged with having committed.

There is also the question of the difference between voluntary and involuntary intoxication. Here all that is required is avoidance of confusion between voluntary drunkenness and intentional drunken-

---

[27] *Cf. Att.-Gen. for Northern Ireland* v. *Gallagher* [1963] A.C. 349, where it was held that if D deliberately induced in himself a state of temporary insanity through intoxication with the object of committing a crime whilst intoxicated, the relevant time for determining whether he was insane was when he started to drink and not when he committed the criminal act.

ness. Intoxication may perfectly well be regarded as voluntary even if it is not strictly intentional, as if a man overestimates his own capacity for withstanding the effects of alcohol. All that is required for a case of voluntary intoxication to arise is that through drinking D place himself in a position where his faculties are materially, although not necessarily drastically, affected by alcohol. Since this is likely to happen at an early stage, the only practical case of involuntary intoxication is if a harmless drink is surreptitiously replaced by an intoxicant which the unsuspecting defendant takes.

Other personal incapacity

Discussing cases of illegal sale, Cussen J. in 1906 said, "I can find no authority in England or Victoria which lays down that, where a person *bona fide* thinks he is selling one article, where in fact he is selling another, that ignorance of that fundamental fact is of no importance. In such a case the article or liquid may be so wrapped up or bottled, and may be so compounded that, even if the seller thought of making an inquiry, it would be difficult or impossible for him to do so. Take, for example, the case of a blind man thinking he is selling a perfectly innocent article."[28] The example is perhaps not very happily chosen, for a blind man must be rare in a business which requires the physical handling of retail articles. Nevertheless it raises the question of physical incapacity not falling under any of the preceding heads.

The recent English case of *Strong* v. *Dawtry*[29] has been referred to earlier.[30] It will be recalled that in that case D was convicted for illegally parking in a metered area when for the whole of the two minutes during which he had left his car in the area he had been occupied trying to get the right piece of small change to put into the meter. The court held that there could not be read into the relevant regulation an implication that the motorist was to be allowed a reasonable period in which to insert the appropriate coin. One wonders what would be the position of a driver suffering from partial paralysis of the legs through polio who drives a car with manual controls. There are many such drivers who are perfectly competent to drive their specially adapted vehicles. It usually takes them quite an appreciable period of time to enter and leave their vehicles. It

[28] *Gleeson* v. *Hobson* [1907] V.L.R. 148, 157.
[29] [1961] 1 W.L.R. 841.
[30] Above, p. 42

might well take more than two minutes before the appropriate coin was inserted into the meter. According to *Strong* v. *Dawtry* such a driver commits an offence every time he parks in a metered area.

It is incredible that the doctrine of strict responsibility should ever be carried so far. If such a case arose there can be no doubt that *Strong* v. *Dawtry* would be distinguished on its facts, very likely being equated with negligence on the part of the driver in not having previously provided himself with small change. In the absence of authority to the contrary it is reasonable to assume that a personal incapacity such as blindness or paralysis would be taken into account even under the doctrine of strict responsibility in passing upon liability to conviction. The theoretical basis for this view appears to be that physical incapacity is really one form of the wider defence of necessity or impossibility, which will be considered next. Of course, if a physically handicapped person were to put himself unreasonably in a position where it was likely that his handicap would occasion a breach of the law, and he committed such a breach, then it might well be proper not to allow him to plead his handicap in excuse.

Necessity, impossibility, inevitable accident

In *McCarthy* v. *Codd*[31] D was charged that, being a licensee, he failed to have every bar door of the licensed premises shut and locked during prohibited hours.[32] The trial judge, Pape J., after citing authority[33] which established that responsibility under the relevant section was "absolute", continued:[34] "Indeed, one may be pardoned for wondering whether it is not too absolute, for as far as I can gather, a licensee could not lawfully open the bar door during prohibited hours for the purpose of extinguishing a fire which had begun in the bar by reason of an electrical fault occurring therein, but would have to let his premises burn down, if he could not extinguish the fire without entering the bar."

His Honour did not go on to deal with the position which would arise if the licensee under these circumstances then claimed under his

---

[31] [1959] V.R. 88.
[32] Licensing Act, 1928 (Vic.), s. 206, as amended by the Licensing (Amendment) Act, 1953 (Vic.), s. 26.
[33] *Thompson* v. *Sampson* [1930] V.L.R. 191; *Richards* v. *Grant* [1958] V.R. 241, 246.
[34] [1959] V.R. 88, 93. Cf. *Buttons* v. *Melbourne Justices* (1890) 16 V.L.R. 604, where D, a licensee charged with wilfully failing to admit a police officer to his licensed premises, defended himself by saying that he believed he was not allowed to let anyone at all in on a Sunday, and had offered the policeman the key so that he could let himself in!

insurance policy. Neither did he consider whether the licensee would be in the same position if members of his family were trapped behind the locked doors in the fire.

In *Kilbride* v. *Lake*[34a] D was charged, in effect, with permitting to be on a road a vehicle which was not carrying a current warrant of fitness. He had parked his car in a normal place and left it for a short while. When he left the car it was bearing an unexpired warrant of fitness but when he returned the warrant had gone and a traffic offence notice, leading to the present prosecution, had been fixed to the windscreen. P conceded that D had known nothing about the removal of the warrant of fitness and in the circumstances could have done nothing about it. Woodhouse J. of the New Zealand Supreme Court held that before any question of *mens rea* or strict responsibility could arise, P had to prove some causal connection between D's conduct and the occurrence of the prohibited state of affairs. Here there was no sufficient causal connection. Therefore the question whether D, once having permitted his car to be on a road, was strictly responsible for its condition, did not arise, and the charge should be dismissed.

In *Canty* v. *Buttrose*[35] D was charged with knowingly permitting a drunken person to remain on licensed premises. The facts were that D, on discovering the drunken man in an advanced state of intoxication, instead of turning him off the premises immediately had sent for the police to remove him instead. She was therefore literally within the wording of the section. It was held, however, that since the object of the section concerned was to protect drunken persons, and since D's action in the circumstances had been in the interests of the drunken man, she had a good defence to the charge. Reliance was placed on the analogy of a drunken man who was hurt or disabled.[36]

In *Beckwith* v. *Nicol Bros.*,[37] D was charged with carrying on business as a dairyman without holding a current licence to do so.[38] He and his brother had carried on a dairying business for some time and had regularly paid the requisite fee for a licence and received their licences without trouble. On this occasion they had sent in their fee in the usual manner, and had heard nothing more. The local authority kept the fee, "for such a time as would entitle any owner to

[34a] [1962] N.Z.L.R. 590.
[35] [1912] V.L.R. 363.
[36] *Ibid.*, 365.
[37] [1916] V.L.R. 261.
[38] Dairy Supervision Act, 1915 (Vic.), s. 44 (*g*).

believe that his money had been accepted and that he had been
accepted and that he was entitled to a licence under the Act".[39] This
being so, the court acted on the view that D was actually entitled to
a licence under the Act. If he was entitled to the issue of a licence, he
was to be put in the same position as if he actually had the licence.
Therefore he could not be convicted. There is a flavour of equity
about this process of reasoning which appears rather oddly in the
criminal law, although the decision was undoubtedly just and correct.

These cases illustrate the element of diversity which has to be taken
into account when considering the extent to which necessity, impossibility and inevitable accident constitute an answer to a charge
based on strict responsibility. If sufficiently striking examples are
chosen, such as people trapped in a locked and burning bar room, one
feels no doubt about the answer: it would be monstrous to convict
the licensee for opening the door during prohibited hours under these
circumstances. Indeed, it would not only be monstrous, it would be
futile. One may therefore safely assert that to some extent necessity,
which includes the necessity of others as well as of the defendant
himself, is a good defence to a charge of this kind. The question is
how far necessity can be carried.

The problem is perhaps seen more clearly with impossibility or
inevitable accident. Suppose, by analogy with *Kilbride* v. *Lake*, that
a motorist has lawfully parked his car in a metered parking area and
returns shortly before the time has expired only to find that another
vehicle has illegally parked alongside, so that, since there are cars
legally parked both in front of and behind his car, he cannot drive
away unless he himself breaks the law by driving over the sidewalk.
Before the vehicle alongside moves away the meter flag drops. This
is a straight case of impossibility through no fault of the defendant.
If the rule for regulatory offences were reasonable behaviour, there
would be no problem. There ought to be no problem with strict
responsibility either, but one cannot assert with confidence that every
court would follow *Kilbride* v. *Lake* and decline to convict.
Larsonneur[40] was also a case of impossibility.

There is no need to distinguish with any great precision between
necessity, impossibility and inevitable accident, or to confine the
latter category of misfortunes to so-called acts of God. A bar room

[39] [1916] V.L.R. 261, 264.
[40] (1933) 24 Cr. App. R. 74. Above, p. 193. Impossibility created by D's own fault is,
of course, no defence: *Narrandera Pastures* v. *Coote* (1961) 78 W.N. (N.S.W.) 697.

door on licensed premises might be unlocked during prohibited hours either because the lock was broken by a violent and unusual storm or because burglars had forced it. From D's point of view both of these occurrences might be classed as accidents. At first sight it seems absurd that a licensee should be criminally responsible for the act of a burglar,[41] a stranger acting unlawfully. Yet such responsibility has frequently been imposed in this part of the law.

To cite only one well-known example, in *Parker* v. *Alder*[42] D was convicted of selling adulterated milk when it was found as a fact that the adulteration had taken place after the milk had left the control of himself and those for whom he was responsible by being consigned to the purchaser by rail. In that case it was perfectly clear that an unknown stranger, acting unlawfully, had brought about the prohibited situation. If a stranger under those circumstances, why not a burglar?

It would be superfluous to multiply instances. What is clear is that if the general defence of necessity or impossibility is pushed far enough, it eliminates strict responsibility altogether, for the very basis of that doctrine is that D should be convicted whether he could have prevented the proscribed occurrence or not. Yet since it is also clear that courts have from time to time, as in *Canty* v. *Buttrose*, *Beckwith* v. *Nichol Bros.*, and *Kilbride* v. *Lake*, declined to push the law as far as they could have done, an uneasy tension between the ground of responsibility and the ground of exculpation is inevitable. One can only say, more by way of rational prophecy than ordered interpretation of the law, that if the facts are sufficiently dramatic, necessity, impossibility and inevitable accident will furnish defences even to strict responsibility prosecutions; but that how dramatic the facts have to be is obscure.

[41] *Cf. Bear* v. *Lynch* (1909) 8 C.L.R. 592, 600, 603. Above, p. 125.
[42] [1899] 1 Q.B. 20.

BIBLIOGRAPHY

The principal sources of reference are cited in the text. They are the following.

BOOKS

Blackstone, *Commentaries on the Law of England* (15th ed.), London, 1809.

Coke, *Institutes of the Law of England*, 1641, reprinted with annotations, London, 1817.

Edwards, *Mens Rea in Statutory Offences*, London, 1955.

Hale, *Pleas of the Crown* (Wilson ed.), London, 1778.

Hall, *General Principles of Criminal Law* (2nd ed.), New York, 1960.

Holdsworth, *History of English Law, vol.* 1 (7th ed.), London, 1956; vol. 2 (3rd ed.), London, 1923.

Holmes, *The Common Law*, London, 1882.

Mueller (ed.), *Essays in Criminal Science*, London, 1961.

Osborne, *Justices of the Peace 1361–1848. A History of our Magistracy during Five Centuries*, Shaftesbury (Dorset, Eng.), 1960.

Perkins, *Criminal Law*, New York, 1957.

Pollock and Maitland, *A History of English Law Before the Time of Edward I*, Cambridge, (Eng.) 1985.

Pound, *Jurisprudence*, St. Paul (Minnesota, U.S.A.), 1959.

——, *The Spirit of the Common Law*, Francestown (New Hampshire, U.S.A.), 1921.

Radzinowicz and Turner, (eds.) *The Modern Approach to Criminal Law*, London, 1945.

Stephen, *A History of the Criminal Law of England*, London, 1883.

Stroud, *Mens Rea*, London, 1914.

Tappan, *Crime, Justice and Correction*, New York, 1960.

Williams, *Criminal Law: The General Part*, (1st ed.) London, 1953; (2nd ed.) London, 1961.

——, *The Proof of Guilt*, London, 1955.

Winfield, *Select Legal Essays*, London, 1952.

PERIODICAL ARTICLES AND NOTES

Anonymous, "Public Torts" (1922) 35 *Harvard Law Review* 462.

Brett, "Manslaughter and the Motorist" (1953), 27 *Australian Law Journal* 6.

Conway, "Is Civil or Criminal Procedure Proper for Enforcement of Traffic Laws?" [1959] *Wisconsin Law Review* 418.

Devlin, "Statutory Offences" (1958), 4 *Journal of the Society of Public Teachers of Law* (New Series) 206.

Dixon, "The Development of the Law of Homicide" (1935), 9 *Australian Law Journal (Supplement)* 64.

Edwards, "Automatism and Criminal Responsibility" (1958), 21 *Modern Law Review* 375.

Enloe, "Criminal Sanctions for the 'Status' of Narcotics Addiction" (1963), 17 *South Western Law Journal* 134.

Gausewitz, "Reclassification of Certain Offences as Civil instead of Criminal" (1937), 12 *Wisconsin Law Review* 365.

Hall, "The Three Fundamental Aspects of Criminal Law" *Essays in Criminal Science*, ed. Mueller (*q.v.*, *supra*), 159.

Hart, "The Aims of the Criminal Law" (1958), 23 *Law and Contemporary Problems* 401.

Jackson, "Absolute Prohibition in Statutory Offences," (1936) 6 *Cambridge Law Journal* 83.

Kadish, "Some Observations on the Use of Criminal Sanctions in Enforcing Economic Regulations" (1963), 30 *University of Chicago Law Review* 423.

Keedy, "Ignorance and Mistake in the Criminal Law" (1908), 22 *Harvard Law Review* 75.

Kirchheimer, "Criminal Omissions" (1942), 55 *Harvard Law Review* 615.

Lacey, "Vagrancy and Other Crimes of Personal Conditions" (1953), 66 *Harvard Law Review* 1203.

Laylin and Tuttle, "Due Process and Punishment" (1922), 20 *Michigan Law Review* 614.

Mannheim, "Mens Rea in German and English Criminal Law" Part III, (1936) 18 *Journal of Comparative Legislation* 78.

Martinon, "Unburdening the Substantive Criminal Law in Wisconsin – Civil Offenses" [1946] *Wisconsin Law Review* 172.

Mueller, "Mens Rea and the Law Without It" (1955), 58 *West Virginia Law Review* 34.

——, "The German Draft Criminal Code 1960 – An Evaluation in Terms of American Criminal Law" [1961] *University of Illinios Law Forum* 25

Packer, "Mens Rea and the Supreme Court" [1962] *Supreme Court Review* 107.

Perkins, "The Civil Offense" (1952), 100 *University of Pennsylvania Law Review* 832.

Prevezer, "Automatism and Involuntary Conduct" [1958] *Criminal Law Review* 361.

Remington, Robinson and Zick, "Liability Without Fault Criminal Statutes" [1956] *Wisconsin Law Review* 625.

Remington and Rosenblum, "The Criminal Law and the Legislative Process" [1960] *University of Illinois Law Forum* 481.

Richardson and Sayles, "Parliaments and Great Councils in Medieval England" (1961), 77 *Law Quarterly Review* 213.

Sayre, "Criminal Responsibility for the Acts of Another" (1930), 43 *Harvard Law Review* 689.

——, "Mens Rea" (1932), 45 *Harvard Law Review* 974.

——, "Public Welfare Offenses" (1933), 33 *Columbia Law Review* 5.

Schwenk, "The Administrative Crime, Its Creation and Punishment by Administrative Agencies" (1943), 42 *Michigan Law Review* 5.

Stallybrass, "The Eclipse of Mens Rea" (1936), 52 *Law Quarterly Review* 60.

Starrs, "The Regulatory Offense in Historical Perspective", *Essays in Criminal Science* ed. Mueller (*q.v. supra*), 235.

Travers and Morris, "Imputed Intent in Murder" (1961), 35 *Australian Law Journal* 154.

Turner, "The Mental Element in Crimes at Common Law" (1936), 6 *Cambridge Law Journal* 31.

Wasserstrom, "Strict Liability in the Criminal Law" (1960), 12 *Stanford Law Review* 731.

Wechsler, "The Challenge of a Model Penal Code" (1952), 65 *Harvard Law Review* 1097.

Wigmore, "Responsibility for Tortious Acts" (1894), 7 *Harvard Law Review* 315.

Williams, "Constructive Malice Revived" (1960), 23 *Modern Law Review* 605.

——, "Homicide and the Supernatural" (1949), 65 *Law Quarterly Review* 491.

Winfield, "The Myth of Absolute Liability" (1926), 42 *Law Quarterly Review* 37.

OFFICIAL PUBLICATIONS

1938 Report of the Departmental Committee on Corporal Punishment (U.K.) Cmd. 5684.

1953 Report of the Royal Commission on Capital Punishment (U.K.) Cmd. 8932.
1959 Report of the Commission of Inquiry on Capital Punishment (Ceylon), Sessional Paper XIV.
1960 Report of the Advisory Council on the Treatment of Offenders (U.K.), Cmd. 1213.
1960 Proceedings of the United Nations Seminar on the Role of Substantive Criminal Law in the Protection of Human Rights and the Purposes and Legitimate Limits of Penal Sanctions, held at Tokyo, Japan, in May 1960, published by the United Nations, New York.

MISCELLANEOUS

The Annual Practice, London, 1962.
Model Penal Code of the American Law Institute, Tentative Drafts Nos. 1, 2, 3, and 4, Philadelphia, 1956; Proposed Official Draft, Philadelphia, 1962.

INDEX

ABSOLUTE RESPONSIBILITY. *See generally*, STRICT RESPONSIBILITY
ACCIDENT, 145
  defence of, inevitable, 204
ACT OF GOD, 206
ACTUS REUS
  automatism, 201
  burden of proof, 43
  defences, 190
  definition, 1, 190
  "knowingly", 65
  mens rea, distinguished, 190
  negligence, 36
  physical act, 123
  status offence, 47, 191
  vicarious responsibility, 191
ADMINISTRATIVE COURTS
  reform by, 84
ADMINISTRATIVE CRIME, 73
ADMINISTRATIVE DISCRETION, 23–24
ALLOW. *See* PARTICULAR WORDS
AMERICAN LAW INSTITUTE MODEL PENAL CODE. *See* MODEL CODE
ARREST
  defence to status offence, 193
ATTEMPT
  synonymous with endeavour, 121
AUSTRALIAN CRIMINAL CODES. *See also* CODES, REFORM
  automatism, 148
  burden of proof, 166
  case law, 156–166
    Queensland, 156–162
    Western Australian, 162–166
  common law, comparison with, 154
    relationship to, 146, 161, 162
  consolidating, whether, 160
  declaratory, whether, 161
  exclusive nature, 146
    effect of, 146–147
  ignorance, 154
  interpretation of sections, 145 *et seq.*
    "accept", 164
    accident, 147

"act", 147
  by-law, effect on, 157
  "excuse", 158
  inconsistency, 159
  "knowingly", 153
  malice, 150
  neutral words, 154
  "omission", 147
  "purporting", 157
  relationship between sections 23 and 24, 151, 153, 159, 161
  section, 23, 147–150
  section, 24, 150–153
  status offences, 154
  "unlawfully, 156
  mens rea, irrelevant, 146
  mistake, 150
  negligence, 145 *et seq.*, 152
  reform by, example, 74
  scope of, 146–147
AUTOMATISM, 199
  Australian Criminal Codes, 148
  mens rea, 201
  Model Code, 182

BIGAMY, 2, 97
BURDEN OF PROOF, generally, 39 *et seq.*
  defendant's, 40
  evidentiary, 40
  ignorance, 44
  mistake, 44, 105–109
    evidentiary burden, 107
    persuasive burden, 107
  Model Code, 187
  persuasive, 40
  probability, balance of, 43
  quantum, 39, 43
  regulatory offences, difficulties, 41
  standard of reasonableness, 42
BY-LAW, 157

CASE-LAW,
  Australian Criminal Codes, on, 156 *et seq.*
  reform by. *See* REFORM

CAUSE. *See* PARTICULAR WORDS
CHANGE, LAW OF. *See* REFORM
CIVIL OFFENCE, 73
CIVIL LAW
decisions, reforming influence, 80
CODES, *see also* AUSTRALIAN CRIMINAL CODES
reform by. *See* REFORM
Model Code, 70
COERCION, MARITAL. *See* COVERTURE
COMMON LAW
Australian Criminal Codes relationship to, 146, 161–162
COMPULSION. *See* COVERTURE, DURESS
CONSTRUCTION. *See also* PARTICULAR WORDS *and* INTERPRETATION
Australian Criminal Codes, 145 *et seq.*
criminal statutes, 11 *et seq.*
particular words, of, 53–67
status offences, 50
illustrations, 51–53
statutory words, generally, 46 *et seq.*
CONTEMPT OF COURT
Australian Criminal Codes, in, 146
CORPORAL PUNISHMENT, 5
COURTS. *See also* MACHINERY, REFORM
construction of words, role of, 66
interference with legislative policy, 10
interpretation of legislative intention, 12
pressure of work, 15
reform by, 78–84
summary trial, 29
trial by jury, 29
COVERTURE, 192
CRIME
classes of,
Model Code, 167
constructive, 30
CRIMINAL STATUTES
codification, 10. *And see* CODES, MODEL CODE
construction, 12
drafting of, 10

interpretation of, generally, 11 *et seq.*
Wisconsin Study (1956), upon, 7, 11
CULPABILITY. *See* MODEL CODE
Reporter's comments, 180

DEATH PENALTY, 5
DEFENCES
accident, inevitable, 204
act of God, 206
arrest, to, status offence, 193
automatism, 199
burden of proof, *See* BURDEN OF PROOF
coverture, 192
duress, 193
mistake, effect of, 197
general, 189 *et seq.*
Sayre's discussion, 189
impossibility, 204
inevitable accident, 204
infancy, 192
insanity, 199
intoxication, 201
mistake. *See* MISTAKE
particular words, and, 113 *et seq.*
neccessity, 204
physical incapacity, 203
precautions, reasonable, 129
sleep, 92
statutory, 143–144
DEPORTATION, 20, 32, 33
DETERRENCE
argument, 24
knowledge, presence of, 25
publicity, 26
refutation of argument, 25
DRUNKENNESS. *See* INTOXICATION
DURESS, 2, 193, 200
defence, enactment of, 10
reasonable belief in, 195

EMPLOYERS. *See* VICARIOUS RESPONSIBILITY
EVADE. *See* PARTICULAR WORDS

FELONY
Model Code, in, 167
FINES. *See also* PUNISHMENT
combination, other punishments, with, 35

Model Code, in, 169
serious punishment, as, 32
FORFEITURE, 32, 33
Model Code, in, 175, 186
FRAUD, *See* PARTICULAR WORDS

HISTORY, 13 *et seq.*
argument for strict responsibility, 13
origin of strict responsibility, 13
refutation of argument, 13

IGNORANCE
Australian Criminal Codes, 154
burden of proof, 44
mistake, compared, 88, 91, 95, 104
Model Code, 168
wilful, mistake and, 150
IMPLEMENTATION
argument for strict responsibility, 18
discretion, policy of, 24
morality, 21 *et seq.*
proof, difficulty of, 18
punishment, role of, 18, 20
refutation of argument, 19
vicarious liability, 23
IMPOSSIBILITY
defence of, 204
IMPRISONMENT, 32
INADVERTENCE, 36
INFANCY, 2, 192
INSANITY, 199
defence, enactment of, 10
mistake, and, 94
time, relevant, 94
INTERPRETATION. *See also* CONSTRUCTION
Australian Criminal Codes, 145
et seq.
Model Code, of, 167 *et seq.*
INTOXICATION, 201

JUSTICES OF THE PEACE, 15

KNOWING. *See* PARTICULAR WORDS

LAW, DEVELOPMENT OF. *See* REFORM
LEGISLATIVE INTENTION. *See also*
CONSTRUCTION, INTERPRETATION
ambiguity, 12

argument for strict responsibility, 9
courts, interference by, 10
information, lack of, 12
judicial conflict, interpretation in, 12
refutation of argument, 10
LEGISLATIVE PURPOSE, 18
Australian Criminal Codes, 145
et seq.
Model Code, of, 167 *et seq.*
LEGISLATURE
intention of, 9. *And see* LEGISLATIVE INTENTION
intention, unproved assumptions, 11
policy, 9 *et seq.*
strict responsibility, policy, 9
LICENCE. *And see* PUNISHMENT
deprivation of, 32, 33

MACHINERY OF CHANGE. *See*
REFORM COURTS
MACHINERY
criminal law, inadequacy of, 14
MALICE
Australian Criminal Codes, in, 150
MAXIMS. *See* WORDS AND PHRASES
MARITAL COERCION. *See* COVERTURE
MENS REA
actus reus, and, 190
Australian Criminal Codes, in, 146 *et seq.*
Australian High Court, in, 85–87
automatism, 201
"cause", 140
codes, in, 75
criminal statute in, 11
defences, and, 190
definition, 1, 36, 190
"evade", 142
"fraudulently", 141
"knowingly", 132
lack of time, 16
mistake, 99 *et seq.*
Model Code, in, 167 *et seq.*
proof of, lack of time, 16
public interest, 7, 36
punishment, and, 31, 33
regulatory offences, background, 3 *et seq.*

MENS REA—*cont.*
  sleep, and, 92
  social importance, 7
  status offences, 47, 125, 191
  statute, criminal, in, 11
  statutory words, 12, 46, 53 *et seq.*
    And see PARTICULAR WORDS
  strict responsibility, generally, 190
  vicarious responsibility, 191
  "wilfully", 132
MENTAL ELEMENT
  crime of. *See* MENS REA
MISDEMEANOR
  Model Code, in, 167
  petty, 167
MISTAKE
  Australian Criminal Code, 150
  Australian High Court, state-of rule, 85
  bigamy, 97
  burden of proof, 44, 105–109
    evidentiary, 107
    persuasive, 107
  Canadian Cases, 110
  characteristics of rule, 88–109
  defences, statutory, 143–144
  duress, 197
  English cases, 109
  fact of, and law, 96 *et seq.*
  honest, ignorance and, 150
  ignorance, compared, 88, 91, 95, 104
  insanity, 94
  law of, and fact, 96 *et seq.*
  Model Code, 168
  negligence, and, 103
  negligence and, rule stated, 138
  neutral words, *See* NEUTRAL WORDS
  New Zealand Cases, 111
  particular words, 113–144. *And see* PARTICULAR WORDS, NEUTRAL WORDS
  quantum of proof, 105–109
  Queensland Case-law, 162
  reasonableness, 99–105
  sleep, 92
  status offences, 125–132. *And see* STATUS OFFENCES
  statutory defences, 143–144
MODEL CODE, 167 *et seq.*
  act, voluntary, 168

aim, 72, 167, 187
  Reporter's comments, 169–171 172
  analysis, 172 *et seq.*
  Australian. *See* AUSTRALIAN CRIMINAL CODES
  automatism, 182
  burden of proof, 187
  causal relationships, 168
  civil penalty, 174, 175, 186
  classification, 167–172
  crime, 167
  criminal responsibility, 168
  culpability, 168, 170, 179–185
    criticism, 180
    necessity, 183
    Reporter's comments, 180
    rules, basic, 179
    status offences, 182–185
    weaknesses, 181
  effect, overall, 185
  elements, offence of, 169, 177
  exclusiveness, 168 *et seq.*
  ignorance, 168
  interpretation, 172 *et seq.*
  "knowingly", 168
  misdemeanor, 167
  mistake, 168
  morality, and, 21
  necessity, 183
  "negligently", 168
  omission, voluntary, 168
  penalty. *See* punishment *infra*
  possession, as act, 168
  punishment, 169, 185–187
    fine, 169, 176, 186
    forfeiture, 175
  "recklessly," 168
  reform by, example, 70–74
  Reporter, *See* WECHSLER, Professor
  scheme, 167
  states of mind, 168
  status offences, 182–185
    Reporter's comments, 182
  violation, 172 *et seq.*
    civil penalties, 175
    classification, 173
    construction, 172–179
    definition, 179
    definition by outside statute, 177
    definition within code, 173

MODEL CODE—*cont.*
   definition with reference to punishment, 175
   identification, 172 *et seq.* 177
MORALITY, 3 *et seq.*
   crime, regulatory offences as part of, 72
   implementation, regulatory offen-offences, of, 21 *et seq.*
   injustice, 23–24

NECESSITY
   argument for strict responsibility, 15
   defence of, 204
   Model Code, 183
   refutation of argument, 16
   sentencing, revelance of, 17
   strict responsibility, doctrine of, 15
NEGLIGENCE
   Australian Criminal Codes, in, 145–150
   basis of responsibility, 79–80
   burden of proof, 39, 44
   criminal, 152
   definition, Australian Criminal Codes, in, 147 *et seq.*
   generally, 38
   inadvertence, 36
   meaning of, 36
   mens rea, 36
   mistake, and, rule stated, 103, 138
   Model Code, in, 168
   Queensland Criminal Code, 75
   recklessness, 36
   reform, strict responsibility, and, 79
   relation to strict responsibility, 6
   social standards, 37
   standard of care, 25
NEUTRAL WORDS
   attempt, 121
   Australian cases, 114
   Australian Criminal Code, 154
   definition, 114
   "endeavour", 121 *et seq.*
   examples, 114
   history,
      mistake, 116
      negligence, 115–116
      pre-1918, 114–119

      1918-1945, 119–122
      post 1945, 122–125
   plain words, 114
NOMENCLATURE
   strict responsibility, of, 1

OFFICE, REMOVAL FROM, 32, 33

PARTICULAR WORDS
   "allow", 55, 56
      civil cases, 137
      mistake, 133 *et seq.*
      qualified by "knowingly", 137
      rule stated, 140
      vicarious responsibility, 137
   Australian Criminal Code, in.
      See AUSTRALIAN CRIMINAL CODES
   "cause", 54
      Australia, in, 141
      mistake, 140–141
      "wilfully", 141
   "evade", 142–143
   "failing", 137
   "fraudulent", 141–142
   generally, 53 *et seq.*
   "knowingly", 62
      Australian cases, 132
      Australian Criminal Codes, 153
      Australian High Court, in, 87
      burden of proof, 63
      construction of, 65, 66
      distinguished "wilfully", 132–133
      mistake, 132–133
      Model Code, 168
      New Zealand rule, 111
      omission of, 63
   mistake and, 113–144
   form of, 113
   neutral words. *See* NEUTRAL WORDS
   negligence, and, 134
   "negligently", Model Code, 168
   "permitting", 55
      another's act, 58
      Australian High Court, in, 87, 88
      ignorance, defence of, 61
      "knowingly", in conjunction with, 66
      mistake, 61, 133 *et seq.*

PARTICULAR WORDS—*cont.*
own act, 55
rule stated, 140
vicarious responsibility, and, 58
"recklessly", Model Code, 168
"suffer", 55
mistake, 133 *et seq.*
rule stated, 140
"wilfully", 62
distinguished "knowingly", 132–133
mistake, defence of, 132–133
PENAL CODE, American, 6. *And see* MODEL CODE
PENAL STATUTES. *See* CRIMINAL STATUTES
PENALTY. *And see* PUNISHMENT
deterrence, 25, 26
PENOLOGY, influence on strict responsibility, 5
PERMITTING, *see* PARTICULAR WORDS
PHRASES. *See* WORDS AND PHRASES
PHYSICAL INCAPACITY. *See* IMPOSSIBILITY, DEFENCES
defence of, 203
PLAIN WORDS, 46, 114
PRECEDENT. *See* REFORM.
reform by, role of, 81–83
PROOF. *See* BURDEN OF PROOF
PUBLIC INTEREST
argument for strict responsibility, 27
injustice, 27
mens rea, 36
refutation of argument, 27
PUBLICITY
deterrence, 26
PUNISHMENT
corporal, 5
death penalty, 5
deportation, 20, 32, 33
deterrent effect, *See* DETERRENCE
effect, 34
fine, Model Code, 185
serious punishment, as, 32
forfeiture, 32, 33
implementation, 18–20
imprisonment, 32
serious punishment, as, 32
licence, deprivation of, 32, 33
livelihood, deprivation of, 34
mens rea, relevance of, 31

Model Code, in, 169, 185 *et seq.*
office, removal from, 32, 33
serious, 32
status offence, 127, 128, 130
value, 34

QUANTUM OF PROOF. *See* BURDEN OF PROOF
QUEENSLAND CRIMINAL CODE. *See also* AUSTRALIAN CRIMINAL CODES, REFORM
case-law, 156 *et seq.*
negligence, 75
scheme, 74

REASONABLENESS, burden of proof, 42
RECKLESSNESS, 36
REFORM, 68 *et seq.*
administrative courts, by, 84
Australia, High Court, present law, 85
case-law, by, 78–84
American, 82
Australian, 81–82
court of appeal, new, 84
English, 79
flexibility, 83
statute, and, 84
codes, by. *See* statutes, by, *infra.*
statutes, by, 68–78
American Model Penal Code, 70–74
Australian Codes, 74
codification, 69
defences, 76
Model Code, 70–74
REGULATORY OFFENCES. *See generally*, STRICT RESPONSIBILITY
classification, Sayre by, 1–2
crimes, as, 70, 72
definition, 44
general law, implied, 11
particular words. *See* PARTICULAR WORDS
status offences, 46 *et seq.*, 182

SANCTIONS, 29 *et seq. And see* PUNISHMENT
relevance, 29
trial by jury, 29

SAYRE, classification of regulatory offences, 1–2, 6
defences, discussion of, 189–190
SEXUAL OFFENCES, age of victim, 2, 67
SLEEP, 92
SOCIAL OBLIGATIONS
  awareness of, 37
  minimum standards, 37
SOCIETY, importance of strict responsibility, 7
STARE DECISIS. *See* PRECEDENT, REFORM
STATUS OFFENCES
  aiding and abetting, of, 47
  Australian Criminal Codes, 154
  "being found", 47
  bigamy, 97
  construction of, 50
    illustration, 51–53
  form of words, 127
  impersonal wording, 125, 130, 133
  mens rea, and, 191
  mistake, 125–132
    Australian cases, 125–132
    Model Code, 182–185
    Reporter's comments, 182
  occupiers, 48
  owners of chattels, 49
  precautions, reasonable, 129
  punishment, 127, 128, 130
  statutory defences, and, 125
  vicarious responsibility, 49, 129
  wording, 46
STATUTORY DEFENCES. *See* DEFENCES
STATUTORY OFFENCES. *See generally*, STRICT RESPONSIBILITY
STATUTORY REFORM. *See* REFORM
STATUTORY WORDS, 46 *et seq. And see* PARTICULAR WORDS
  absolute wording, 42
  construction, canons of, effect, 46
  legal implications, 12
  plain words, 46
  status offences, 46
STRICT RESPONSIBILITY
  accident, inevitable, 204
  AMERICAN LAW INSTITUTE MODEL CODE. *See* MODEL CODE
  Australian Criminal Codes, 145 *et seq.*

automatism, 199
background, 3
burden of proof, 39
change, machinery of, 68 *et seq.*
codes, 96 *et seq.*, 167 *et seq.*
compulsion, 193
constituents of, 1
coverture, 192
defences, generally, 189 *et seq.*
definition, 1
deterrence, 24 *et seq.*
development, 68 *et seq.*
drunkenness, 201
duress, 193
ethical considerations, 3 *et seq.*
generally, 1 *et seq.*
history, 3, 13
impossibility, 204
inevitable accident, 204
infancy, 192
insanity, 199
intoxication, 201
justification of, 9–28
legislative intention, 9
literature, 1n, 2n
machinery of change, 68 *et seq.*
  case-law, by, 78 *et seq.*
  courts, by, 84 *et seq.*
  statute, by, 68 *et seq.*
mental element, 190 *et seq.*
mistake, 85 *et seq. And see* MISTAKE
  statutory words, 113 *et seq.*
Model Code, 167 *et seq.*
moral guilt, 3
necessity, defence of, 204
necessity of, 15
need for, arguments, 8 *et seq.*
negligence, 36, 38
nomenclature, 1
public interest, 27
punishment, 5
  mental element, 31
reform, 68 *et seq. And see* machinery *supra*
sanctions, 29
social importance, 7
status offences, 46 *et seq.*
statutory words, 46 *et seq.*
  mistake, 113 *et seq.*
Wisconsin Depth Study of. *See* WISCONSIN STUDY
SUFFER. *See* PARTICULAR WORDS

TASMANIAN CRIMINAL CODE, 74
TRIAL BY JURY, 29

VICARIOUS LIABILITY, 23, 164
VICARIOUS RESPONSIBILITY
mens rea, and, 191
"permitting", distinguished, 58
status offences, 49, 50, 129
VIOLATION. *See also* MODEL CODE
STRICT RESPONSIBILITY
classification, 173
definition, 1, 70, 172–179
moral stigma, 21
punishment, 169
strict responsibility, for, 71

WECHSLER, Professor
Reporter, Model Code
culpability, comments, 180
general comments, 169
status offences, comment, 182
WESTERN AUSTRALIAN CRIMINAL
CODE. *See also* AUSTRALIAN
CRIMINAL CODES
case-law, 162
WILFULNESS, 62
WISCONSIN STUDY (1956)
criminal statutes, in, 11
findings, 7
WORDS AND PHRASES
"accept", 164
"act", 147
*actus non facit reum nisi mens sit
rea*, 4
actus reus. See ACTUS REUS
administrative crime, 73
"any person who", 114
"being found", 47
civil offence, 73

civil penalty, 174, 175
"criminal cause or matter", 81
culpability requirements, 179
ejusdem generis, 123, 137, 175
"endeavour", 121, 123
"expressed impersonally", offences, 130
*expressio unius est exclusio
alterius*, 113, 143
"failing to prevent, " 137
"holding out", 164
"honest ignorance, " 112
"inconsistency", 159
"intrinsically nefarious", 127
mala in se, 73
mala prohibita, 73
mens rea. See MENS REA
"negligent act or omission", 147
neutral words. *See* NEUTRAL
WORDS
"no person shall", 114, 181
"omission", 147
"operate", 165
"physical act", 123
plain words, 46, 114
"provisions of the law relating to
subject", 152
punishment, serious, 32
reasonable man, 150
reddendo singula singulis, 174
respondeat superior, 23
serious punishment, 32
"shall not use", 160
stare decisis, 83. *And see* PRECE-
DENT
statutory words, generally, 46
et seq.
subjective fault, 11
"unlawfully", 156